The Career Book

Help for the Restless Realist

Jane Downes

Foreword by Edward de Bono

KITE BOOKS

Published by Kite Books
an imprint of Blackhall Publishing
Lonsdale House
Avoca Avenue
Blackrock
Co. Dublin
Ireland

e-mail: info@blackhallpublishing.com
www.blackhallpublishing.com

ISBN: 978-1-84218-197-3

A catalogue record for this book is available from the British Library.

Printed in Ireland by ColourBooks Ltd.

About the Author

Jane Downes is founder of the Clearview Coaching Group (www.clearviewcoachgroup.com), which she established in 2004 following an extensive career working within the area of recruitment and IIR consulting. She co-owns Ireland's first Assessment and Coaching Centre for Emotional Intelligence – www.EIIreland.com – and is the resident interview coach expert on Ireland's top jobs websites, www.irishjobs.ie and www.jobs.ie. She facilitates numerous workshops around the country in the areas of career change management, effective interviewing and post-redundancy career management. She is married with one child and lives in Dublin.

This book is dedicated to four very special people:
My late father, Tony
My amazing mother, Terry
My darling husband, Clive
My beautiful daughter, Anna-Jane

Foreword

This book is unusual because it is both original and practical.

It is important to remember that it is written by an experienced career coach who calls on her experience as needed. The author believes that 20 per cent of people need minimal career advice but that 80 per cent need something more.

In the first part of the book the author puts forward nine basic types of people based on personalities or simply attitudes towards career choices. She lays out these types in detail so that readers can identify with them in whole or in part. The range is very broad so by no means is the reader made feel restricted or 'put in a box'. The author explains how each type impacts or inhibits career decisions and actions.

The author then explains in detail how to overcome the inhibitions set up by each type in order to move forward. In some cases, realisation may be enough.

The second part of the book lays out practical advice relating to putting yourself on the career market. In this way, the book encourages reflection before action.

I would strongly recommend this book to anyone who is experiencing any doubts or difficulties in their career path.

Edward de Bono
February 2010

Contents

Contents

Acknowledgements

My beloved late father, Tony, was the first to spot my talent for helping people to help themselves to career success. It is to him I owe my own choice of career – and so much else besides. I only wish he were here to give me his thoughts on this book.

The unconditional love and support of my mother, Terry, has been an amazing grace in my life. While I don't propose to embarrass her (and me!) by listing everything she's done for me over the years, I cannot let this opportunity pass without letting her know one thing: not a day goes by that I don't scratch my head and wonder all over again what I did to deserve such an incredible, incredible mother. The world is a warmer place because she's in it.

My darling husband, Clive, responded with heroic patience and tolerance to all the 'time out' and 'commitment' which the writing of this book demanded. His unwavering encouragement and enthusiasm at every step of the way are deeply appreciated.

My brother, Daragh Downes, gave me invaluable critical feedback on the various draft chapters of this book. My thanks to him for delivering so much bad news with so much good grace.

Cartoonist Ronan McIntyre did a sterling job of translating silly scenarios into hilarious cartoons. I thank him nine times over.

Not alone did Blackhall Publishing give me the opportunity of writing this book, they were also an absolute pleasure to work

Acknowledgements

with. A special thank you to Elizabeth Brennan for having shown such faith in my initial vision for the book and for having been so helpful and insightful at all stages of its production. Thanks also to Eileen O'Brien for her 'on-the-ball' editing of the finished script and her quite remarkable stylistic antennae.

I would like to thank my first professional coaching mentor, Maureen Hewitt, who helped me get established in the field by teaching me so much about the 'nuts and bolts' of effective coaching.

Finally, this book simply would not have been written without the extraordinary clients and groups I have had the privilege of working with over the years. They have inspired me with their own personal stories of career challenge and career success. To say that I have learned a huge amount from them would be a crass understatement. But it's the best I can do.

Jane Downes
March 2010

Preface

Q: How many career coaches does it take to change a lightbulb?
A: Are you sure that changing this particular lightbulb is the most proactive, impactful and values-aligned step you could be taking right now?

My name is Jane Downes and I am a career coach. Let me start by telling you a nice little story.

§

Larry was a 35-year-old mid-management-level administration manager from Limerick working in a telecoms operation. He came to me because he wanted to move on from his current job. What did he want from his next job? He had a simple shopping list:

- To earn enough money to have a modest life
- To enjoy interacting with people at work
- Not be over-challenged intellectually, which he felt would stress him out
- To work in an administrative capacity in a stand-alone role that would give him ownership and a sense of responsibility

What area did Larry see himself going into? He wasn't too pushed. Anything from a similar industry to a chemical waste facility would be fine – as long as the above needs were being met. Larry had a healthy work ethic but never saw work as anything more than a means to an end – that end being basic freedom from financial care. He had a really good social and personal life; loads of friends; plenty of hobbies; sports activities. Last but not least, he had a great fiancée with whom he had been going out for the past six years and with whom he was very much in love. This guy, in short, was as well-rounded and happy as they come.

Having taken Larry through some values, work motivators and transferable skills exercises, I put him on a two-week fact-finding mission. The aim of this was to help him narrow his long list of possible career options down to a shortlist of just five. This involved him putting in a couple of intensive weeks of online research, trips to the ILAC library in Dublin, scouring of the classified ads sections, exploratory cups of coffee with friends and acquaintances (and friends of friends and acquaintances of acquaintances...) with connections in various career areas. And much else besides. Larry came back to my office, as agreed, with his shortlist of five options typed up. After some discussion, and a further week of research and reflection, he had his shortlist narrowed down to just one item: a middle management position in the ESB that had just been advertised.

Having put this option through one last rigorous vetting exercise, and having discussed it at length with his fiancée, Larry sent in a meticulously prepared job application. He got called for interview. We did an intensive interview coaching session, the aim of which was to ensure that Larry managed to stay on script without coming across as scripted. That afternoon, Larry went and did the interview proper. He got the job. He was as happy as – well, Larry.

§

I would estimate that around 20 per cent of my clients are 'Larry' types. They have a good idea of what it is they want, and they are willing to do what it takes to get it. They almost always succeed. In the rare event that they don't, they show effortless resilience, bouncing back to put Plan B into operation. One way or another, they come away with a successful career upgrade.

The other 80 per cent of my clients are not 'Larry' types. Perhaps they have a good idea of what they want but are unwilling to do what it takes to get it. Perhaps they have a good idea of what they want and are willing to do what it takes to get it – but end up not actually *doing* what it takes to get it. Perhaps they have a good idea of what they want, are willing to do what it takes to get it, and actually do go and get it, only to find themselves as discontented as ever. Perhaps they *think* they have a good idea of what they want but really don't. Or perhaps they have absolutely no idea of what they want and have come to the conclusion that they never will.

While Ireland's Larrys (the members of the lucky 20 per cent group) will certainly learn a great deal from this book by way of strategies and tips for managing career and career change, it is not in truth written *primarily* with them in mind. The past few months have seen a positive rash of rush-released job-search books hitting the shelves in response to the recession. Some are good, many dreadful. There have also been many career manuals out there on the market for some time. Some are good, many dreadful. Nearly all these books seem to have one thing in common however: they take it as read that the reader is a Larry – someone who just needs some sound practical advice to set them on their way.

This book takes a different tack altogether. It starts from the understanding that *upgrading one's career is not just a technical or logistical affair.* It involves *YOU* – your psychology, your personality, your strengths, your weaknesses, your hopes, your dreams, your fears, your habits, your worldview, your story, your value system. This book is heavily biased in favour of meeting the needs of the 80 per cent group, i.e. all those people out there who find that things are never quite so *textbook* for them as they seem to be for the Larrys of this world.

When it comes to the careers field, these members of the silent majority are The Disappointed.

§

Disappointment

It's the verse, chorus, instrumental break and repeat chorus I hear over and over again in my work as a career coach.

Not that an 80 per cent group client will necessarily use the word 'disappointment' in every case. They may complain of:

- Boredom
- Frustration
- Thwarted ambition
- Stress
- Resentment
- Exhaustion

or – particularly since the economic downturn –

• Fear

But the hidden sponsor of these emotions is more often than not a horrible feeling that life and career are turning into one long purgatorial anti-climax. Whether talking about:

• Job
• Lack of job
• Life outside job

or

• Lack of life outside job

these people feel imprisoned, constrained, *stuck*. Many are waiting on some financial, professional or personal event, known or unknown, to come along and somehow throw their world into technicolour. But this magical event has that godawful Godot quality of never, ever arriving. As one young lady recently remarked to me in our first executive coaching session together, 'I have an almighty dread in the pit of my stomach that when I'm on my deathbed looking back over my life I'll find myself thinking, *"was that it?"*' This, mark you, from one of Ireland's 'success stories' – high achieving, high earning, high status. And haunted by a sense of deep personal failure. In many other cases, the client feels unhappy with their lack of visible professional status, in some cases even their lack of profession.

The Disappointed have one thing in common: a sense of *failure*. By this word is meant simply *any* dismal scenario whereby a person finds themselves living a life contrary to *their* values, *their* hopes, *their* goals. This may entail working a job that is alienating and unsatisfying. It may entail not being able to ascend the career ladder. Or it may entail not knowing where to start in putting together a career for oneself.

§

The good news: the strong majority of 80 per cent group people who have come to me tormented by this feeling of disappointment have managed to turn their careers around as a result of intensive coaching. This has been the case not just during the Celtic Tiger years but also more recently.

The very good news: in a significant number of cases the turnaround has come within a dramatically short timeframe, with solutions usually proving a *lot* less complicated than the original obstacles had appeared to be.

The bad news: a minority of clients have managed to improve their careers only sluggishly and to a severely limited degree.

The very bad news: a certain – albeit small – number have failed *completely* to turn their careers around.

§

Now I'm probably not supposed to have mentioned those last two items. I'm supposed to have given you a nice feelgood tale about one unhappy starting point (disappointment) invariably leading to one happy outcome (transformation). By the end of the next paragraph, I'm supposed to have sold this book to you on the promise and premise that it will change your life – guaranteed.

Sorry, but no can do. Such phoney-baloney positivity is precisely the kind of thing we need to drop in these post-Celtic Tiger times. If the otherwise profoundly traumatic bursting of Ireland's boom bubble has had one upside it has been to sharpen our collective BS detector. Reality, all of a sudden, is very much back on the agenda. People are that bit less afraid to tell the truth about where they are at – and that bit slower to accept other people's self-serving spin on things. As a check on what the US columnist Barbara Ehrenreich has called the 'delusional optimism' of a credit-fuelled 'boom' economy,* the 'power of negative thinking' is very much back on the agenda. And thank God for it.

So ... sorry to ruin a good story with awkward facts. The work I have done with clients over the past few years has seen one unhappy starting point lead to *four* different outcomes:

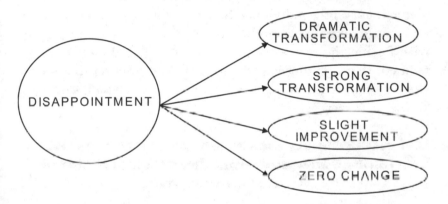

One simple element has made the key difference. My input? No. The rapport between myself and the client? No. The age, education, gender, class or professional grade of the client? No. The client's ability to rattle off feel-good clichés? *No.* The key variable has been the ability of the client to realise that *they themselves* were the person they had been waiting for, *they themselves* were the person who needed to show up for things to kick off. Once *this* idea has gone 'click', something profound has taken place –

---

* The *New York Times*, 23 September 2008

every time. Lasting change has suddenly become an attainable goal. Not an attained one, mind. *Attainable.* Without this attitudinal shift from passive aspiration to active self-direction, however, change has remained dispiritingly unlikely. And even if it has come about in the short term, it has proven a lot less likely to stick.

Please don't misunderstand me. I am not inviting you to buy into the very Celtic Tiger notion that a person's destiny is *nothing more than* a function of their 'attitude'. Such a simplistic worldview won't get us very far here. Poverty, structural unfairness, unearned misfortune, recession – no amount of positive psychology can wish these harsh realities away or blame them on the individual. Self-responsibility, however, has nothing to do with pretending otherwise. It has nothing to do with fleeing the real world. It has nothing to do with telling yourself that thinking happy thoughts and praying to the universe to deliver the goodies will get you where you need to go. On the contrary:

Self-responsibility means *embracing the real world* – taking sober and objective stock of it and of your situation in it.

§

This book is written as a guide to breaking your appointment with disappointment on the career front. Accordingly, I am most anxious that it not *add* to your litany of disappointments by itself disappointing you. So I must ask you not to bring to this book a set of false expectations. Perhaps you have already gone through a veritable forest of 'self-help' books. If so, then how about we try to make this your last, OK?

Here, then, is the deal. Please – *please* – read carefully:

Preface

- This book is not written to help you. It is written to help you help yourself.
- This book is not written to soothe you. It is written to energise you.
- This book will not show much respect for your comfort zones. It will attempt to make you allergic to the sensation of comfortable numbness.
- This book will not invite you to Make a Wish, Hand It Over to the Cosmos and Wait for It to Come True. Nor, however, will it invite you, in the name of some shrivelled idea of 'the real world', to settle for an existence of mediocrity, drudgery and diminished expectations.
- This book will not tell you that life will be easy if only you can start drilling some Happy Thoughts into your head five hundred times a day. Nor, however, will it let you away with the negative thought patterns that may be slowly crucifying you.
- This book will not pass judgement on your life. Nor, however, will it encourage you to ignore the impulse *within you* that you are failing to live up to your potential.
- This book will not presume to tell you what 'success' is. Nor, however, will it try to talk you into 'reframing' your current unsatisfactory situation as the best of all possible worlds.
- This book will not reassure you that you're doing just fine despite all your feelings of disappointment and anxiety. Nor, however, will it assume as correct any interpretation you may have of your life as one long fifteen-act tragedy.
- This book will not indulge your fantasies. Nor, however, will it underestimate the powerful role your imagination can play in helping you break out of the disappointing 'reality' you have constructed around yourself.
- This book will not insult you by minimising the scale of your problems. Nor, however, will it uncritically endorse your own cherished analysis of those problems.

Preface

- This book will not give you one Big Idea that will unlock your Infinite Potential and lead you to Infinite Abundance and Perfect Positivity. Nor, however, will it withhold from you a repertoire of simple insights and strategies that may in fact revolutionise your life if you deploy them well.

- This book will not offer you false shortcuts out of your difficulties. Nor, however, will it let you mistake drift for progress.

- This book will not give you a short-lived buzz by telling you Disneyfied stories of individuals who have realised their dreams. Nor, however, will it be silent on the exemplary heroism which its author has encountered in the many people she has met in the course of her work as a career coach and recruitment consultant.

- This book will not offer you cut-price theology by telling you that success is what automatically happens to people who are in harmony with God's will for them. Nor, however, will it let you off the hook by telling you that people who renounce their happiness or success in this life are on schedule to earn brownie points in the hereafter.

- This book will not assume that you believe in God. Nor, however, will it assume that you don't.

- This book will not equate wealth with virtue. Nor, however, will it equate poverty with virtue.

- This book will not tell you that you can be absolutely anything you want to be. Nor, however, will it fail to point out that there is nothing you can do that can't be done.

- This book will not patronise you with the fiction that the world is a happy, unpolitical place in which ego trips, power trips and greed never mess with people's lives to an often disgusting extent. Nor, however, will it let you take cover behind a conveniently sociological explanation for your own underachievement or unhappiness.

- This book will not invite you to reduce your wonderfully complex and messy self to the status of a 'brand'. Nor, however, will it hide from you the importance of astute self-presentation in attaining the career you want.

You like where all this is going? Good. This book is probably for you.

You don't like where all this is going? Great. This book is definitely for you.

§

Introduction

For career change to become a real possibility, your level of discomfort must temporarily rise. You come to this book with a gnawing sense that you are somehow selling yourself short. Underachieving. Apologising for your existence instead of living your life. Surviving instead of thriving. *This gnawing sense is not your enemy. It is your dearest, dearest friend.* Learn to understand it, and you can convert it into positive action. Convert it into positive action, and your life will never be the same again. The man or woman who has come to grips with the 'grammar' of their own discontent and underachievement is nothing short of a force of nature. Whatever their circumstances, they are primed for real change.

Yes: whatever their circumstances. I don't use this phrase lightly. Your personal circumstances may well be severely challenging. You may be one of the many casualties of the current economic downturn. You may have a personal, family or financial situation that places you under severe strain. You may feel that every escape route from your problems is impossibly and impassably blocked. I have not met you, let alone walked a single mile in your shoes, so how can I blithely and abstractly talk about your 'circumstances' and your capacity to transcend them? In one sense, of course, I cannot, and it would be obnoxious of me to claim any differently. This book, however, is based on a simple wager:

The challenges you face have given your perception a negative bias, leaving you with an unrealistically narrow estimate of the room for manoeuvre currently open to you.

Pessimism can be every bit as delusional as optimism. My years as a practising coach have shown me many, many times that seemingly helpless and trapped individuals really can beat fearsome odds to bring about real and lasting change in their lives. Maybe I just happen to have lucked out on an utterly anomalous, freak cluster of almost supernaturally fortunate clients? Or ... maybe, just maybe, life really does support us in surprising ways as soon as we give ourselves a fair shot.

Don't take my word for any of this. Don't go making a leap of faith just yet. All that's required of you for now is a leap of *decision*. Decide to give this book a chance by letting it ask some hard questions of you. As you face into the *temporary* discomforts which this book has in store for you, try to cultivate a background mood of *ultimate* optimism. Be quietly defiant in the face of your current challenges. Trust in the process and I am confident that you will soon find yourself moving from a condition of learned self-helplessness to one of educated self-help. Your optimism will be informed, not facile, your goals viable, not pie-in-the-sky. You will be ready to help yourself to help yourself to more of what life has to offer.

§

Introduction

This book has two chief aims:

1. To help those of you in the 80 per cent group examine the ways in which you may be sabotaging your own prospects in life.
2. To help you develop a sound and detailed practical strategy for making the realisation of your career potential a realistic goal.

There are two sides to this: principles and practices. Neither can be neglected.

Targeted action that is founded upon self-limiting belief patterns and habits will ultimately prove fruitless. You may polish up your CV to a state of knock-'em-dead perfection. You may play a stormer in the interview. Heck, you may even get the job. But the person you will be bringing to work every day will still be ... you. Your unacknowledged gremlins will, one way or another, find a way to mess with you (and probably those around you too). Too many career manuals neglect this elementary fact. They tell you lots about *what to do* in going for your ideal job, but little or nothing about *who you are*. This is like a doctor trying to solve a patient's chronic digestive problems by telling them to eat more and more food. It may go down alright but will end up delivering all the nutritional benefits of a piece of bubblegum.

By the same token, there is little point in principles if they are not followed by a laser-beam focus on practices. No amount of introspection and motivational focus will effect change if it is not accompanied by real-world, nitty-gritty application. My office has seen too many 'refugees' from what I call *meta-career literature* – that is, self-help books which get the reader all pepped up with vague talk of breaking free of the captivity of negativity, optimising performance and upgrading your career, only to leave them high and dry when it comes to, well, actually doing something with all this positive energy. Sometimes these books even try to pass off banal fortune cookie wisdom as deep spiritual insight. Sadly, many people actually become addicted to such vacuous 'self-help' books because *they make the idea of change so much sexier than change itself.* As a passionate believer in the self-help movement, this kind of thing makes me downright angry. I have long since come to the conclusion that self-help advocates can be divided into two opposing camps:

- *Cheerleaders* – 'feel-good factor' spoofers who ultimately disempower their client/reader by selling them a bogus form of positivity.
- *Empowerers* – specialists who endeavour in good faith to offer principled and practical insights into the process by which real and lasting career change can come about.

I wish emphatically to align myself with the second category. This book has not been written as an academic or intellectual exercise. Nor has it been written for your entertainment. Either it helps you to help yourself, or it has been a royal waste of time, money and paper.

§

At the risk of stating the bleeding obvious, *this is a career coaching book, not a career coaching session.* Coaching takes place in real time, allowing an on-the-spot give-and-take between coach and client. The client must be encouraged to engage, challenge and keep the interaction real.

If this book is to be of any real use to you, then, you need to read it in as *wakeful* a manner as possible. Be critical. Be alert. Don't let me sneak cheap Pollyanna myths past you. Don't let me oversimplify the known world for the sake of keeping things upbeat. Don't let me abbreviate the complications of real life for the sake of a soundbite. Measure *everything* I say against the integrity of your own experience. Be humble enough to consider the possibility that I may have new insights to offer you. But don't let me be arrogant enough to impose my own ideas – or ideology – on you.

Our physical absence from one another as you read this book means that the communication will be one-way, from me to you and not back again. I will not have access to the specifics of your story or the unique phenomenon of your personality. This double information deficit will result in an unavoidable loss of nuance. By necessity, I will have to paint certain things in broad brushstrokes. While you should be open to letting some of your mental pictures be altered by those brushstrokes, please, whatever you do, don't relinquish your powers of intellectual self-defence. In return, I will try my best not to pontificate on things I don't understand.

This means, amongst other things, dropping what I call The Authority Fallacy: the absurd fiction that I, The Author, have The Meaning of Life Sussed.

Fiddlesticks and nonsense. Like you, I often find life bewildering and heartbreaking. The strong optimism which I bring to my job is founded not on a blindness to life's messiness but on having watched people – loved ones, friends, colleagues and clients – negotiate their way through often formidable challenges *without forfeiting their humanity, dignity and vitality*. What inspires me to be the best coach I can possibly be, and what has persuaded me to write this book, is the uneasy knowledge that there are so many unhappy people out there whose spirit, originality and *charisma* have somehow gotten suppressed by life.

What does success mean for you? *You* decide, not me. You are not a photocopy of my last client, nor they a photocopy of the one before. It is my fervent hope that this book will serve as a ladder to help you climb to *your* definition of success, whatever that definition may be. If and when you get there, kick the ladder away.

§

One of the great joys of being a career coach is that you get to work with clients from all walks of life. Amongst the people who have visited my office have been:

- Teachers
- Recently retired pensioners
- Corporate high-fliers
- College students
- Secondary school students
- Academics
- Foreign nationals living in Ireland
- Graphic designers
- Journalists
- Individuals who are long-term or short-term unemployed
- Civil servants
- Housewives and househusbands
- Sales assistants
- Professional sportspeople
- Ex-soldiers
- Public transport workers
- People with disabilities
- Musicians and artists
- Writers
- IT specialists
- Nurses
- Road hauliers

- Figures in the public eye
- Heirs to a family fortune
- Taxi drivers
- Recent divorcé(e)s
- Special needs assistants
- People wanting to set up their own business
- Workers just made redundant

Amidst all the variables of age, income, status, class, nationality and temperament (not to mention hairstyle), however, I have noticed a quite amazing regularity when it comes to *the errors which hold the 80 per cent group of self-disappointing clients back.*

I have come to believe that these errors can be boiled down to just nine core types. I call them The Disappointers:

i.	The Faulter Ego
ii.	The Walter Ego
iii.	The Halter Ego
iv.	The Altar Ego
v.	The Vaulter Ego
vi.	The Alterior Ego
vii.	The Salter Ego
viii.	The Exalter Ego
ix.	The Voltaire Ego

Before we go into what each of these Disappointers is, let's get one thing straight. Contrary to what the above variations on the phrase 'alter ego' might suggest, a Disappointer is not like some mind-altering drug or hippy state of consciousness. A Disappointer is actually a lot less exotic than that, but every bit as potent.

A Disappointer does exactly what it says on the tin: it leads to disappointing outcomes, again and again and again. It is an unhelpful temptation, tendency or role into which we habitually fall and which alters our expectations, behaviour and destiny. Because of the influence of one or more of these often unconscious saboteurs, we second-guess our naturally intelligent response to life's challenges, thus blocking our instinctive problem-solving capacity.

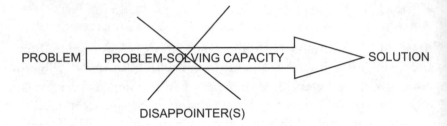

The result? We 'somehow' keep getting stuck as a result of the choices we make.

§

It is the core theory of this book that members of the 80 per cent group will never break their appointment with disappointment unless they:

    a. Become conscious of the ways in which one, some or all of the Nine Disappointers may be sabotaging their progress

    b. Learn to disenthrall themselves from their dominant Disappointers so that they can be free to draw on their and others' influence in more benign ways

It is crucial that you take note of the second half of point b here. Each of the nine 'alter ego' types listed above has a positive 'Appointer' dimension as well as a negative 'Disappointer' one. Put simply, tendency in Appointer mode is a tendency that empowers you. It literally helps you to disappoint disappointment.

DISAPPOINTER — DIS-APPOINTING THE DISAPPOINTER → APPOINTER

(a sabotaging tendency)   (an empowering tendency)

For members of the 80 per cent group – the non-Larrys of this world – the *initial* focus must be on *who they are* rather than *what they are to do*. Psychological insight, in other words, must precede concrete operations. Getting to know one's own psychological make-up is not some self-indulgent, wishy-washy luxury. It is absolutely indispensable. Without it, no amount of practical action, however constructive or well-conceived, will ultimately get an 80 per cent group individual out of their current 'stuckness'. Even if that person succeeds in changing their circumstances, they are still headed for trouble down the line – because the self they have brought along for the ride will be the same self that has gotten into difficulties over and over again in the past. Sooner or later, the patterns of old will reassert themselves.

Unless a person's Disappointer is identified, challenged and converted into an Appointer, it will continue to schedule appointments with disappointment on behalf of that person.

§

So, 'what *are* these Nine Disappointers?' I hear you ask. By way of introduction, let's watch each in action as it goes about a simple task – driving a car....*

---

* All nine cartoons below have been drawn by the scandalously talented Ronan McIntyre. If you like Ronan's work, you can reach him at ronanmc intyrecartoons@gmail.com

I.

THE FAULTER EGO

A woman gets into a car. As she is about to put the key in the ignition, an unsettling thought comes into her head: 'I'm such an eejit, I'll probably crash.' With a sigh, she gets out and walks.

DEFINITION: The Faulter Ego is named after the tendency to find fault – with others, with life but most especially with ourselves. It is the inner critic run amok.

DISAPPOINTER MODE: undue pessimism, negativity, anxiety.

MOTTO: 'Always look on the sh*te side of life.'

APPOINTER MODE: critical intelligence, healthy scepticism, modesty, eyes-open realism.

II.
THE WALTER EGO

A man gets into a car. Driving along at 27km an hour, he imagines himself on the Meditteranean island he recently bought on the royalties from his debut novel, a thriller that was the highest-selling fiction book in the world last year. Now working on the follow-up, he finds that the best ideas come from these gentle spins round his private island. He presses his foot on the accelerator – gotta cut this spin short, Dan Brown is dropping in on the chopper in five minutes.

Damn. That was the turn off for Donaghmede library. They close in five minutes. And they won't renew the book over the phone because it's already been renewed ten times. The wife will kill me if I get another bloody fine.

DEFINITION: The Walter Ego is the tendency to resort to fantasy as a way of escaping one's unsatisfyingly ordinary life. It is named in honour of Walter Mitty, the anti-hero of James Thurber's classic 1939 short story, *The Secret Life of Walter Mitty*. (It was later made into a wonderful film starring Danny Kaye.) In the story, Mitty futilely tries to escape his humdrum and henpecked existence by spending his time daydreaming of one grandiose adventure after another.

DISAPPOINTER MODE: escapism, magical thinking, unrealistic goals.

MOTTO: 'All I gotta do is dream, dream, dream, dream.'

APPOINTER MODE: imaginative restlessness, thinking big, sense of possibility.

III.

THE HALTER EGO

A woman gets into a car. She goes for a quick spin round the local estate. This is where her driving lessons took place fifteen years ago. Since passing her test, she has never taken any other route. Those main roads with all the horrible accidents you hear about? No thanks! Besides, why risk getting lost when you have a route that works just fine?

DEFINITION: The Halter Ego is named after the leather headgear device used to restrain and guide animals, usually workhorses. Accordingly, the Halter Ego never looks at options to the left or right. Instead it is governed by the timid belief that life is a matter of unquestioningly and uncomplainingly ploughing the furrow that has been laid out straight ahead of you. The Halter Ego tells you that you must at all costs play safe in life.

DISAPPOINTER MODE: conservatism, low expectations, extreme risk aversion.

MOTTO: 'Aim low, aim low, it's off to work we go.'

APPOINTER MODE: work ethic, reliability, freedom from glory-glory-hallelujah egotism.

IV.
THE ALTAR EGO

A man gets into a car. He puts the key in the ignition, but the car won't start. 'That's strange', he thinks to himself, 'I put a fresh tank of holy water in only this morning.' Just then, a van drives by with the words CALL NOW emblazoned on its side. A sign! Closing his eyes, the man bows his head and prays: 'O Infinite Cosmic Power, I gratefully accept Thy invitation and humbly call on Thee for a miracle. Please make this car move!' Nothing happens. After a few moments of mute perplexity, the man finally realises what is happening. 'O Infinite Cosmic Power, I thank Thee for this message which Thou hast sent me from the Realms of Infinite and Pure Potentiality. I now realise it is Thy Will that I not drive this car. Thou wiltst miraculously get me to my destination some other way.' The man serenely gets out of the car, sits down on the pavement and waits. And waits.

DEFINITION: The Altar Ego is named after the tendency to take refuge in spirituality – or rather, in the sickly, unreal 'spirituality' promoted in so much New Age 'self-help' literature. The Altar Ego is typically a covert egotist whose devotion to the 'Gospel of Prosperity' leads him or her to a crass equation of material success with godliness. The fact that said material success never seems to transpire for the Altar Ego-inspired individual prompts not puzzlement but a further round of mystification and gobbeldy-gook.

DISAPPOINTER MODE: using religion or spirituality as an opium to block out personal fears and failings, dressing up one's ambitiousness in cod-spiritual garb.

MOTTO: 'The Lord is my shepherd, I want, I want.'

APPOINTER MODE: sense of life's mystery, existential leap of faith, appreciation that there may be more things in heaven and earth than are dreamt of in the practical world's philosophy.

V.
THE VAULTER EGO

A woman gets into a car. She puts the key in the ignition, goes straight into fifth gear and revs up. The engine makes a horrible screeching noise – but doesn't budge. So she gives it even more gas. Same result, only worse.

DEFINITION: The Vaulter Ego is named after the tendency to try to vault one's way over obstacles in order to reach a goal A!S!A!P! It harasses you with a belief that time is perptually running out. This tricks you into bypassing the logic of next-step thinking, which is needed for careful management of progress and change.

DISAPPOINTER MODE: misplaced impatience, leaping before looking, demand for instantaneous results.

MOTTO: 'It's now or never.'

APPOINTER MODE: drive, urgency, resistance to drift.

VI.
THE ALTERIOR EGO

A man gets into a car. When he gets to the first set of traffic lights, he rolls down the window and asks a driver in the next lane, 'Excuse me, I'm out for a drive. Can you tell me where I should go?'

DEFINITION: The Alterior Ego is named by fusing two words: *alter*, meaning 'other', and *ulterior*, meaning 'beyond what is seen or shown'. The Alterior Ego is the tendency to let oneself be controlled by what *others* think. Someone with an ulterior motive acts in bad faith, according to some hidden agenda. Someone with an *alterior* motive acts in bad faith also, but in this case the bad faith resides in the fact that the motive does not ultimately belong to them. A life dominated by the relentless effort to please, placate or impress others is a prolonged act of profound self-betrayal. The true engine of my Alterior Ego decisions – the internalised belief system of others – usually remains ulterior, hidden even to myself. This enables me to think of myself as an independent individual, all the while handing over my key life decisions to others.

DISAPPOINTER MODE: loss of personal autonomy and self-direction, timidity, obsession with what others think.

MOTTO: 'I just can't get you out of my head ....'

APPOINTER MODE: openness to the views and input of others, capacity to see oneself objectively.

VII.
THE SALTER EGO

A woman gets into a car. Listening to melancholy opera music on RTÉ lyric fm, she drives down a dead-end lane and crashes into a stone wall. Getting out to survey the damage, she sobs, 'Why oh why did they have to put this damned wall HERE? When am I going to get a BREAK??'

DEFINITION: The Salter Ego is named after two things: the the act of rubbing salt into one's own wounds, and the salty tears which flow as a result of doing this. The Salter Ego enjoys playing the victim. It gets an almost masochistic buzz out of converting experiences into tragic narratives.

DISAPPOINTER MODE: self-pitying narcissism, addiction to painful outcomes, martyr complex, insensitive use of one's own 'sensitivity'.

MOTTO: 'Poor me.'

APPOINTER MODE: emotional sensitivity, openness to the sadness of life and the suffering of others.

VIII.

THE EXALTER EGO

A man gets into his brand new, top-of-the-range Porsche with cream leather seats. He dons a pair of Gucci shades, rolls down the windows, yanks the music up to eleven and speeds down the road. Each time he overtakes another car, he lets out a jubilant roar: 'Out of the way, loser!' The adrenaline pumping through his system, he soon hits the motorway and lets rip. But he doesn't have any friends.

DEFINITION: The Exalter Ego represents the very Celtic Tiger temptation to exalt oneself at the expense of others and of one's empathy with others. In its quest for an alienated and narrow form of success, the Exalter Ego performs a sad reduction of the self to competitive and narcissistic categories. As such, it usually masks profound insecurities about true self-worth.

DISAPPOINTER MODE: over-competitiveness, lack of personal or professional ethics, money madness, contempt for anyone perceived as weak or useless.

MOTTO: 'Baby I can drive my car, and baby I love me. Beep beep'm beep beep yeah.'

APPOINTER MODE: ambition, healthy competitiveness, refusal to sell oneself short or simply 'fit in', entrepreneurial dynamism.

IX.
THE VOLTAIRE EGO

A woman gets into a car. She puts the key in the ignition, turns the heater up and switches the radio on. 'Now isn't this comfy', she says as she leans back and closes her eyes. The car has been parked in the back garden for the past ten years.

DEFINITION: The Voltaire Ego is named after the famous eighteenth century French philosopher, Voltaire, who once famously declared that 'it is our duty to cultivate our garden'. The Voltaire Ego represents the temptation to focus on a tiny private realm – sometimes even a literal garden – outside of which nothing really registers as interesting or worthy of attention.

DISAPPOINTER MODE: retreat from the world, smugness, conservatism, narrow horizons.

MOTTO: 'There's no place like home.'

APPOINTER MODE: embrace of the small is beautiful philosophy, love of home and family, enjoyment of the simpler things in life, enjoyment of one's own space and one's own company.

On the page opposite is a Wheel of Disappointment. With nothing else to go on but the brief impression you have just got from reading the nine sketches above, rank the influence of each Disappointer on you *as you are here and now, at this point in your life*. We're going to use a simple ranking scale of 1 (strongest influence) to 9 (least strong influence). Each Disappointer should receive one number between 1 and 9, and no number is to be used twice. Thus, for example, if you instinctively experienced strongest self-recognition as you read the Walter Ego scenario above, put a '1' in the Walter Ego segment of the circle. If, on the contrary, you found yourself identifying with Walter Ego behaviour less than with any of the other behaviours, put a '9' in that segment. And so on.

Be honest with yourself as you do this quick exercise. Above all, go with your gut. Don't try to second-guess your answers too carefully. I find that most people have a pretty good spontaneous idea of how the key Disappointers rank for them. You will probably find it easy enough to identify your top two and bottom two, but pretty difficult to get the order right around the middle. That's fine and normal, just do the best you can without spending more than two minutes on the exercise. It's not an exam!

Nor should you worry that you are pigeonholing yourself by ranking your Disappointers. The Nine Disappointers, rather like Edward de Bono's Six Thinking Hats or his Six Frames for Thinking about Information,* are merely a useful shorthand for certain tendencies or styles. These manifest themselves to widely varying degrees in different individuals. I would never say that 'X *is* a Walter Ego', merely that (s)he is prone to Walter

---

* See Edward de Bono, *Six Thinking Hats: An Essential Guide to Clearer Thinking in Business Management from the Creator of Lateral Thinking* (Harmondsworth: Viking, 1986) and *Six Frames for Thinking about Information* (London: Vermilion, 2008).

Ego thinking or behaviour. If X is alerted to this circumstance, there is no good reason why (s)he cannot choose to drop the pattern and try something else on for size.

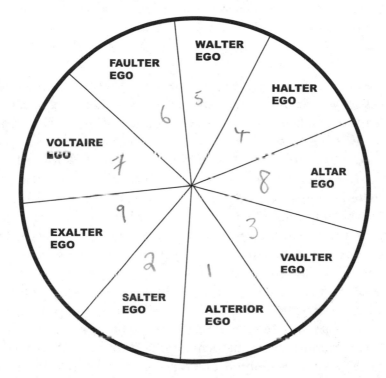

The point of this exercise is simple: to give yourself a suggested reading order for the in-depth Disappointer profiles which follow. When you get to the end of this Introduction, you should turn first to the Disappointer to which you gave your number 1 vote. After that, read about your number 2, then your number 3, etc., all the way down to your number 9.

Why, you might reasonably ask, should you even bother reading about those Disappointers near the bottom of your list? After all, they barely seem to affect you, right? Well, there are no hard and fast rules here. If you just want to read the profiles of Disappointers that seem most relevant to you, that's OK. There is a good chance you will be spurred on to corrective action by what you read. That alone will have more than justified your purchase of this book. So be my guest.

There are however three strong reasons why you may be well advised *not* to skip over the remaining Disappointers.

1. You may have underestimated the role of certain Disappointers in your own life. As already indicated, one of the key features of a Disappointer is that it often does its work on you undercover, so to speak. You may not yet be aware that you are in thrall to your Alterior Ego, say, or your Vaulter Ego. So be open to the possibility that reading in more detail about these Disappointers may trigger some surprising insights.

2. It is good to remind yourself that *each Disappointer has the potential to be converted into an Appointer*. Hence if a particular Disappointer ranked only seventh or eighth or ninth with you it is quite possible that you are *lacking* something which it has to offer. Thus, to take just one example, you may *need* a little touch of the Walter Ego as you start asking the question, *What am I going to do with the rest of my life?* Perhaps a bit of Walter Ego brainstorming might counteract your Halter Ego's prohibition on even *imagining* new adventures in life. Perhaps it might challenge your Faulter Ego's insistence that a neglected artistic talent must remain suppressed if you are to avoid making a fool of yourself. Or perhaps it might get you fired up with post-Alterior Ego ideas of a life lived on *your* terms rather than other people's.

3. These Disappointer profiles are packed with case histories from my coaching practice.* Most reveal a given Disap-

---

* Names and key details have of course been changed throughout to protect client confidentiality.

pointer mode in unusually obvious form. This is for the purpose of clarity rather than typicality. A key part of my coaching technique in this book is to get you to read aspects of yourself in the stories of others. You are certain to find several of these stories triggering an idea or realisation in you about your own career, even if the situation of the individual in the story does not match your own situation particularly closely. These stories are also peppered with insights into how career and career change can be managed in the real world. You could thus be making a big mistake by skipping over some of the profiles.

§

All of this will become much clearer as you encounter each Disappointer in depth. For now, all you need do is read the sections in your chosen sequence, all the time observing your own reactions carefully as you read. In particular, *be alert to any pangs of unease these Disappointer profiles may trigger.* Those pangs will be a very precious signal to you that what I am writing is touching a raw nerve. One of my jobs as a coach is to watch out for such signals in a client's language and gestures. I can't do that with you. So your task as you read about other people's struggles will be one of *self-recognition.* If you find that a Disappointer profile is making for uncomfortable reading – smile for the camera! *You are tuning in to the propoganda of that Disappointer. It is already beginning to lose its hold over your psyche.*

Stick with this indirect method of self-analysis and, by the time you come to focus on the practical question of your own career options in Part II of this book, you will find yourself in an immeasurably stronger position. As we shall see when we get to Part II, the fine art of career management involves a sequence of stages:

1. Self-assessment
2. Narrowing down of options
3. Further research and reflection
4. Decision
5. Action

In order to reach a new accommodation between yourself and the world of work, you must first reach a new accommodation between yourself and yourself. This is what the self-assessment stage is all about. If you rush Part I of this book, therefore, there is every risk that mastery of the nuts and bolts of career self-management, as presented in detail in Part II, will elude you.

§

Part I

Disappointment

1

The Faulter Ego

'Always look on the sh*te side of life'

I'm such an eejit, I'll never make a decent driver …. The Faulter Ego just loves to sabotage your plans, your thoughts of change, your attempts to upgrade your life. It is the seat of low self-esteem and high self-doubt. I am quite deliberately putting the Faulter Ego first in our rogues' gallery of Disappointers because it is by far – and I mean *by far* – the most common of the nine I have come across in coaching. Perhaps it was your own number 1 or 2?

The Faulter Ego goes into overdrive whenever we face a challenge. It is the inner critic or 'gremlin' to whom so many of us become beholden. When allowed to take over, it becomes nothing less than our own personal saboteur, drilling thoughts of failure and inadequacy into our brains and wrecking our attempts to improve our lives. The Faulter Ego's weapon of choice is the self-limiting belief – any over-critical thought about ourselves or about life generally that artificially and needlessly holds us back from fulfilling our true potential.

§

The Faulter Ego likes to make you think it is basing its assessments on objective criteria. It isn't.

Let me tell you about two clients who came to me around the same time.

Shirley looked at her CV and all she could see were the mistakes she had made and the lack of transferable skills available to her. She was very uncomfortable with her weaknesses and skills gaps, and put herself down constantly. She had never asserted herself at appraisal or salary review time in her current job. This kept her on a low salary even as others at her level earned more. She had never set expectations with her bosses for what she needed in order to do her job and be happy. Her bosses were only too happy to leave her stagnate. Shirley was no longer willing to tolerate this state of affairs. She felt she had to do something to upgrade her career. But every time we focused on specifics, she'd make it clear that she didn't feel like she deserved a career upgrade. Examining job specifications, she would say things like, 'I can't do that … I don't have the right experience for this … What if I am exposed for not being able to do that?' The very idea of job interviews filled her with pure dread. Interviewers had one goal and one goal alone: to see through her and catch her out.

Joanne, my other client, had a great energy about her. She talked positively about herself and her skills gained to date. Crucially, she was perfectly comfortable about her weaknesses and skills gaps. They were a fact and, if need be, could be dealt with one by one. Joanne was crystal clear that she was not willing to tolerate staying in a role that she had been finding increasingly unstimulating. She wanted a job that represented more about what she was and that tapped into her key strengths. While she acknowledged it was a scary time in the market to make a change, she chose to embrace the challenge from a position of power. She was not remotely arrogant. She merely possessed healthy self-esteem. She had always made a point of stretching herself and refusing to sell herself short. Measured risks were for her a way of life. When we examined Joanne's CV she got excited discussing her achievements to date. She knew what she had got from each role and could verbalise what these transferable skills were. When we looked at potential job specs together she saw only possibilities, getting excited in a nervous way about new challenges in new fields. Her analytical style typically involved identifying a problem full-on and *immediately* taking the attitude that it would prove solvable: 'I've never covered that but I am sure I could learn it quickly as I learnt X fast in the past ... I'm not sure about that area, to be honest, but I can do some research to get up to date ...'. As we discussed interviews for these roles, Joanne would get animated and say things like, 'You know what? I blinking *deserve* this! ... I have earned the right to be taken very seriously for this job ... This is my showdown, it's time to knock 'em dead.'

Joanne was facing similar market conditions to Shirley. In fact they worked similar roles within a similar industry. Their qualifications and skills were also strikingly comparable. Yet they could hardly have been more different. Joanne was a happy member of the 20 per cent group, while Shirley was in danger of letting her Faulter Ego style of thinking sabotage her chances of a career upgrade. So busy was she finding fault with herself that she doesn't realise that this was itself her greatest fault – and one which, if not addressed, would put her out of contention on the jobs market.

§

The Faulter Ego can be a pretty addictive tendency. To say 'I can't' and find oneself flooded with thoughts of self-doubt and hopelessness can actually be quite a buzz, particularly if the habit is ingrained. Indeed, this is one of the key strategies of the Faulter Ego: it teaches you to invest your very sense of self in the role of 'loser' or underachiever. The thought of actually succeeding becomes deeply threatening to your self-image.

The Faulter Ego is a big fan of the self-fulfilling prophecy. When our Faulter Ego woman gets into her car she tells herself she is never going to be a decent driver. What happens? She doesn't. Magic, right? *The imaginative anticipation of an unfavourable outcome massively raises the real-world likelihood of that unfavourable outcome coming to pass.* If I bring a pessimistic and self-critical bias to bear on a challenge, then one of two things is going to happen. Either I will take to that task in a dysfunctional fashion or I will run away from it altogether. In either case, success will prove beyond my reach. This in turn will give the Faulter Ego further ammunition against me when it comes to facing new challenges. Bit by bit a sustained narrative of failure and defeat is being built up, until even the most promising and straightforward situation becomes fraught with anxiety.

The logic at work here is pure heads-you-win, tails-I-lose. If the situation appears unfavourable, then you will anticipate defeat as the probable outcome. Fair enough, you might say. But the Faulter Ego's bad faith is exposed in the alternative scenario. If the situation is *favourable*, then the prospect of defeat will seem even more deliciously inevitable. In this strange way, the person in thrall to their Faulter Ego gets hooked on the *narrative pay-off* of failure. The experience of *not* meeting a challenge, or of meeting it only in a half-hearted and inadequate way, becomes as reassuringly familiar as the big kiss at the end of a romantic comedy. By telling ourselves we don't make the grade we end up succeeding – by not succeeding. Sometimes, the Faulter Ego gets us to identify with our negative self-image so strongly that it actually becomes a matter of *pride* for us to *not succeed*!

The Faulter Ego

§

Catherine was just six months away from sitting her Engineering finals at college. Her mother had contacted me in a panic. 'Jane, we're at the end of our tether. Catherine is talking about throwing in the towel without even sitting the papers!'

It turned out that Catherine had an impressive track record of exam marks going back to her school days. But over the past year or so something had gone terribly wrong.

I gently insisted to Catherine's mother that Catherine must herself take the next step in contacting me. I don't do involuntary referrals! When Catherine finally did ring, the first thing I noticed was the series of Faulter Ego mantras that peppered her conversation: 'Knowing me, I'll make a hames of it ... I just can't keep up with the coursework ... The finals are a hundred times more difficult than any exams I've done before ...'. When we met for our first session, I suggested that we stop treating the finals as one monstrous block of work and instead break it down into detailed subject-by-subject mini-blocks. What emerged very quickly was that Catherine's picture of not being on top of things was perfectly valid, *but only for about 3 per cent of the course material.* What had happened was that this 3 per cent had taken on totemic status in her mind, absorbing 90 per cent of her attention and yielding a grossly distorted picture of how the exams were likely to go.

Although all this was interesting enough in itself, it is not the chief reason I am telling you Catherine's story here. I pointed out to Catherine that she was generalising from a small area of difficulty to her entire finals. I was met by an unexpected reaction: 'What the *hell* do you know about it? When did you last have to sit an engineering exam? Sorry, but you haven't a clue what you're on about!' Now Catherine was the farthest thing from a petulant brat you could ever hope to find. Her outburst was as untypical as it was revealing. It articulated a fear deeper even than that of getting poor marks. Catherine's deepest fear was that she might be *proven wrong* in her overly pessimistic analysis. What the detailed breakdown of her subjects had done was to smoke her Faulter Ego out of its lair, challenging its lazy three-part strategy of:

- *Generalisation* (my difficulty with aspects A and B represents my inability to cope with the entire course)
- *Catastrophisation* (the fact that one or two small areas of the course are proving hugely challenging to me is a clear signal that I'm heading for complete meltdown in May)
- *Black-and-white thinking* (the possibility that I may not do spectacularly well in the exams really means that I'm going to humiliate myself)

Having cooperated with me in taking a close and *differentiated* look at her subject requirements, Catherine was now making it clear that she really did not appreciate the way I was confusing the issue with awkward facts. So invested was she in her Faulter Ego narrative of most dire failure, that she actually resented being offered a viable counter-narrative. So habituated had she become to the idea that she was a failure and an inadequate student that the very possibility of this not being true seemed disheartening! *If there is one thing the Faulter Ego fears, it is the prospect of having any of its dogmas disconfirmed in real life.* At some level, Catherine did not *want* to do well in her finals. Above all else she wanted to be right. Her talk of boycotting the exams altogether had stemmed from an unconscious desire to get her Faulter Ego off the hook by keeping its cherished black-and-white scenario of impending catastrophe intact. Better to pull out than ruin a good hard-luck story by failing to fail.

What was going on here? It was not as though Catherine had a history of low self-esteem and under-achievement.

Bit by bit, Catherine started to let her defences down with me, allowing the true picture to emerge. What had given her Faulter Ego its opening to sabotage her exam preparation was a deeper fear that, no matter how hard she studied or how well she performed, she would never be as successful an engineer as her father. Once this issue was named and placed out in the open, Catherine and I were able to work through it together, *free of the Faulter Ego's sly masking techniques.* The problem was not the exams but what came after the exams. The problem with what came after the exams was what had led Catherine to study Engineering in the first place. *This* was what needed attention. For it quickly became clear that Catherine's going into extreme Faulter Ego mode with regard to her exams was a delayed reaction to her Alterior Ego decision back in sixth year at school to choose Engineering as a way of pleasing her father. A simple timeline made this clear:

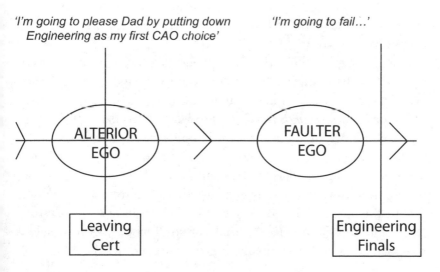

Catherine had become obsessed with the Faulter Ego idea of failing her finals because she did not want to face an even more fearful prospect: that of being in her father's shadow for the rest of her professional life. Having recognised this fact, she was now free to deal with the real problem. After careful discussion, Catherine and I worked out the following strategy: she would give her Engineering finals the best shot she could, after which she would come back to me and we would focus on how she might carve out a career that would be *hers* rather than a photo-copy of her father's. This would involve careful scrutiny of her values, work motivators and transferable skills.

As it turned out, Catherine did great in the exams and went on to diversify into graphic design, a field for which she was an absolute natural.

§

Catherine was an example of someone who had fallen into the classic Faulter Ego trap of focusing with obsessive energy on areas of perceived weakness to the almost total exclusion of areas of strength.

There is a related Faulter Ego phenomenon whereby a person is held back from high achievement not by a cluster of flaws, nor even by a cluster of *perceived* flaws, but by what they erroneously consider their *one single, symbolic, fatal flaw*. This is the belief that X (a job, a goal, an achievement, happiness, anything desirable) could be mine *if only* I did not have *this* flaw, Y. Nothing being more powerful psychologically than the single-cause explanation, the Faulter Ego really scores a significant victory if it enslaves you to this notion. By getting you to pay obsessive attention to one detail, the Faulter Ego is making you forget that your selective focus is completely distorting the true picture.

- Martin wanted to become a journalist but was too mortified by his stammer to do anything about it.
- Anna could not hold down a relationship because she felt her 'big ears' rendered her so ugly that the only reason any man could possibly go out with her would be out of pity.
- Jenny found it incredibly difficult to socialise because she was functionally illiterate. This made even simple social transactions like buying a cinema ticket or ordering food in a restaurant terrifying. Just one slip, and her secret would be out.
- Mark wanted to go into local politics but assumed he would never get elected because he was gay.
- Glen had earned himself an extra night degree at business college but could not bring himself to go for a promotion in his company because he had suffered a nervous breakdown eleven years previously and believed that this would automatically disqualify him in his employer's eye.
- Sharon could not learn to drive because her exquisitely embarrassing tendency to blush made her dread any awkward situation which might arise in traffic.
- Gary's dream of being a rock singer was backed up by a fine voice but threatened by the fact that his hairline had begun to recede prematurely (he was all of 22). What record label, he reasoned, would give a deal to a band fronted by a balding singer?
- Rachel, a retired woman in her early sixties, wanted to go back to college as a mature student to study Italian but was terrified that her age would make her stick out like a sore thumb.

Do you have your very own 'tragic flaw'? Is there one self-limiting belief which you can never quite shake, no matter how hard you try to get it out of your system? Well, if so, you will find what I'm about to say hard to believe:

It is almost certain that this 'reason' you keep reminding yourself of is <u>not</u> the real reason you are being held back.

I am *not* telling you your 'flaw' is necessarily all in your head. You may indeed have identified a genuine problem or shortcoming. Even if that is the case, however, I ask you to consider the possibility that something else may be going on here, something involving Faulter Ego sabotage.

The Faulter Ego gains control over you if it can allow a self-limiting belief to harden into an established narrative. We might reduce this to a formula for Faulter Ego disappointment:

Where a *self-limiting belief* is left unchallenged by a *real-world counter-action*, the result is an *established pattern of failure*. This in turn gives rise to a new set of *self-limiting beliefs*.

Clearly, time is a critical factor in this dynamic. A person's negative self-image feeds on the passage of *empty time*, by which I mean time in which no new data or experiences have been introduced to challenge that person's Faulter Ego beliefs. Self-limiting beliefs, in other words, are self-sustaining and self-reinforcing beliefs. The longer they go unchallenged, the more reliably they seem to represent the truth. This fact allows the Faulter Ego to lure us into a downward spiral of self-doubt and self-recrimination.

§

The Faulter Ego takes the wholly accurate fact that imperfection lies at the heart of the human condition and uses this fact to accuse you of being especially faulty.

Especially faulty.

The Faulter Ego

Have you spotted the covert egotism here? In some cases, finding fault with ourselves to an unhealthy degree can be an oh-so-subtle way of making ourselves feel *special, exceptional, different*. It takes a certain degree of self-absorption to pay such close attention to one's own perceived failings. Sometimes people will allow their Faulter Ego to design a truly lousy self-image for them *because a part of them fears that this is the only way they will ever have a strong, individual self-image at all*. Strange as it might sound, a really negative self-image can be more gratifying than a nondescript, unspectacularly positive one.

§

This brings us to the Faulter Ego error of perfectionism (an error it shares with the Exalter Ego). Some people refuse to forgive themselves for being human. Instead of accepting themselves warts and all, they try to airbrush the warts out of their self-image. This leads only to denial and an even greater fixation on the warts. It also commonly leads to fixation on *other* people's warts. The refusal to forgive oneself for being human gets deflected and projected onto others. Many perfectionists are extremely judgemental about other people. The one thing that always seems to fall outside the scope of this judgementalism, however, is ... the judgementalism itself. The Faulter Ego doesn't really care *which* target is chosen for fault-finding. The only thing that matters is that *someone somewhere* be criticised.

Sometimes the Faulter Ego's fault-finding habit goes even beyond targeting others. It can develop into a generalised pessimism about life and the world. This in turn leads the individual to visualise the future – their own, their family's, their friends', 'society's', 'the human race's' – as a site of utter chaos, conflict and misery. I had a client once who had spent years positively refusing to plan for his future on the basis that the world was going to hell in a handbasket. Why should I upgrade my qualifications when we're all going to be under water in a few years anyway? This was neither social concern, political idealism nor philosophical depth. It was an extreme Faulter Ego cop-out (with a little help from the Salter Ego).

§

The Faulter Ego, then, represents the pessimistic mindset. If you have an over-dominant Faulter Ego, it will try to persuade you that pessimism is the thinking person's realism. It will present you with a cartoon definition of optimism and assure you that only a fool would swear allegiance to it.

In their primer on emotional intelligence, *The EQ Edge*, Steven J. Stein and Howard E. Book address this topic well:

> [O]ptimism is very often misunderstood. It's not a tendency to believe that things are going to turn out for the best no matter what. That inclination reflects a weakness in our reality testing. It is also abdicating our part in the equation – risky behaviour that can blind us to the real challenges that must be faced and overcome. Nor is it the capacity to indulge in a perpetual pep talk – to keep repeating positive things about yourself. This too can lead you up a blind alley. Rather, it's the ability to stop thinking or saying destructive things about yourself and the world around you, especially when you're suffering personal setbacks. True optimism is a comprehensive and hopeful but realistic approach to daily living.*

---

* Steven J. Stein and Howard E. Book, *The EQ Edge: Emotional Intelligence and Your Success* (Mississauga, ON: John Wiley & Sons Canada, 2006), p. 232.

If you are prone to a pessimistic Faulter Ego mindset, it is *crucial* that you go beyond the treacherous double equation:

OPTIMISM = WISHFUL THINKING
PESSIMISM = REALISTIC THINKING

What a crock!

Contrary to popular belief, optimism and pessimism do not simply refer to what I expect to happen in the future. Rather they represent two distinctive *mental styles.*

The optimist may see the same outer situation that the pessimist sees, but (s)he will arrange the facts in a different manner in order to extract encouragement and possibility rather than loss of heart. To put this in shorthand, the optimist will look at a situation past, present or future through a hope-tinted lens, the pessimist through a fear-tinted one. Make no mistake: in each case a certain bias is at work. The question is, in which direction do I *choose* to bias my perception? Hope or fear? It is the premise of positive psychology that the hopeful bias is not merely the more pleasant option, *it is also the more useful one.*

How can this be so? No great mystery. If I allow my Faulter Ego to be in the ascendant as I look at 'Event X', it will be only too happy to impose a negative, fearful style of interpretation on that event. This style of interpretation will in turn affect my interaction with that event – *whether that event is in the past, present or future.* You don't need to be a quantum physicist to spot that the observer *will* affect the thing being observed.

§

Sometimes the best antidote to Faulter Ego paralysis is spontaneous *action.*

Maria was a worrier. She came to me on the threshold of a new job, which she was due to start in less than a month's time. This approaching date injected a note of urgency into our first session. For Maria was terrified that she had made a dreadful mistake in going for the position, let alone accepting it. 'It was a moment of madness. I was on my lunch break from the bank, having a panini and coffee in the café around the corner, when my eye was caught by an ad in the paper for a finance director with an insurance company. Just for the heck of it, I decided to throw my hat in the ring. I didn't dream I'd actually be called for interview.' But she did get called. And, by her own account, she played an absolute blinder in the interview, displaying a charm and self-assurance she didn't even realise she had. The reason? 'I knew I didn't have anything to lose, so I just said, "Feck it, I'm going to enjoy myself here."' When, to her shock, she actually got offered the job, her best friend and flatmate told her she'd be crazy not to take it. Without giving the matter further thought, she rang the company back and confirmed her acceptance of the position.

Here's what's interesting about Maria's story. The act of sending off her CV, doing the interview and accepting the job had happened too quickly for her Faulter Ego to intervene and block the process as it would normally have done. By *not* indulging in too much reflection, Maria had *spontaneously allowed deeds to overrule misgivings*, thereby breaking over ten years of complete professional stasis.

So far so remarkable. But now, with the start date on the new job looming, Maria was in emotional turmoil. Why? Because her Faulter Ego had had time to regroup. It now had convinced her that *this was too good to be true*. Maria's negative tape loops had kicked in with appalling ferocity. *It can't be this easy ... They're probably going to be really bad employers ... Staff turnover must be really high ... There must be some mistake ....* When I heard Maria going on in this vein, it was clear to me that her Faulter Ego was trying frantically to win her back to her habitual pessimism before it was too late, i.e. before the new situation gained sufficient *objective reality* to overrule Maria's *subjective pessimism.*

Rather bizarrely, Maria did not actually doubt that she was up to the responsibilities as outlined on the job specification. Her pessimism emanated rather from a barely articulated belief that life was something which never quite worked out the way we planned it. Indeed this verged at times on Altar Ego superstition, as Maria talked about being 'jinxed' whenever she wanted to do something constructive. The hard work of helping Maria to get beyond this ingrained pessimism began with getting her to see that it had grown not so much out of past experiences as out of her *interpretive style* in processing these past experiences. On several occasions when she was growing up, Maria had become excited about a certain prospect, such as a planned family holiday, being asked out by a boy she liked at school, making the school hockey team. When the hoped-for event did not transpire, she had unconsciously made a memo to self: *Don't get your hopes up in life, don't set yourself up for disappointment again.* It so happened that this memo was countersigned by her parents, whose philosophy in life was conservative and based on low expectations. Maria needed to withdraw allegiance from her parents' script.

§

Time for a personal confession here. The Faulter Ego cartoon woman who refuses to drive her car is someone I know pretty well. Her name is … Jane Downes! It took me *ages* to get my first provisional driver's licence. Every time I pictured myself at the wheel of a car, I would visualise an accident or a nasty incident with some bully on the road. I had received a grand total of one lesson when I was eighteen, but it had been a nightmare. The instructor kept telling me to 'engage the clutch'. I tried to explain to him that I had no idea what he was talking about. So he 'engaged the clutch' for me with his special instructor's pedal-board, and off we went. Except off we didn't go .... My steering was a joke, a circumstance not wholly unrelated to the fact that I was too scared to look at the road. By the time the hour was up, I was a nervous wreck. That the instructor seemed curiously unpushed about setting a date for our follow-up lesson was not lost on me.

Long story short, I failed to book further lessons for another year. Every time I contemplated applying for a provisional licence, the memory of that tragi-comic first lesson would short-circuit the idea. This was pure Faulter Ego pessimism. *One hour of stress had expanded into one year of fear.* Those sixty minutes behind the wheel had stamped on my brain an automatic association of 'driving' with 'disaster'. At no point did I even spot the pessimistic bias of my interpretations:

*   The reason I didn't drive well that day was that I don't have the makings of a competent driver. *(Faulter Ego generalisation: one incident is eternalised in order to establish <u>my inadequacy</u>.)*
*   The instructor was in no way to blame for my cluelessness at the wheel that day. *(Faulter Ego black-and-white thinking: no complicating factors are allowed intrude on the simple narrative of <u>my failure</u>.)*
*   The fear I felt at the wheel came from an intuition that I cannot be trusted behind the wheel of a car. *(Faulter Ego judgementalism: the possibility that the fear was a perfectly normal and common reaction of a first-time driver is not entertained.)*

My fear of driving had led me as an eighteen-year-old into a traumatic first lesson. Instead of asserting myself with the instructor as soon as he began giving me unintelligible instructions, I had clammed up and fulfilled the self-imposed prophecy: Thou Shalt Not Drive. So disempowered did I feel coming out of this 'lesson' – I use the term generously – that it became a settled narrative in my memory: The Time I Nearly Crashed the Car Over and Over Again. By failing to challenge that narrative with follow-up lessons (and a new instructor), I gave my Faulter Ego an easy victory. My pessimistic mindset was in overdrive* at every stage in this process:

- Going into the lesson (*I'm going to fail*)
- Coming out of the lesson (*I failed*)
- Fleeing the prospect of other lessons (*I don't want to fail again*)
- Giving myself a hard time for fleeing the prospect of other lessons (*I'm such a chicken*)

My Faulter Ego gave me a bad *preview* before the lesson, a bad *purview* at the wheel of the car during the lesson and a bad *review* after the lesson – all of which in turn led to an even worse *preview* of any future lessons. And so the wheel of pessimism turned.

I did eventually learn to drive. One day, when I was nineteen, my mother just said to me:

'Jane, you're going to drive. We're going into town right now to get your licence sorted out. When we get home, we're booking some lessons.'

'I can't do it, Mam.'

---

* Sorry.

'Yes you can. You're going to do it by doing it.'

She was right. *I did it by doing it.*
  Only for my mother's intervention, I would have fallen victim to my Faulter Ego's favourite ploy, mentioned at the start of this chapter: the self-fulfilling prophecy.

I expect not to drive ⟹ I end up not driving

The way I defeated this logic – and the only way I *could* defeat this logic – was to stop second-guessing myself and move from discourse to action.

§

I know of no more devastating way to defeat the Faulter Ego's attempts at sabotaging our progress than to follow this formula:

If you are in a pessimistic mindset, do not grant *objective reality* to your fear by acting upon it.

Instead, let the action you take create *an objective reality of its own* which will overrule your fear.

Arguing with your Faulter Ego will only get you so far. There comes a point when you have to allow the deed do the talking for you. If there is one thing the Faulter Ego loves, it is endless Hamlet-style agonising on the theme of *Can I Or Can't I?* If there is one thing it hates, it is to be overruled by the devastating simplicity of a constructive action. To misquote the poet T.S. Eliot, *between the thought and the deed lies the shadow.* The best way to defeat the tricks of the Faulter Ego is to allow your pessimistic thought to cast no shadow over your deed. *Do it not by thinking about doing it but by doing it.* This does not mean falling into the opposite extreme of Vaulter Ego recklessness, mind. It merely means recognising that there are times when the only thing that can overrule a Faulter Ego mindset is a positive deed.

§

Some Typical Faulter Ego Traps

- Giving in to defeatist thoughts about even the smallest things
- Focusing on possible pessimistic scenarios instead of real istically predicting outcomes
- Seeing every little challenge in life as a referendum on one's ultimate inner worth
- Leaving things to the last minute and getting in a panic
- Giving yourself a relentlessly negative review whilst over-estimating the abilities of those around you
- Not addressing problems (e.g. financial) as they arise but burying them and hoping they will go away
- Indulging in bitchy criticism of others as a way of alleviating your own self-doubts
- Focusing on what one is lacking rather than what one has to offer
- Feeling like an imposter as you go about your work
- Mistaking setbacks for failure

2

The Walter Ego

'All I Gotta Do Is Dream,
Dream, Dream, Dream…'

The psychological key to the Walter Ego mode is grandiosity. Instead of basing my self-regard on the things I do, on my relationships and on my inner character, I worship at the shrine of a fictional version of myself. This fictional Me lives in what a grammarian would call the subjunctive mood – a land of possibility, where the only limit on what can be achieved is the limit of my imagination. Happy to see me luxuriating in this fool's paradise of unchecked possibilities, the Walter Ego keeps me from facing the challenges of practical reality. It is forever getting me to make big plans and dream big dreams. Rarely, if ever, does it let me do anything constructive towards bringing any of these to fruition.

Behind such ineffectual grandiosity lie fear and insecurity. If I habitually build castles in the air, it is not because I feel like a queen or a king – it is precisely because deep down I feel like a royal nobody. So I build an airy realm where I can enthrone myself and reign supreme. In this way I suppress my true fears – of trying to achieve something and failing miserably and conspicuously; of setting an ambitious goal but losing myself immediately in the boredom or strenuousness of the first concrete steps; of subjecting a Big Idea to a slow, painful Reality Check.

A couple of years back I co-founded Emotional Intelligence Ireland, a company dedicated to taking the pioneering work from the 1980s of the American-born Israeli psychologist Dr Reuven Bar-On and applying it to work and life issues in an Irish context.* Our company has offered so-called 'EQ' (emotional quotient) evaluations, which have become an increasingly widespread tool in assessing the 'soft skills' necessary for balanced and emotionally integrated living and working. Amongst the key skills that an EQ assessment measures are:

* *Self-regard*, the capacity to respect oneself in an authentic way
* *Self-actualisation*, the capacity to fulfil one's potential
* *Reality testing*, the ability to size up a situation objectively

These three skills are precisely the skills which are most disastrously underdeveloped in someone in thrall to their Walter Ego. The link between the three is of course anything but arbitrary. If I do not have healthy self-regard, then I will not have confidence in my ability to achieve things in life. This may send my Faulter Ego underground, leading me into the Walter Ego temptation of seeking bogus validation in the land of dreamy wish fulfilment. By taking flight from reality into a fictional world of subjective and subjunctive fantasies, I trick myself into believing that my low self-regard is being healed and that my poor self-actualisation skills are not really so poor after all.

§

* Daniel Goleman, who is generally given credit for emotional intelligence, was in fact responsible for popularising the method rather than discovering it. His books are engagingly written and well worth getting your hands on.

It is telling that Walter Mitty, the patron saint of the Walter Ego, does not simply lose himself in daydreams. In each scenario he also makes sure to appoint himself top dog: heroic navy boat pilot, renowned surgeon, icy assassin, RAF pilot on a daredevil bombing mission. Only in these fantasies can Walter enjoy the psychological release that disinhibition brings. Only in grandiosity can he make up for the sad lack of grandeur in his real life. Only in fiction can he feel real.

The Walter Ego gets us in its clutches by heightening the contrast between our inner and our outer worlds. Recall our Walter Ego driver who daydreams about being rich and famous as a novelist. Note the massive *surplus of internal experience over external event.* The man visualises so many triumphant things going on – best-selling novel, ownership of Mediterranean island, visit of *Da Vinci Code* author Dan Browne – that it is easy to forget just how little is actually happening on the external plane. He is driving to the local library to get a book renewed. The very fact that the book has been renewed ten times already is yet another index of his failure to *get things done.* Not alone does this guy fail to write books, he even fails to *read* them! Day in, day out, he displaces his attention from the world around him to the effortlessly constructed worlds of his imagination. He may be physically present in the car, but he is psychologically absent. Hence the missed turn for the library. Instead of investing his cognitive and imaginative resources in the task at hand, he has been squandering his energy on the cheap thrills of fictional glory.

§

Am I dismissing all positive visualisation as a dead end? *No.* The whole school of neuro-linguistic programming (NLP), which I am an enthusiastic supporter of, stems from an insight into just how powerful a tool visualisation can be. If I can get a client to visualise a successful scenario and 'programme' their very nervous system to expect it, then I have helped them to take a useful step towards actualising that scenario. I frequently use NLP techniques to help clients experience a psychological shift away from low expectations and under-achievement. So why is it that the Walter Ego is not a sponsor of success? Surely it is giving us a free course in NLP by continually flooding us with positive visualisations?

Would that it were so simple. Positive visualisation is a *necessary but insufficient condition* of success. That is to say, it constitutes a really important *preliminary* step on the road. The Walter Ego is only too happy to have us take this step, as long as it can hoodwink us into thinking that this alone will suffice to get us places. In NLP, my client positively visualises a successful outcome so that it will energise them to take the all-important *action steps* that must follow. The point is not to get high on one positive visualisation after another. It is to release energy needed for the actualisation stage. The Walter Ego abuses visualisation as an end in itself, turning its victim into a visualisation junkie.

Perhaps you have spotted the intimate link here between the Faulter Ego and the Walter Ego? *Both use the power of visualisation to sabotage our progress.* The Faulter Ego uses negative visualisation, the Walter Ego positive. Each sees to it that we get stuck in visualisation mode without making any serious dent in the real world. The Faulter Ego stops us from challenging our negative visualisations with concrete action. It thereby secures negative outcomes for us. The Walter Ego stops us from challenging our positive visualisations with concrete action. It thereby secures equally negative outcomes for us. In both cases, the *imagined scenario* is granted complete supremacy over any real or potential scenario.

So why, you might ask, does the law of self-fulfilling prophecy apply to our Faulter Ego visualisations but not to our Walter Ego visualisations? Simple: pessimism goes with the downward flow of falling energy, of defeat. If I so desire, I can think negatively, sit back and watch things crumble around me without me stirring. Optimism, by contrast, goes against this downward flow – *as long as it is accompanied by effort.* A positive mental attitude *must* be supported by positive action if entropy is to be reversed. To put it bluntly, nothing works like good hard work.

Let me give a brief and simple illustration of this principle. Whenever I am having a low-energy day, I know immediately what the reason is: I have let a few days slip without getting some decent exercise in. My feet feel cold. My head has a heaviness which borders on the downright unpleasant. My body feels strangely constricted and under-oxygenated. I have two choices here: either I go with the downward flow of energy and get more and more sluggish, or I fight back by going for a jog or a swim. Isn't it an extraordinary physiological fact that the expenditure of energy through vigorous exercise doesn't deplete our energy stocks even further, but actually replenishes them? This replenishment is totally different to the synthetic, artificial, cut-price energy boost I might get out of a cup of coffee or a bar of chocolate. To gain real energy, I need to expend some. What better metaphor for achieving our goals in life?

Progress takes work. Entropy takes acquiescence.

They say if you want to get something done, you should ask a busy person. Ain't it the truth? Turn to someone with nothing but time on their hands, and chances are they will take an age to rev up into motion. The busy person, on the other hand, has the momentum of action on their side, so they are already up and moving in fourth or fifth gear. For that person, adding an extra task to their list will not involve them having to bring themselves from a state of inactivity into one of activity.

§

The Walter Ego hates verbs but loves verbiage. It is happy for you to think the thought, talk the talk, but never to walk the walk. To paraphrase Woody Allen, it makes you a failure – but only in actuality.

This brings us to another telling detail in the man-drives-to-the-library vignette. Not alone is our Walter Ego-dominated man not focused on the job at hand, which is getting to the library before closing time. Even his daydream has little or nothing to do with his avowed dream of writing books. What excites him is *the ego-trip of being a best-selling author.* This is another giveaway clue to the grandiosity which is really behind the Walter Ego. It tends to get us fixated on a dream not in terms of any intrinsic interest in that dream but in terms of the collateral pay-off which would come from achieving it. Thus our friend dreams not of writing great novels but of being acclaimed as a great novelist. This is a sure sign of a Walter Ego trip rather than a true vocation. If, for example, I dream of being an entrepreneur but have no real interest in the workings of industry or the minutiae of money, then this is probably a cheap Walter Ego fantasy rather than a genuine ambition. Whenever a client of mine waxes lyrical about a goal but evinces little or no interest in the *process* by which that goal might be achieved, alarm bells go off in my head: Walter Ego.

§

The Walter Ego likes to get you to write extravagant cheques to yourself, but hopes you will never stop and wonder why they keep bouncing at the bank of reality. Derek, a 27-year-old Dubliner, booked some interview coaching sessions with me. He was currently working in a bookshop, having returned from two years' temping as a waiter in Barcelona. He wanted to find a better-paying job, though he was adamant that it must be part-time. The reason was that Derek wanted 'head space' in order to follow his dream of becoming a successsful actor. He desperately wanted to escape the tedious world of wage labour for the glamour of showbusiness.

When we explored his acting dream at our first session, however, it quickly became evident that something was not right. 'This is going to sound full of it,' Derek said rather bashfully at one point, 'but I truly believe I am destined to be a star.' I asked him where this conviction came from. 'Because it is my burning ambition,' he said in an even more self-conscious way, 'and I am not taking no for an answer from the world.' The problem was that Derek had been not taking no for an answer for over five years now, and seemed no closer to his dream. When I asked him what actual steps he had taken to date towards getting into the acting business, he at once became defensive. 'Look, the right opportunities haven't come my way yet. I know how this looks from the outside, but I don't care what you think, I know this is going to happen.' Reassuring him that I admired his conviction, I nevertheless pressed the point. What had he actually done in the past five years to match his conviction with action? 'I have studied the greats.'

You're no doubt getting the picture. This young man, who was sensitive, intelligent and to all appearances genuinely full of potential in life, had come under the *X-Factor* spell of his Walter Ego. His strategy for becoming an acting star amounted to little more than Waiting for Something Marvelous to Happen. So pie-in-the-sky was this 'strategy' that he rarely even went for parts in amateur dramatic productions. This was a simple case of fear. To enter the realm of reality would be to taint his pristine dream and risk exposing it to an unbearable truth. Imagine being rejected even for bit parts in tiny local productions? That would be a step too far into Joey-from-*Friends* territory. Instead of either a) taking real steps to break into the acting business or b) taking stock and opting for a less glorious but perhaps more amenable goal in life, Derek was existing in the no-man's-land of unsatisfying temp jobs. The gulf between Dream and Everyday Reality was massive, and made all the more unbearable by the way in which colleagues, friends and family would ask him insinuatingly patronising questions about 'how the acting was going'.

It was clear that, barring some dramatic (!) change, Derek was never going to make his dream come true. This made it all the more important that I let him know that the tough questions I was asking him were not simply a coded hint that I thought his dream worthless. So I reassured him that I had no hidden, sceptical agenda: 'Look, Derek, I have absolutely no idea whether you can act or not. How could I? I've never seen you in performance. It's quite possible that you have the makings of a brilliant stage or screen star. By the same token, it's quite possible that you don't. But I am stone cold certain that the question will remain completely academic if you don't *put it to the test* again and again and again.' Derek listened and began dropping his defences a little. Initially he found it excruciating to have to subject his dream to critical appraisal. It took a lot of patient toing and froing before he would take on good faith my assurances that I was not trying to get him to give up his acting dream. I merely wanted to hear him tell his story.

Here was that story. After his Leaving Cert, Derek had done an Arts degree, majoring in Drama. He had been part of a very tight-knit group in college. Derek spoke with fond nostalgia of the collective sense of anticipation with which they had projected

great things for themselves in the future. He recalled one particularly symbolic moment shortly before the final year exams.
The class had gone out for a big dinner, after which they had
repaired to the pub. There, with a few drinks in their system, he
and five good friends had made a pact: they would meet up again
in that very pub as soon as one of them had starred in his or her
first international feature film. This pact took on a near-mystical
importance in Derek's mind. Something told him it would be in
his honour that they would be meeting again in that pub. The
thought of that reunion drink became totemic of his goal. The
drunken pact, which was probably soon forgotten by Derek's
five companions, had sponsored his absolute obsession with
becoming a movie star.

Derek had found leaving college quite traumatic. All of a sudden the mutually sustaining dreams of the class members had
evaporated, leaving the group splintered off into a collection of
individuals feeling the hard bite of the real world. Some left Ireland, most gave up drama, while a surprisingly small number
actually went into some form of acting work. None made an
international screen début. Having reminisced to me about his
college days, Derek now displayed obvious grief about this post-
college period. He had keenly felt the anti-climax of those
'quarter life crisis' years when he found himself no longer a student but just another nondescript citizen. The more keenly
Derek had registered this anti-climax, the more insistently his
Walter Ego had told him not to compromise on his dream. That
in itself was not necessarily a bad thing. Sometimes you do need
to hold your nerve when the outside world doesn't give a damn.
The trouble was that this defiance was also restraining Derek
from either taking proactive steps to realise that dream or
reassessing it altogether. When I asked Derek whether he might
be interested in using our sessions not simply to examine ways
of finding less frustrating temp work but also to take a good

look at his future plans, he initially put up strong resistance. It was obvious that his Walter Ego was terrified at having its sacred subjunctive space profaned by critical inquiry.

What happened in our fourth session was momentous for Derek. Having reassured him yet again that I did not have any prejudice against his going into acting, I was encouraged when he finally agreed to broaden the scope of our exploration to include his acting dream. I asked Derek to tell me what had attracted him to acting in the first place. He took me back once again to his college days and the camaraderie of the group – a camaraderie which had been so deliciously spiced up by a hint of competitiveness and ambition. He told me about some of the characters in the class and shared some of the anecdotes which had really stuck with him. Then he went on to the (very) few amateur dramatic productions he had taken part in since leaving college five years ago. Finally he talked about how much he would enjoy being a movie star – the lifestyle, the kudos and, yes, the money.

I was struck by how much he talked about *being an actor* and how little about *the act of acting*. I shared my puzzlement on this score with him. Extraordinarily, tears welled up in his eyes. They were, it turned out, tears of realisation, recognition and relief. My comment had expressed a thought which he *had not permitted to come to consciousness* for at least five years. What was that taboo thought? *That he didn't really enjoy acting.* His dreams of becoming a movie star centred on three things: making good on the delicious sense of possibility he had tasted during his college years, proving himself to his former college classmates and *being special.* Derek, it turned out, had been using acting as an escape clause from the challenges of life and work. He had a deep-seated need to stand out from the crowd, for the simple reason that he feared being thought ordinary. His self-regard being low, he had handed over his plight to his Walter Ego, which was more than happy to slip him a promissory note: *One day, my lad, you'll be a star and everyone will see how special you are.* Acting just happened to be the vehicle for this hollow promise.

Low self-regard, as we established in the last chapter, is the province of the Faulter Ego. We might say that the Walter Ego likes to take up where the Faulter Ego leaves off. If, like Derek, I feel insecure and suffer from low self-esteem, I will be at risk of being tempted *away from* the hard but necessary work of self-development in those areas and *in the direction of* the banal extraordinariness of the Walter Ego's never-never-land. *The Walter Ego distracts us from the crisis laid by the Faulter Ego.*

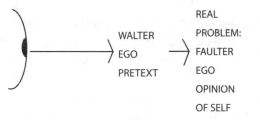

It was a huge step for Derek to see that his Walter Ego had been hiding his true master – the Faulter Ego. As soon as this was brought out into the open, he was able to displace his Walter Ego fixation and start renegotiating his relationship with his Faulter Ego. Concretely, this meant working on the sources of his low self-esteem and the resultant dreams of grandiosity and specialness. Along with this deepening of Derek's self-awareness came a fresh look at his career options. We soon found that he was far from a blank slate when it came to talents, aptitudes and interests. Having come to the rather startling recognition that acting was in fact a red herring, he was now free to look at other, more authentic options. In the end, he settled on radio journalism as his preferred avenue. It allowed him to develop an interest in current affairs which had been quietly simmering away since college. This time round, he didn't make any grand announcement. He just put the head down in good Halter Ego fashion and got himself sorted with a course in broadcast journalism in the UK.

§

One of the most horrible errors into which the Walter Ego can lead us is the assumption that others can magically see how utterly special we really are. This I call

THE SPECIAL TREATMENT FALLACY:

There is something so special about me that different, kinder, gentler rules apply to me than to everyone else.

When the world does not indulge this spoiled-child fantasy, the reaction can be one of deep resentment and confusion.

I remember one client – we shall call her Clare – showing me the CV which she had recently submitted for a pretty high-level admin position in television. She simply couldn't understand why she hadn't been called for interview. One look at the CV, and the mystery evaporated. It turned out that Clare had absolutely no experience in the media sector. In fact, the only significant work experience she had to her name was working as a receptionist! When I pointed this out to her, she responded in a tone of pained protest:

'But anyone who knows me will tell you that I can take to a new task like a duck to water!'

'That may well be true, Clare, but how on earth do you expect an employer to know this? Telepathy?'

'No, but everyone knows there's more to life than a bloody CV.'

'Sure. It's an awful thing to have to reduce yourself to a few items on a sheet of paper. But like it or not, that's how employers filter job applications. You've got to play the game.'

'Well, I know I would have been brilliant at this job.'

'How can you be so sure? What exactly did the job entail?'

'Working in TV.'

'Doing what?'

'Oh I would have picked up the specifics no problem once I got stuck in.'

This otherwise engaging and bright young lady was here operating according to the Walter Ego equation:

$$SUBJECTIVE = OBJECTIVE$$

It is enough for me to feel I am right for this job for this job to be right for me. Instead of honest and healthy self-assessment, all Clare could engage in was vague self-inflation. Instead of taking constructive steps towards a goal, she could only indulge in rhetoric. And instead of a strategy she had a wishy-washy Walter Ego aspiration.

The CV is a cruel instrument. It forces us to put down in black and white what we have achieved career-wise, what qualifications and training we have attained and what experience we have that might be relevant to the current job. In one sense, this really is an obscene reduction of our human complexity. Is it not almost offensive to honour such a document with the title *Curriculum Vitae* (*Course of Life*)? On this point, I sympathised with Clare as far as her argument went. She was one of many clients I had met who deplored the CV mentality because they saw it as modern culture's way of reducing us to the level of soulless function and utility. But it was quite apparent that with Clare something else was going on. Her Walter Ego was hijacking a legitimate humanistic critique of the CV and using it to protect her own illusions. The CV offered a litmus test that exposed the total drift of Clare's past few years. What Clare's Walter Ego really loathed about having to put together a CV was that it left so little wriggle room for her to make excuses for her lack of proactivity and dynamism. It asked her for the very things which are most terrifying to anyone dominated by their Walter Ego: *verbs*. To be forced to lay out one's external achievements without waffle or fudge is a brutal assignment for anyone who has been on the run from those criteria for a long time. And make no mistake, an experienced employer, HR manager or recruiter can spot CV padding a mile away. The rich interior spaces of subjective experience are ruthlessly pushed aside in favour of a more one-dimensional question: what have you actually *done*? I repeat: from a broad human point of view this is indeed an appallingly narrow way to look at a person's life. However, if truth be told, it is also a clinically effective method of sorting wheat from chaff when a batch of job applications comes in the mailbox.

I had to point out to Clare that the impression given by her CV – that she was signally unsuited to the job being advertised – was *accurate*. She needed to have this fact brought home to her gently, but firmly. She was *suffering* when she first came to me – from the humiliating rejection of a potential employer, from the barely acknowledged realisation that she was going nowhere fast in terms of career and from the deep fear she had of a world that treated her as just another person. No favours, no indulgences, no special treatment.

What was interesting here was that Clare, for the first time in her life, had at least shown *some* interest in self-advancement. But she had aimed much *too* high much *too* soon, and had fallen flat on her face. Like most Walter Ego individuals she was, underneath the surface bravura, awfully thin-skinned. And her Walter Ego was now using her failure to get called for interview as evidence that she would be better off reverting to her prior pattern of simply waiting for something great to fall into her lap.

Providentially, Clare's self-esteem had taken such a knock that she was now finding it increasingly difficult to keep falling for the Walter Ego's game. She was only half-believing its assurances that everything was going swimmingly. The other half of her was beginning to connect with her Faulter Ego, that deeper, hitherto hidden dread she had of being inadequate for the tasks of life. Clare was, in brief, ready to start moving beyond the control of her Walter Ego. My hope was that she would soon be ready, like Derek, to start dealing head-on with the lies of her Faulter Ego.

Before things could progress on either front, however, Clare needed to have the *personal sting* taken out of her rejection by the TV company. Not alone did it do her no good to read the incident as a personal insult, it was also important that she learn to *look at herself a lot more impersonally*. The great Danish philosopher, Søren Kierkegaard, once wrote that most people are subjective towards themselves but objective towards others – whereas the real trick in life is to become objective towards ourselves and subjective towards others. I suggested to Clare that she try out a technique I had developed under inspiration from Kierkegaard's luminous insight. I call it the Third Person Technique. Put simply, the technique involves thinking, talking and writing about yourself not as an 'I' but as a 'he' or 'she'. Thus for instance:

> *Jane is sitting at her laptop in the office, typing away at her new book. Beside her is a cup of coffee, which she sips from time to time. She is explaining how the Third Person Technique works ....*

And so forth. Pretty banal stuff, eh? Yet you would be amazed how effectively this simple linguistic technique can train us into the mental habit of *seeing ourselves as others might see us*. It coaxes us out of the habit of special pleading on our own behalf. It teaches us to apply the same standards to ourselves that we would apply to others.

Once Clare started experimenting with this technique of suspending her ego-identification, a space was cleared for her to be more objective about herself without feeling threatened by the coldness of that objectivity. Here is one example of a Third Person exercise she did one evening:

> This afternoon, Clare went into town and wandered around the shops. She enjoyed the hustle and bustle of town, it made her feel part of something. A little less lonely. She usually did this when the weekend was beginning to drag out. It was a way of avoiding chores and boredom.

This showed a kind of novelist's awareness on Clare's part of her activities. She actually *enjoyed* being able to spot her own 'erroneous zones' at a distance. There was not a trace of defensiveness about her self-criticism. Taking a break from the world of 'me, myself and I', she suddenly became remarkably clear-eyed about herself.

I also encouraged Clare to try a related technique: the First Person Technique. In Clare's case, this involved talking from the point of view of the recruitment manager of the TV company which had rejected her application. Clare found this exercise in being subjective on behalf of a perceived antagonist tremendously liberating. Here is what she wrote:

I don't think Clare is a serious candidate. She has no experience, no training, and gives us no evidence whatsoever that she is applying for this position on anything but a whim. Why should we waste our time on a candidate with such an irrelevant CV?

The beauty of this exercise was that, *for the minute or two that she was playing the role of the recruitment manager*, Clare actually agreed with every word she* said! She *saw* how absurd her job application had been. She *saw* how disastrously wrong she would have been in the job. She *saw* how insultingly poor her CV was. She *saw* that there was an almost pleasing *impersonality* in the process by which the decision against her was taken. She found it impossible to continue harbouring her grudge against the company.

These simple exercises in Third Person and First Person role-reversal transformed Clare's outlook. At one point she even got a kick out of satirising her earlier self's Walter Ego assumption that she should be given a special pass by the world. She did this by playing the role of the recruitment manager *as the old Clare had originally assumed she would be*:

Clare's CV is really fascinating. She hasn't got a whole lot of work experience, which suggests that she is a really deep and thoughtful person. I have a funny feeling from the font she's using that she's in possession of huge talents which

---

* Interestingly, Clare assumed that the recruitment manager in question was female.

just haven't been brought to the surface yet. And there's something about her quirky photo that leads me to believe she's kinda special. Maybe I'm wrong, but I think we should grab Clare before someone else gets her!

Being able to laugh at oneself is a great gift – in fact, it is a highly refined form of Third Person thinking. As Clare found out to her benefit, there are two fundamentally different ways of looking at oneself: from the inside out and the outside in. If you've ever watched yourself in a home movie, you'll know what I'm talking about. It can be quite a shock to relive the scene, only this time from outside your skin. Many people find it excruciating, even worse than hearing their voice back on tape. If someone is dominated by their Walter Ego, then they need to be shown that objectivity is nothing to be frightened of. This will only happen if they first become aware of the pain they are causing themselves by allowing their subjective side to lose its moorings in real experience. The Walter Ego's vacuous, fantasy-spinning, faux-grandiose self is a parody of that rich interior subjectivity which deepens life and allows us to engage authentically with the outside world. The more objective you are, the more you will flourish subjectively. It's not a zero sum game.

§

Many people who have an out-of-control Walter Ego are addicted to self-help books, motivational seminars and other such phenomena. If they are such hopeless underachievers, why is it that they are so attracted to the literature of success? Simple. Most self-help literature concentrates on things like attitude, can-do mentality and optimism. These are indeed crucial components of success. However, they are only components. They are never enough on their own.

By way of example, let's return to the act of driving a car. Imagine someone is determined to learn how to drive. They buy motivational books which tell them all the right things: visualise success, tell yourself you can do it, imagine all the benefits which will flow from learning how to drive, work on the negative tape loop which is holding you back. Now imagine a person doing all this *but nothing else*. They still won't have learned how to drive. They still won't have taken a single step *specific to the art of driving*. They will have spent all their time *circling around the task* without ever actually engaging in it.

Such people are stuck in what I call *about*-mode. Instead of ever actually getting round to doing X, they content themselves with just thinking *about* it, talking *about* it, psyching themselves up *about* it. In other words, they get the *mood music* right, but totally neglect the *deed*. It's like Rocky Balboa listening to *Eye of the Tiger* but not getting up off his backside to go out and train for the fight. Or Harry Potter pepping himself up with can-do spells but failing to turn up for the Quidditch match. I am reminded here of a classic wisecrack made by comedian (and Father Dougal actor) Ardal O'Hanlon when he was compering a TV stand-up comedy contest a few years ago. He asked the judges beforehand what they were looking for in a contestant. One judge waffled on about having a go-for-it attitude and not taking any prisoners. Should contestants also try to be funny? wondered Ardal. Ouch.

The Walter Ego will often try to get us hooked on self-help literature because it is by and large *the literature of motivational mood music*. Our Walter Ego bluff is called when the time comes for us to actually move from general attitude to detailed action (in the case of our wannabe driver – how to control the gears, fill the tank, judge traffic, etc.). I have met so many people who love to give themselves a rush of adrenalin just thinking about achieving something. But this is often just *about*-adrenalin –

adrenalin released at a safe distance from the deed itself. Fearing to get their hands dirty, these people confine themselves to mood music – and consign themselves to failure.

It is also worth noting that the Walter Ego does not always work by getting us hooked on just one big dream which never seems to go anywhere. It can also manifest itself in dilettantism – the phenomenon of being jack of all trades and master of none, of having lots of irons in the fire but not one that is red hot, of drifting from one half-arsed possibility to the next. This type of individual is afraid to place *limits* on themselves – the kinds of limits that make it possible to really hone one's talents in one particular sphere.

§

Lauren was a 26-year-old secondary school teacher who, as she made it clear to me in her introductory email, detested her job. She knew she was temperamentally unsuited to teaching, but had gone and done the H.Dip. for want of any better alternative. She had graduated from college four years before that with a 2:2 Arts degree.

Lauren had a vague sense that she must be destined for some-thing more than *this*. Nearly every evening she would stop off at her local DVD library and take out a movie, often two. Her life outside of school consisted of going home to the small flat she was renting, putting on some food and turning her room into a private mini-cinema. She needed to escape into the fic-tional worlds of these films just to 'stay sane'. So humdrum and soul-destroying did she find her working life – 'I'm literally back at school and it feels like the resumption of a prison sentence' – that she needed a film fix to even out the balance between bore-dom and excitement.

But of course the excitement of watching a film is a pale, pas-sive and vicarious shadow of the excitement of having a life.

Bingeing on DVDs was the only way Lauren knew of clinging on to a sense of life's grandeur. For at least a couple of hours every evening, she could feel the energy of adventure, romance and intrigue pulse through her system.

If only she could take some of the time and energy she was putting into watching films and channel it into activities in the real world. But she hated the real world. It was the site of her 'crucifixion', as she put it herself. By her own admission, her teaching was deteriorating. Amongst the aggravating factors in her inability to perform effectively in the classroom was the insomnia which had become a bigger and bigger problem over the past year. Lauren's low energy and poor mood were obviously being picked up by her students. Class discipline had been breaking down. It turned out that several nights a week Lauren would wake up in the early hours after maybe just an hour or two of sleep. She would feel an irresistible urge to get up, make a strong coffee and settle down in front of the telly for another movie. Sometimes she even rented out *three* movies a night to have a third to fall back on in case of 2 a.m. insomnia. Not surprisingly, her body clock was totally out of sync with her work routine.

Lauren was typical of the Walter Ego-dominated personality in that her everyday life felt unreal and devoid of authenticity while her fantasy life felt like the only site of meaningful experiences. When she was at school, her body and mind went numb. She was on autopilot. But when she was engrossed in a good film, she would find herself accessing all those emotions that were being blocked by the need to present a stable and equable daytime persona to her students and colleagues. She would get teary in the sad scenes, joyous in the uplifting ones and pumped with adrenalin in the exciting ones. Significantly enough, it was inspirational films which attracted Lauren the most. Tales of the underdog fulfilling a dream against the odds. Tales of extraordinary courage under pressure. Tales of heroic nobility in the face of mistreatment and injustice. Where James Thurber's Walter Mitty escapes dull reality by generating his own heroic narratives (albeit narratives modelled on adventure story clichés), Lauren was going a step further into passive fantasy by 'disappearing' into ready-made narratives. Obviously, she needed to make some changes, and big time.

First off, she agreed to start by cutting her weekly ration of DVDs down to just one midweek movie. She resisted this idea at first, but ultimately agreed to the plan. Next, we took stock of her job situation. It was clear that teaching was not for her. She had never really had any interest in it as a vocation. It gave her no satisfaction to face a group of teenage students every day and confront their open apathy. By her own admission, she was a 'charisma-free zone' in the classroom. The only reason she had done the H.Dip. was that the hours were relatively humane and the holidays good. I had no reason not to take Lauren's professional self-assessment at face value. Her accounts of classroom chaos were hardly faked. She even showed me scraps of paper she had confiscated from students. They bore extremely offensive comments about, and cartoons of, *her*. Such items indicated a serious lack of respect.

It was important to disenthrall Lauren from her escapist Walter Ego way of living (or half-living). She needed to take control of her life again, starting with her career. I carried out a 'Signature Strengths' assessment on Lauren. Developed by the 'positive psychology' pioneer Martin Seligman, the Signature Strengths assessment seeks first to identify those areas in which a person excels and then to find career possibilities that might match those strengths.* To the surprise of neither Lauren nor

---

* Go to http://www.authentichappiness.sas.upenn.edu/Default.aspx and do a Brief Strengths Test online! Also check out Chapter 9 of Seligman's book, *Authentic Happiness: Using the New Positive Psychology to Realize Your Potential for Lasting Fulfillment* (London: Nicholas Brealey, 2002).

myself, the results of the Signature Strengths assessment confirmed just how unsuitable she was to teaching. Put simply, classroom teaching played to none of her strengths: independence, creative strategising, problem-solving and solo project work. So what might provide a better 'fit' for these skills?

The answer emerged gloriously within a couple of sessions: *entrepreneurship*. Lauren was like a caged bird in the classroom, unable to spread her wings. She had zip-all drive as a teacher, and had been dissipating all her considerable energy at home by going into couch potato mode. We looked at how she might go about setting up her own business. She began to research the area of event management, specifically wedding planning. It turned out that she had a contact who worked in the field and had generously remarked a while back that Lauren would be a natural at it herself. At Lauren's request, this contact met her for a coffee and took her through some of the ins and outs of wedding planning. I could tell from Lauren's face at our next session that she was totally energised by what she was discovering. We agreed that it would be unfeasible for Lauren to just drop out of her teaching job and try to set up her own business from scratch. Instead, we developed a more gradualist approach: she would keep up the day job for the time being and use her weekends to accompany her wedding planner contact to weddings, where she would get some work experience for a reduced wage. This proved to be an invaluable first step, for it grounded Lauren's dream in the minutiae of event planning. By moving quickly into 'concrete operations', she avoided the Walter Ego trap of getting stuck in *about*-mode.

As I had hoped, Lauren found her brain sparking with ideas on how to improve her contact's wedding planner business. So dynamic and creative were her suggestions that within six months her contact (and now of course part-time boss) offered to bring her in on the company as a junior partner. Lauren gracefully thanked her for the high compliment, but declined the invitation. She was determined to set up on her own. Independence was, after all, her single greatest signature strength.

In the end, Lauren moved to Scotland, where she had family, and set up her own events planning company. She developed innovative ways of meeting the needs of clients for their wedding day. Typically things can be painfully slow in the start-up phase of a small business. For Lauren, however, her new enterprise did a roaring trade almost from day one. Within a month she was turning customers away, as word of mouth spread as to how efficient, value-for-money and original her services were. Within just over half a year, Lauren had gone from being a depressed, lonely and frustrated DVD addict who was falling to pieces in her job to a successful entrepreneur running her own business and thriving on both a professional and a personal level. The last I heard from her, in an email a few months ago, she had gotten engaged to a young man she had met while organising a wedding bash! You won't believe what *he* does for a living …. That's right – he's a secondary school teacher. Talk about yin and yang!

Looking back, Lauren is able to see that *her unhappiness in the classroom was actually her salvation.* It was this unhappiness that finally forced her to outgrow her narcotic Walter Ego lifestyle and rejoin the human race. Rarely have I seen such a startlingly fast turnaround in a person's fortunes as in the case of Lauren. And rarely have I taken such pleasure in watching a client conquer their Walter Ego. This breakthrough was possible because Lauren was fundamentally very healthy. Her flight into the insanity of DVD addiction was her Walter Ego's inappropriate response to the fact that she had chosen the wrong career. Teaching is *way* too important to be left to people who are temperamentally unsuited to it. It should *never, ever* be considered a soft or default option.

Lauren's ultimate defeat of her Walter Ego demonstrated that
she had *infinitely* more to live for than the hollow substitute
offered by Hollywood fantasies.

§

Some Typical Walter Ego Traps

- Responding to less-than-satisfactory situations with fantasy solutions
- Wildly overestimating your talents in a given field
- Being inspired by successful role models but filtering out any complications in the story of their rise to the top
- Turning to novels, films and TV programmes for meaning in life
- Fantasising about the glory of some great achievement while not doing a tap of work to achieve it
- Adopting an all-or-nothing attitude to success
- Lack of basic reality testing and goal setting
- Not attending to details of daily living (financial, practical, etc.)

3

The Halter Ego

'Aim low, aim low,
It's off to work we go'

One of my favourite books as a little girl was Anna Sewell's *Black Beauty*. It must have been this bewitching story of a sensitive and intelligent horse's trials, tribulations and eventual triumph that sensitised me to get really upset one day in town. I saw a horse drawing a tourist carriage down the street. The poor creature looked thin and exhausted but what distressed me most were the halter and blinkers in which it was harnessed. How horrible to be blinded to the life going on around! How cruel to be forced into a route of your master's choosing! How unthinkable to have your room for manoeuvre reduced to zilch! Being a bolshie little seven-year-old, I raised the issue with my teacher in school the next day. She reassured me that the halter and blinkers were there for the horse's own good. The halter kept the horse safe from accidents, while the blinkers protected it from getting startled by sudden movements. I wasn't having any of the teacher's explanation however. It was quite obvious to me that the real point of these monstrous contraptions was to stop the animal from being tempted to run away. Only by keeping it unaware of the big world around it, I reasoned, could you keep it in such miserable slavery.

It is in honour of that horse, now presumably long since gone where all the good horsies go, that I have given the name *Halter Ego* to our tendency to accept excessive limits on our choices in life.

I must stress the word *excessive* here. Life, alas, is full of real limits. It is not, despite the hippy urgings of the Walter Ego, an arena of effortless wish-fulfilment. The Halter Ego takes this truth and distorts it beyond recognition by making it fearful and all-encompassing. According to the Halter Ego's lights, the only way to *be* safe in this life is to *play* safe in every department of it. Ironically, this philosophy can be an extremely dangerous one to follow.

One more cautionary note about the appropriate and inappropriate recognition of real-life limits is in order. It is a sad and outrageous fact that for the overwhelming majority of human beings on earth at this time, the limits on their freedom *are* excessively real. For millions and millions of people, brute economics dictate that the only thing keeping body and soul together will be back-breaking and soul-destroying labour. What the average person in Burma, Brazil or Burundi needs is not coaching but emancipation. The drudgery and powerlessness of their lives are due not to their individual lack of dynamism in shaping their own destiny but to their appalling lack of *structural* status as economic and political agents. They are not victims of the Halter Ego, they are victims of the Halter which the system has strapped on them. Some rather smug New Age writers would have us believe that these unfortunate people's fundamental problem is 'scarcity consciousness'. It is not. It is scarcity – and on such a formidable scale that the self-appointed gurus who gloss over it so blithely would lose their reason if they had to experience it personally for twenty-four hours.

So, out of basic human decency, let's be careful here how we talk about the Halter Ego. When I use that phrase in a career context, I am thinking very concretely of that body of citizenry in the West which enjoys the unusual privilege of having at least *some* degree of *economic and personal room for manoeuvre.* To *have* this freedom and not *enjoy* it is a tragedy. A critique of the Halter Ego mentality can*not* be levelled at all those excluded from the minimal economic security enjoyed by most of us in the West. All over the world, there are mothers and fathers sacrificing their every waking hour just to put food in their children's bellies. They are heroes.

And speaking of heroes, why were there no life coaches for our parents' or grandparents' generation? Because back then it was generally assumed that one had to find *one* trade or profession and *cling on for dear life.* What dictated one's entry into the labour market was not choice, ambition or vocation but *fear* and *social expectation.* The outlook of the average citizen thirty or more years ago *corresponded to the reality of their world at that time.* If they had scarcity consciousness, it was because, like most humans still living around the world, they were conscious of an all-too-real scarcity of options in the socio-economic sphere. They were more often than not *right* to feel fearful about the future, *right* to play it safe, *right* to value holding down a job above deeper quality-of-life considerations. They did not have the luxury of approaching their career in a more creative way. The relative prosperity of the present generation is built in no small part on the fact that earlier generations met the challenge of putting on halters and *doing one thing as well as they could.*

Perhaps you grew up in the world I am describing? If so, then you will probably be keenly aware of just how much the world has changed. The assumption that playing it safe is the safest option *no longer corresponds to the real world.* It is a cultural hangover from a bygone era. The new economy, with its increased short-termism, casualisation and pace of change positively demands fluidity and flexibility on a hitherto unimaginable scale. Do we respond to this new fluidity as a threat or as an opportunity? The choice is ours.

§

Patrick had recently retired after twenty-seven years working in an academic library. He came across almost as a caricature of your stereotypical librarian. Slightly pedantic in manner and anxious at all times to be correct and in control, he had thoroughly internalised his working environment. He even spoke in the near-whisper appropriate to a library ambience. When I offered him a cuppa to kick off our first session, the fact that he wanted it 'weak, with lots of milk and no sugar' felt kind of symbolic.

Having given a quarter of a century of his life to the cataloguing and delivery of books that other people needed to read, Patrick now found himself completely alienated from life outside the library. The shock of retirement was still raw when he came along for his first coaching session. He felt deeply upset by the manner in which his colleagues and employers had handled his departure. They threw a nice send-off party in his honour, gave him a mantlepiece clock (how original) and told him not to be a stranger. He took them at their word, dropping in a couple of times a week to say hello. At first, everyone was friendly. Then the friendliness turned to politeness. Within a fortnight, Patrick found himself being received with barely concealed irritation.

It was only then that the reality hit him: *it's over*. A wave of panic and grief hit him, as he went into vocational cold turkey alone in the small suburban house he had inherited from his mother. His neglect of the world outside of work was coming back to haunt him. He felt savagely betrayed. With real hurt in his face, he described to me how he had looked on his fellow library staff as nothing less than a surrogate family. So many years had passed in the job that it had taken on the character of a permanent way of life, a stable comfort zone, a safe world. Now he was having to face the appalling reality that he had been missing all these years: this was a job, not a life. The friendliness of his colleagues, including those younger staff whom he had put a lot of time into mentoring, had never been anything other than functional, context-specific, impersonal even. These people just happened to work in the same place as Patrick. Now that he no longer worked there himself, he no longer featured in their hearts and minds.

This was a rude awakening indeed. Suddenly Patrick found himself forced to revise his assessment of the value of his work in the library over the previous twenty-seven years. The thought that tormented him most of all was that he had spent all this time serving a function that could just as easily have been served by someone else. He had been a cypher. Where previously the impersonal nature of his tasks had given him a certain psychological security, it now turned on him, mocking him for having loaded it with such personal meaning. This is a common problem for people who invest excessive emotional energy into becoming the model employee. The very conscientiousness which turns them into such a reliable pair of hands at work can, if not balanced by other interests and outlets, lead to an excessive inhibition of authentic personality. The *self* disappears gradually behind the *work persona*. Forgetting that this mask I put on when I first started working here is only ever a mask, a fiction, a role, I lose contact with the wellsprings of spontaneity, individuality and integrity.

At Patrick's first coaching session, it was obvious that he had lost the plot that had been sustaining him all these years. His Halter Ego had lured him into a totally predictable routine.

With that routine now gone, he felt completely disoriented. He was going through withdrawal symptoms, having not a clue what to do with all the time he had on his hands. When he told me he had started a project at home, I was delighted. When he explained that said project involved cataloguing his own personal library by means of a filing cabinet and a clear, user-friendly index card system, my heart sank.

Patrick was now sixty-five years of age. A bachelor with no close friends to speak of, he was convinced his life was over. He was going through nothing less than a full-blown existential crisis.

Patrick managed to turn things around, but not until he had been brought to the realisation that the pain he was experiencing was due to the fact that he was *waking up*. The sand in the hour-glass had run out on his Halter Ego comfort zone. Having long ago bought into the myth that the world would stop turning if he missed a day at work, he was now having his head ruthlessly purged of that myth. This, I helped him recognise, was a *necessary process* which had to be gone through if there was to be any hope of creating a more compelling future for himself. The almost clinical behaviour of his former colleagues could now be reframed as a painful but ultimately helpful wake-up call: *Leave this place behind and get on with the rest of your life, for goodness' sake!* Patrick was being pressed into a much more accurate picture of where he was and where he needed to go – see diagram on opposite page.

Patrick learned to put his immersion in the world of books to constructive and social use by getting involved in adult literacy. We worked together to brainstorm his transferable skills, work motivators and his new value system. From this we decided adult literacy work could potentially suit him really well. He put his name down for a course on teaching basic literacy to adult learners. At a very early stage in the course, he had a chance to

The Halter Ego

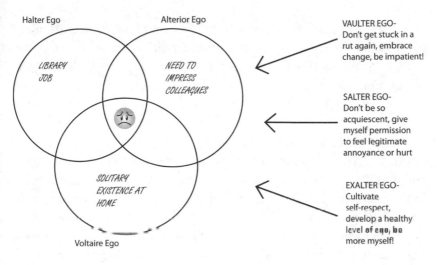

Halter Ego

LIBRARY JOB

Alterior Ego

NEED TO IMPRESS COLLEAGUES

SOLITARY EXISTENCE AT HOME

Voltaire Ego

VAULTER EGO- Don't get stuck in a rut again, embrace change, be impatient!

SALTER EGO- Don't be so acquiescent, give myself permission to feel legitimate annoyance or hurt

EXALTER EGO- Cultivate self-respect, develop a healthy level of ego, be more myself!

do some actual teaching practice. He was absolutely charmed by the experience! Helping others overcome a massive barrier in their lives also had an interesting side effect: it reawakened dormant feelings which had been associated with his library job. For many years he had found the attitude of some of the academics and students towards him condescending and snobbish. 'Behind their surface politeness I often picked up a kind of quiet contempt for someone like me, a lowly functionary.' Mr Weak Tea was getting his bite back! The stories that some of his students were now telling him about people's insensitivity towards illiteracy gave him real fire in his belly to empower them with the gift of reading and writing. In the space of just a couple of months, Patrick went from seeing his retirement as a humiliating defeat to embracing it as a long-overdue release from his Halter Ego prison. Empowered by his new role of empowering others, he went from a space of poor self-esteem to one of rejuvenation and self-confidence. Instead of spending the rest of his life getting lost in self-recrimination for what he now saw as wasted years, he took the instinctive support for the underdog which those years had nurtured in him and put it to good use.

Having experienced low self-confidence and based his workaday personality on institutionalised timidity, he was now able to spot such characteristics in others with uncanny intuition – a gift which made him a brilliant and popular teacher.

§

Most people still treat their career like a train journey. You purchase the ticket and climb aboard. The train is scheduled to travel down one specific track. The moment you get on the train, both route and destination are already decided. Of course you have the option of getting off at a station along the way, but if you do so then your options are still very limited: either stay in that town, wait for the next train or catch a connecting train to a different destination.

In today's economy, this is sheer lunacy. A far more useful metaphor for embarking on a career is driving your own car. You are no longer the passive passenger whose one and only job is to buy a ticket and turn up on time. You are now the *decision-maker* at the wheel. Sure, there are still limits and parameters, such as the basic rules of the road and the need for fuel, but the way you map the world in your head is completely different. Instead of commuting back and forth on a single track, you have the freedom to consider alternative routes and alternative directions. Your ability as a driver will require you to read the road map carefully. You have both the privilege and the pressure of being master of your course.

But it gets better, for we need to add a nicely surreal detail: *The car you are driving doesn't just take you down established roads, it has the special feature of being able to build a new road wherever you drive.*

The Halter Ego tells you that driving is dangerous. Look at all the road fatalities! It tells you that you can't relax when you're driving. How much less stressful to place all the responsibility on the shoulders of an anonymous train driver. That way you can sit back and enjoy the ride. If you absolutely insist on going by car, the Halter Ego will give you a phoney map that shows only a tiny fraction of the roads available to you, never mind the new roads you could be opening up for yourself. If you somehow manage to discover the double secret that your map is faulty and that new routes can be created, your Halter Ego will enlist your Faulter Ego in a desperate attempt to convince you that someone as unspecial as *you* could never make a competent driver of such a special car.

§

The Walter Ego seduces us with empty possibilities that serve to distract us from the real coordinates of our situation. The Halter Ego, by contrast, doesn't want us even *thinking* about possibilities. One of the first things I like to gauge when I meet a new client is their attitude to this notion of 'possibility'. Do they see life as basically open or closed? Do they see themselves as creators or followers? Which do they prize more: adventure or security? If you were to ask me which Ego tendency wreaks more havoc in people's lives, the Walter Ego or the Halter Ego, I would be hard-pressed to give you an answer. On balance, however, I would probably have to say that the only thing more corrosive than dreaming too much is dreaming too little. As Edward de Bono cautions in *How to Have a Beautiful Mind*:

> In a sense, having an adequate way of doing something is as much of a problem as a traditional problem. Is this adequate way the best? Should we be blocked from further thinking because we already have a way of doing something (or looking at something)?*

---

* *How To Have A Beautiful Mind* (London: Vermilion, 2004), p.123.

As U2 put in when they're working on a song in the studio, 'If it ain't broke, break it!'

Do you find that your life has shrunk to a routine that crushes your spirit with its predictability? Do you feel angry with yourself for having let yourself get trapped in this job? Do you go through a miserable time en route to work every morning? Do you feel tension in the pit of your stomach when you are at work? Do you feel that your job requires you to suppress your real personality and prepare a face to meet the faces that you meet? Do you make your way home from work feeling demoralised and in dread of tomorrow? Does the thought of changing jobs strike terror into you?

If you tick any or all of the above boxes, then I must ask you to consider the following propositions, none of which I put to you flippantly:

1. YOU DON'T NEED THIS.
2. Your unhappiness is a *healthy reaction to an unhealthy situation.*
3. Your failure to adapt happily to your job is no failure at all. It is a legitimate inner protest against the prison into which your Halter Ego has led you.
4. There are no medals for staying in this job, *unless your doing so is absolutely the only way for you to sustain yourself or your dependants.*
5. Even if this last is the case, there is a *serious possibility* that your assumption that this job represents the *only way* for you to generate enough income to get by is flawed. You may well be working off a false map of available routes.
6. Even if for some unusual reason your assumption is *not flawed*, and you *absolutely must stay in this job*, it is critical that you add the following qualification: *This is my current <u>situation</u>, not my ultimate <u>destination</u>*. Change *can* be placed on the long-term agenda.

7. I have never – *never* – met anyone who left a job that was slowly killing them only to look back in later years and experience regret at their decision.
8. This is not to say that I have never met anyone who has looked back and wished they had managed the leap more intelligently.
9. Still and all – please read number 7 again.
10. *It will probably be riskier for you in the long run to stay where you are than to break out of your current 'safety' zone.*

Don't fool yourself into thinking you are being realistic by putting up with this reduced way of living. *The pinched 'realism' of the Halter Ego is delusional and irresponsible.* Your sacrificing yourself on the altar of unsatisfying work *is doing no one any good – least of all yourself.*

§

'Discontent is the first step in the progress of a man or a nation.' Oscar Wilde's famous maxim often comes into my head when I am dealing with clients imprisoned by Halter Ego assumptions. Their feelings of discontent and disappointment always turn out to be their saving grace, for it is these feelings that make their comfort zone uncomfortable enough for them to start asking awkward questions. The great danger with the Halter Ego is that it will make us quiescent and acquiescent. It is so sad to meet people who have become so thoroughly institutionalised in their jobs, and so utterly disconnected from their own personal uniqueness, that they do not even realise how limited their life has become. So stuck in the rut have they become, they cannot imagine living any other way. Their situation, which was once upon a time in flux, has long since cooled down to the hardness of a geological formation.

But might it not be objected that these people are happy by their own lights? I don't believe so. Lack of overt discontent is not the same as happiness. Look more closely at someone who has disappeared into their job and you will find a demoralised self. Spontaneity has long since been traded for routine, personality for function, possibility for predictability. For some people in this unhappy mode of living, their latent despair only gets flushed out when something unexpected comes along, like illness, redundancy or even a mere restructuring within their firm. Any challenge to their carefully constructed world becomes deeply threatening, showing just how strongly established the Halter Ego mindset was all along. As we have seen in the case of Patrick above, even a seemingly benign change like retirement can prove traumatic for someone who has never looked beyond the immediate horizon of their job.

§

Patricia, a young lady of 32, phoned me to book some career coaching sessions. Her vocal style on that first phonecall was clipped, minimalist, almost rudely to the point:

'I am looking for career coaching.'

'No problem, Patricia. Is there any particular area you'll be wanting to focus on?'

'My career.'

I chuckled at the dry statement of the obvious. But there was no corresponding chuckle at the other end of the line. Just silence.

'Oh, ok. Well, can you give me an idea of your current situation so we can hit the ground running when we meet?'

'I'm currently a Group Finance Director with _____.'

'Oh, the coffee people?'

'Yes.'

'And how long have you been with them?'

'Six years.'

A no-nonsense lady.
Patricia arrived for our first session dressed sharply in a dark
business suit and wearing jet-black shades (it was, needless to
say, a cloudy day outside). Her unsmiling mouth, rigid posture
in the chair and blank refusal to engage in small talk signalled
an almost hypertense personality. Rather than heighten Patricia's tension further by challenging this patently defensive
coldness, I brought her onto safer ground by asking her to run
me through the basic facts of her career history.

The coffee company mentioned in our phone conversation had
headhunted her six years ago from a leading soft drinks manu-
facturer, with whom she had been for the guts of three years.
She came to both jobs brilliantly qualified: first in the class in
her Chartered Accountancy exams followed by a Masters in
Business Management. She was looking for coaching because
she could feel herself stagnating in her current job.

'Six years without an upward move is not acceptable.'

'Do you feel underappreciated by the company?'

'They appreciate the job I'm doing, but they don't seem to
have any notion of moving me up to a new position anytime
soon.'

Over the next couple of sessions we tried to tease out the reasons for her lack of advancement. But, to the considerable frustration of both of us, we seemed to be getting nowhere. Then, in the third session, Patricia came out with an enigmatic comment: 'Maybe they just haven't forgiven me for London.'

It turned out that Patricia had had a pretty traumatic experience nearly two years previously in London. She had 'mortified' herself by bursting into tears over dinner in front of a group of male colleagues. It was the last night of a week-long business trip. As her colleagues talked over dinner about the need to drive down labour costs in their South American suppliers, Patricia couldn't help feeling appalled by the coldness of the ledger-sheet abstractions being traded over the dinner table. She started challenging the assumptions of the conversation. To her own surprise as much as that of her fellow diners, her eyes started filling with tears of exasperation at her fellow diners' mocking dismissal of her concerns. 'I just excused myself and went off to "powder my nose". But the damage was done. From that point on I was marked out as "unstable", "over-emotional", "Ms Time-of-the-Month" – take your pick.'

Two things had shifted for Patricia at this dinner. First, she was henceforth perceived differently by her colleagues. News of the incident had spread like a virus once the delegation got back home. Secondly, Patricia found herself relating differently to her job. For the first time she found herself feeling *consciously* alienated from the ethos of the company she was working for. She had inadvertently stumbled upon an ethical sensitivity she had not experienced since her voluntary work with Amnesty International at college over a decade earlier. Despite her best efforts to quell her unease by retreating to head-down Halter Ego hard work back in Dublin, the incident and what had prompted it could not be deleted from her memory. Nor could the latent misogyny which the incident had made manifest. Patricia continued to smart from the new awareness that her values simply were not consistent with those of her employers.

I asked Patricia why she had not mentioned these ethical qualms to me at the outset.

'I didn't think it was relevant. If I wanted to talk moral philosophy I could join an online forum, couldn't I?'

'But is this just some abstract moral question? Maybe London was a wake-up call, forcing you to face up to the question of what you really want to do with your life, your time, your talents?'

'It's funny,' she said after *nearly a minute's* silence. 'I've spent the past couple of years trying to dismiss this feeling of unease as a luxury I can't indulge in.' This was one of the quickest turn-arounds I had ever seen in a client's persona.

What came across was just how dampened down Patricia's real personality had been all this time. Now I have worked with many, many clients who positively thrive on the buzz of corporate life, with personalities perfectly honed to the lifestyle and culture. For them, the rewards are not merely financial but also experiential. I would not dream of second-guessing the obvious temperamental suitability of such people to their chosen career field. My job is never to tell people what their values and work motivators are. It is to help them determine these things for themselves and then design smart career moves accordingly. I have also met people who have tried to give up the corporate life and suffered extremely distressing withdrawal symptoms. Patricia, though, was clearly not in this category. In her zeal to hit the corporate highs, she had gradually lost touch with those sides of herself that did not relate to number-crunching, strategising and networking. Her impressive skills in those departments had turned on her and reduced her, in her own phrase, to a 'walking caricature' of the cold, driven career woman. Her 'performance optimisation' was all in the service of a goal that was out of whack with her personality and values. What quickly emerged as she verbalised her discontent was that her ethical scruples about her current employer were just one dimension of a more general alienation from the corporate culture. Put simply, this did not feel like a case of right job, wrong company. This felt more like wrong career.

I suggested to Patricia that we do a Wheel of Life together. This simple but brilliantly effective technique is a coaching staple, offering as it does a much-needed overview of how one is faring in terms of work–life balance. Here's how Patricia's Wheel of Life came out:

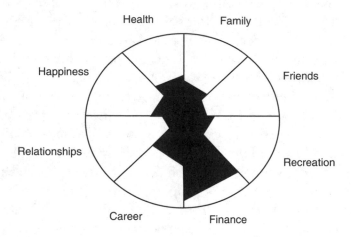

Patricia looked with some shock at the results of this exercise. Imagine trying to ride a bike with this as your front wheel! Clearly her current way of life was hopelessly skewed towards securing her financial security, with all other categories showing signs of pretty extreme neglect. Although she was on the face of it successful in her job, she couldn't in all honesty give the career segment a high satisfaction rating. Delving into the imbalance made graphic by this Wheel of Life, we established that Patricia was suffering from a truly disastrous cocktail of ambition and guilt. Combined, these impulses had:

a. Narrowed her self-regard down to the single area of practical performance at work
b. Robbed her of any sense of real achievement from this same work

To feel that one excels in just one area of life is bad enough. But to feel deep down that that area has little or no intrinsic value is positively soul-destroying.

To her credit, Patricia did not try to hide from me the realisation that her high performance at work masked a severe lack of self-esteem in other respects. The thick skin she had had to develop in the overwhelmingly male corporate world had become undetachable outside the context of work, with the result that it had become an intrinsic part of her social persona.

Patricia mentioned a telling little anecdote which illustrated just how chronically her work had been colonising every aspect of her life. The office had recently held a birthday party for a colleague. Someone had videoed the occasion and given a DVD of the highlights as a memento for everyone who had attended. Watching the playback, Patricia was horrified to see herself checking the time on her mobile phone *three times* while 'Happy Birthday' was being sung. Such behaviour struck her as bordering on the obsessive compulsive. The incident was emblematic of Patricia's uptight relationship with time. Far from being something that could be *enjoyed* or *passed* in a relaxed mode, time had become for her a phenomenon which must be monitored and quantified. The concept of 'going with the flow' and experiencing time psychologically rather than by the clock was utterly alien to the corporate environment in which Patricia lived, moved and had her being. Hardly unrelated to this busy-busy ethos was Patricia's addiction to caffeine: just forty minutes into our first session, she had complained in passing of an oncoming headache due to the fact that it was over an hour since her last double espresso.

Patricia's raising of the London episode proved the all-important turning point in our sessions. For the next few weeks, she and I worked together on the theme of 'The Heart's Logic' and how it had been so grievously neglected over the past few years. As Patricia began to get back in touch with her emotional side, her compassionate and fiercely philosophical nature begin to blossom before me.

We turned our attention gradually to the future. Patricia shared with me that an old dream of hers had been to run, of all things, a health farm. With this one piece of information, she introduced me to her hitherto submerged Walter Ego. Not that she made it easy for me to get to know said Walter Ego. As soon as I attempted to get her to expand on the dream, she clammed up and rebutted me with a sequence of textbook Halter Ego mantras: 'I've got to be practical ... You can't just up sticks and follow some crazy scheme ... It would take years to get something like that off the ground ...'.

I decided to tackle this black-and-white thinking head on:

'Patricia, you came to me four weeks ago looking for job-search and interview prep coaching. You were perfectly clear that you wanted to move up in the corporate world by leaving your current firm for a higher position elsewhere. It soon became clear that you had absolutely no genuine appetite to go even deeper into what you yourself called "the belly of the beast". None of that stuff came from me, it had been churning away inside of you. Do you see where I'm going with this? *If you can turn your intentions around 180 degrees in just a couple of coaching sessions, just imagine what you could achieve within five years.'*

'Yes, but it's one thing to say what you *don't* want, another to achieve what you *do*.'

'If you were a daydreamer, Patricia, with your Walter Ego running amok with your life, I wouldn't be saying any of this to you. But you have a proven track record of setting and achieving concrete results. The Halter Ego has served you well by helping you develop your work ethic. But your Halter Ego badly needs to enter into coalition with your Walter Ego. Because what I'm seeing here is an extremely bright and able young lady who, if she draws up a business plan, would be more likely than anyone I can think of to bring it to fruition.'

'But I can't just jack in the job. I've financial commitments to consider.'

This was progress. At least Patricia was bringing her Halter Ego objections down to size by *naming them*. We were moving from a generalised 'no can do' to a bouquet of smaller problems which could be examined one by one.

We did some focused work on how to manage a hypothetical transition from Patricia's current job to the dream job of setting up a health farm. The solution lay in a word which I have found to have alchemical potency in many career coaching sessions:

PORTFOLIO

I myself came to career coaching from a background in recruitment. One of the downsides of that field is that it tends to foster an all-or-nothing approach to jobs. Should you go for this job or that one? This is pure Halter Ego thinking. One of the joys of coaching, by contrast, is that it is not tied down to any such ludicrous single option. Often what a client really needs is not one 'magic bullet' solution to their career needs but a portfolio or medley of part-time or contract-based jobs that will combine to provide a viable, enjoyable and balanced lifestyle. This may be on a long-term or interim basis. Where the Halter Ego thinks in terms of single options (the train journey), portfolio thinking introduces a liberating *plurality* into the equation (car journey(s)).

I suggested to Patricia that a portfolio-style transition phase might give her a viable exit strategy from her job and an equally viable route to the setting up of a health farm. Although sceptical at first, she ran with the ball and did some sterling research into possible options. It turned out – as it very often does once we have made the leap in our head and heart – that her local Chamber of Commerce was seeking a full-time financial adviser. The position was well below Patricia's current pay grade. She would, to put it mildly, be quite a catch. I suggested to her that she go away and *unilaterally design* the kind of constructive *part-time* role she could offer the Chamber of Commerce and approach them with a ready-made job proposal. She liked the cheekiness of this strategy and went at the assignment with relish. Within two weeks, she had informally approached the Chamber of Commerce with an offer to work three half-days a week for a healthy but not extortionate pay packet. Even she was taken aback by the eagerness with which they bit. Clearly her experience to date and the soundness of her prep work had impressed them hugely. She even got the impression that her limiting of her time to just three half-days a week made her seem even more valuable in their eyes.

With this important first piece of the portfolio in place, Patricia rode the psychological momentum and immediately set about filling in the gaps. Within three months, she had left the coffee company and was doing part-time work for three different groups. True, the income drop was sharp enough, but Patricia had anticipated this by downsizing her consumer 'needs' and working out a viable credit-flow plan.

I got an email from her some six months after our final session (we had eight in all). The adjustment had not been easy. She had moved from a spacious house to a modest apartment, and had found the switch a little panic-inducing at first. Was she crazy to be doing this? Had she just traded security for a hand-to-mouth existence? Thankfully, however, the moment of panic passed. She quickly came to see that her quality of life had risen beyond compare. She was still living on her own but was happy enough to have her own space for the time being. 'I'm going to enjoy this low-pressure front for a little while anyway', she wrote in the email. 'The health farm is still very much on the cards, but I'm going to do it right or not at all. Don't hold me to this, Jane, but if your complementary voucher hasn't arrived by 2012 at the latest, then I'll be as surprised as you!' She signed herself off as 'Patricia Walters'. Walters? This was not her surname! Knowing that she hadn't gotten married in the last six months, and that even if she had she'd be the last person I'd expect to trade in her maiden name, I laughed out loud at the cheeky little in-joke. She had learned to control her Halter Ego and, for the first time in years, give her Walter Ego a fair hearing.

§

When is the Halter Ego our friend? Whenever we need to roll up our sleeves and *get something done*. If I have a project I have to bring in on schedule, I cannot mess around. The Halter Ego, if harnessed properly, can help us to *overrule our moods with our decisions*. It will not let us stray self-indulgently from the task at hand. This is benign and necessary – *as long as that task is one which we can stand back and identify as valuable.* When ex-librarian Patrick started giving literacy classes, for instance, he put to superb use the head-down, no-nonsense work ethic which his years in the library had nurtured. Once restored to its place in a more balanced view of work and life, this Halter Ego work ethic made Patrick an unusually task-oriented and effective teacher in a job which he felt had an occasional tendency to attract well-meaning but ultimately ineffectual idealists. This work had a meaningfulness for him that had been almost wholly lacking in his library job. The Halter Ego habits of hard work and relia-bility were now *integrated* in a role that also called for such qualities as caring, helpfulness and approachability. Once out of a Halter Ego prison, it can be a real joy to befriend one's Halter Ego all over again – though this time with a firm sense of who's in charge.

§

Some Typical Halter Ego Traps

- Playing super-safe in all things
- Taking comfort in routine
- Taking wry note of people who fall to Earth after attempting ambitious things but not of people who attempt ambitious things and succeed
- Reducing all of life to one goal: avoiding embarrassment
- Imposing your own narrow horizons on children and loved ones
- Becoming a 'soft enemy' to friends who share their hopes and dreams with you – by demoralising them with scepticism and patronising 'advice'

The Halter Ego

- Failing to assert yourself with bosses or colleagues
- Lack of initiative and self-direction at work
- Disinclination to ever seek a pay rise or a promotion
- Timidity at work

4

The Altar Ego

'The Lord is my shepherd, I want, I want'

The Altar Ego presents its victim with a picture of the world that is naïve, superstitious and sometimes ridiculously disconnected from reality. When it gets an extreme grip on someone, it can actually be the most devastating Disappointer of all.

Sheila, a fortysomething lady from Ennis, had worked in four different call centres in as many years. She absolutely detested the work but needed the cash to keep body and soul together. Not that she was at all happy about admitting that she hated the work, mind. Her New Age ethos, cultivated from a large number of (mostly American) 'Mind, Body, Spirit' books, prohibited her from being so openly 'negative'. In our first session, she tried to put a sugar coating on the bitter pill she was forced to swallow every day: 'I feel so blessed to be able to connect with the customers ... Whenever anyone is rude to me, I silently send them good vibes down the phone knowing that they are perfect at the soul level ... Sure, the pay could be better, but I trust to the universe to manifest my intentions at a perfect time and in a perfect way.' This was robotic stuff, made all the more unconvincing by the look of poorly concealed stress on Sheila's face as she tried to squeeze trite consolation out of a job that was obviously not satisfying her on any level. It was quite plain that she had turned to this brand of deeply spurious New Age 'spirituality' for one simple reason: it offered a way of converting real-life unpleasantness into vague feelings of hope, connectedness and empowerment.

Not surprisingly, it took quite a bit of work on my part to get Sheila just to give herself permission to assess the here and now in an uncensored and authentic way. Once her initial reluctance to do this was overcome – and it took two sessions to get to this point – the floodgates of frustration and disappointment opened. Sheila's professional life had not worked out at all as she had hoped it would. The fact that she had diddly squat to show for all the positive intentions she had been 'sending out to the universe' only added a further layer of pain to the situation. To see through the New Age mantras she had been parroting for the past few years of her life, to recognise that the authors of her cherished books had been nothing more than cynical snake-oil merchants, to realise that she had effectively wasted precious years on mere pipe dreams – all of this Sheila found painful and embarrassing to do.

Once her resistance was overcome, however, the unvarnished facts came out thick and fast. Here is what emerged:

1. People walked all over Sheila, both at work and out of it. Thus, for example, the behaviour of her landlord. He had been repeatedly ignoring her requests to attend to basic maintenance issues with her bedsit, all the while jacking up the rent with downright unscrupulous frequency. This left Sheila living in an overpriced flat whose deluxe features included a leaking ceiling, a toilet that didn't flush properly and a fridge whose cooling system was completely unreliable. Instead of just admitting to herself that she was scared of standing up to her bastard of a landlord, Sheila had been trying to

convince herself that his failure to meet his basic responsibilities was in reality some sort of gentle lesson in self-denial and perseverance sent to *her* by a benevolent cosmos. This bizarre rationalisation kept her from either confronting her landlord or (perish the thought) actually looking for a new place to live. To do either of these things would have been to admit that all was not well with the world. And to admit *that* would be to 'let in' all sorts of 'negative energies'.

2. Sheila really, really hated her job in the call centre. She would wake up every morning with feelings of dread and despair: dread over the miserable nine hours that lay ahead, despair over her long-term financial and professional future. She could feel herself getting older, but was scared to admit to herself just how scary she found the prospect. The only thing keeping panic at bay was the opium of Altar Ego thinking.

3. Sheila was hopeless with money. God knows, her job didn't leave her with much surplus cash after rent and essentials were spoken for, but whatever she did have over was quickly wasted on various bric-à-brac New Age items like angel statues and expensive aromatic oils – as well, of course, as the very latest in overpriced Make-A-Wish-Come-True books. One further expense was especially telling: Lotto tickets. It turned out that Sheila had been spending up to *thirty euro a week* on them. She had actually convinced herself that the power of positive intention was about to bag her a big win that would, with one stroke, release her from her purgatory of straitened circumstances. She even had a 'magick' ritual for choosing her Lotto numbers. It involved incense, dolphin music and a pair of dice.

4. Sheila had been basing her key life decisions on 'signs'. She had chosen her present employer because their HQ was in an industrial estate whose name was a near-anagram of Sheila's late mother's name. (I kid you not.) Sheila had recently passed

up an interesting job opportunity thrown her way by an old school friend because said friend had rung outside the time-frame stipulated by Sheila's latest 'intention visualisation' exercise. She had impetuously given a short-term loan of money she could ill spare to another old school friend who just happened to have bumped into her in the same week that Sheila had come across an old class photo. The old school 'friend' repaid the kindness by doing a runner with the money.

You are getting the picture, and will no doubt find it as thoroughly depressing as I did when Sheila first started painting it for me. What had made the Altar Ego so dangerous to Sheila's prospects in life was the fact that it operated within a closed circle of logic. Failure? Success in disguise! Disappointment? God's delays are not God's denials! Stress? A sign that the spirit moves in mysterious ways! Cash-flow problems? A symptom of my need to let go and trust even more to the cosmic process! Loneliness? I am not alone, I am all-one! A bullying boss? A soul in need of my silent blessing! Pressed to such an absurd extreme, Sheila's Altar Ego logic was getting her to see mystical significance in *everything*, and rudimentary life lessons in *nothing*. This disabled her from making wise or even halfway practical decisions on a day-to-day basis, let alone strategic choices on a mid- to long-term basis. The poor decisions that *did* flow from the Altar Ego way of thinking only led Sheila into a fresh round of mystification, as she sought the hand of providence in the unhappy results of her latest piece of gormless behaviour.

§

In one sense, of course, Sheila represented a rather extreme case of the Altar Ego-dominated personality. That said, I have in my coaching practice come across an unholy number of what I call 'refugees' from the 'Mind, Body, Spirit' movement. We are not talking victims of religious cults here, just ordinary decent people who have been drawn into a way of approaching life's challenges that is unrealistic, faux-spiritual and propelled by wishful thinking. This is *not*, I hasten to add, to disparage religion or spirituality as such. In discussing the Altar Ego, I am specifically targetting the peculiar New Age mindset which turns these phenomena into a banal box of tricks that can be pawned off to vulnerable people, i.e. anyone who finds the modern world so complex and cut-throat that it cannot be faced without feelgood mystification. While true religion and spirituality can often deepen a person's commitment to personal authenticity, Altar Ego 'spirituality' offers nothing more than a phoney way out of one's fears and insecurities. Its victims are often gentle and kind souls. The authors who push its agenda, however, are (in my professional opinion) greedy and exploitative charlatans who know exactly which buttons to press in order to turn their readers into repeat customers.

It is important to be clear on one thing here: the Altar Ego doesn't always need to involve overt 'spiritual' philosophy to get us to do its bidding.

I once had a client who decided to give up on a CV application because his printer kept jamming on the morning of the deadline. Thus was an annoying stroke of bad luck amplified into a wild conclusion: 'This job just isn't meant for me.' It can be so tempting to decode simple events in life in terms of some deeper significance. What this man was doing was simple: he was letting his Altar Ego talk him out of the job application by handing him an 'act of God' that he could point to as an excuse for his failed application.

Another client felt guilty about ever fighting for anything in life. He worked in a bank and was tempted when an attractive vacancy was advertised internally. He put in his application, even got called for interview – but withdrew his name at the last minute. Why? Because a pushy colleague had indicated to him in no uncertain terms that this job had *her* name written all over it. My client had recently read in a couple of New Age 'success' books that one must always 'go with the flow' and trust that a positive mentality will turn one into a magnet that will all on its own attract the right things in life. *Competing* with someone for a job vacancy did not fit in with this soft-centred notion, so my client chose the line of zero 'conflict'. His Altar Ego had tricked him into confusing integrity with passivity.

§

The Altar Ego likes making extravagant promises to us. You will become rich if you send out positive vibes. You will achieve professional glory if you bring in Jesus as your business partner. You will leave behind your feelings of dissatisfaction if you think happy thoughts. It is almost unbelievable that this kind of nonsense has infected so many people in Ireland.

The Altar Ego is a first cousin of the Walter Ego. Both Disappointers set us up for disappointment by feeding us the idea that things don't ever have to be arduous or hard won. Dream of great things and they shall be given unto you. Each Disappointer makes sure to keep us trapped at the dream-a-dream stage. What differentiates the two modes is this: the Walter Ego keeps us distracted indefinitely with castles in the air, whereas the Altar Ego sets a deeper trap for us by inviting us to be *fatalistic* about whatever happens. By 'fatalism' I mean any temptation to see the hand of fate (or destiny or God or spirit guides – take your pick) in what happens to us. *Fatalism, please note, does not just apply to negative things.* It can be just as seductive an explanatory tool for experiences deemed positive. I think to myself over the lunch break that I'd love to change jobs. The phone rings. It's a friend who casually mentions a job opportunity at the local fitness club. Under normal circumstances I wouldn't be remotely interested. But the uncanny timing of my friend's call is too good not to be true. I apply for the job. Even when I learn that the hours are crap and the pay poor, I still go for it. Was it not meant to be? This type of thinking goes on *all the time – even in people who wouldn't call themselves religious or spiritual in a month of Sundays.* We like to see patterns where sometimes there are none. When we make key strategic decisions on this basis, we more often than not end up making a royal mess of things.

The Walter Ego is not fatalistic, it is just escapist. A person dominated by Walter Ego thinking can find themselves dreaming of wondrous things while experiencing none of them in real life – without necessarily seeing any contradiction between the two realms. A person in thrall to their Altar Ego, by contrast, *does* see the contradiction. The 'success' mantras *are not working.* The promised wealth *is not materialising.* The real world is *not going away.* What makes this contradiction so potentially dangerous is that it can push the Altar Ego victim into a new phase: fatalistic resignation. I asked for X but God didn't give it to me. Therefore God doesn't want me to have X. I am marked out for failure and loser status. (This is not a million miles away from the old Eastern tendency to see poverty or illness as the result of bad karma from a previous lifetime. Why do anything about it, right?) The person who comes to such a bleakly fatalistic view of things is at least showing enough intelligence and courage to see the Altar Ego philosophy through to its logical conclusion. After this, their thinking can go one of two ways. Either they get utterly demoralised by the perceived lack of grace in their lives, or they start to question the wisdom of their Altar Ego. The first route spells further disaster, the second a way out.

§

The Altar Ego, as we have seen, can play havoc at every step of the way:

- If you dislike your job, it tries to persuade you that all is well. *(Avoid the captivity of negativity!)*
- If you feel such normal human emotions as annoyance, frustration, competitiveness, disappointment or anxiety, it makes you feel guilty about them and tries to get you to give them a deep meaningful gloss. *(Avoid all conflict!)*
- If none of this works, it tells you that something marvellous is just around the corner. *(Keep praying!)*
- If that doesn't work, it entraps you by getting you to make bad choices based on the notion that purely accidental things have some fatalistic significance. *(A sign!)*
- If *that* doesn't work, and you actually get up off your backside and try to upgrade your career on your own initiative, it robs you of your ability to cope with any setback or unpleasantness that might come your way. *(Everything happens for a reason!)*

The Altar Ego cripples us in our ability to respond to life's challenges by giving us a simplistic and fatalistic picture of the world. Even when the solution to a problem is positively staring us in the face, our Altar Ego can make us second-guess our own common sense. 'That's all very well in practice,' it seems to whisper to us, 'but how does it work out in theory?'

§

Perhaps you think yourself safe from the wiles of the Altar Ego? Perhaps you are religious, but have never been hooked by New Age mumbo jumbo? Perhaps you are a proud atheist who despises all irrationalism and superstition?

Think again. Can you say, hand on heart, that you have never ever felt yourself the victim of that old devil called 'bad luck'? If not, then you are, well, lucky. When all else fails, the Altar Ego may well resort to the idea of 'bad luck' as the very last card it can play on a resistant subject. Let's not be under any illusion here. The concept of luck, whether good or bad, is as metaphysical and superstitious a concept as any we have met above.

Niall came to me for life coaching. He was thirty – and eaten up by the idea that his life was being wrecked by misfortune. 'Just my ****ing luck' seemed to be his constant mantra.

Niall was a chronic underachiever: highly talented in his field of expertise, French literary studies, but somehow never quite seeming to live up to his potential. When he came to me, he was half-heartedly teaching English as a foreign language in one of the many small language schools which had recently sprung up in Dublin over the past few years. He found the work soulless and exploitative, both of himself and of the mainly Chinese students in his classes. He had opted for TEFL (Teaching English as a Foreign Language) as a 'stopgap' job which would keep him solvent as he worked on an academic book. He had been passed over for an academic scholarship a couple of years previously as a result of an 'unfortunate' technical flaw in his application for funding. The book was now taking forever to get finished, let alone published. With rising panic, Niall had watched two-and-a-half years go by, during which the supposed stopgap job had begun to take on a scarily permanent character.

We talked about the concept of luck. I asked Niall if he felt that luck was just something that people either have or didn't have. Although rationally he knew that this didn't make sense, Niall couldn't deny the impression he had formed that some people do indeed tend to fall on their feet through happy fluke while others (like himself) get 's**t upon' (his words). In the academic appointment stakes, for instance, he felt that a medley of bad luck and departmental politics had conspired to stall his advancement to the rank of lecturer. It really galled him to have to earn his keep day-in day-out by doing teaching work he found intellectually numbing, professionally unsatisfying and ethically dubious.

Niall had mentioned that he was a keen snooker player. On a gut feeling, I went for a 'blurt' and asked him to talk to me about the phenomenon of *luck* as one might encounter it in snooker – a game about which I, like most females in this good world, knew next to nothing. With an eloquence you're likely to find only in a devotee of French poetry and philosophy, Niall explained that the beauty of snooker lies in the delicate balance between skill, tactics and luck. His eyes shone as he painstakingly talked me through the unique ecosytem of the green felt. When he had finished, I pointed out a curious fact to him. When talking about bad luck in snooker, he never seemed to see it in terms of *unfairness.* He seemed instead to detect a kind of aggregate justice in operation.

This comment piqued Niall's interest, so we probed the enigma of luck in snooker a little further. If a player gets a bad 'kiss' or 'kick' on the cue ball, then he just has to put it behind him and either keep his break going or await his next opportunity to visit the table. But if a player finds that time and time again he is going out of position or missing pots by apparent misfortune, then something else beyond random bad luck must be going on. Snooker is not roulette. It is a complex system in which you have to maximise your chances of a happy outcome. If Ronnie O'Sullivan or Ken Doherty were to cite bad luck as the reason for losing a match, people might sympathise. But if they were to cite *repeated* bad luck as the reason for a lousy season on the circuit, no one would take them seriously. Snooker, in short, involves a delicate interplay between what happens *to* me and what happens *from* me.

Niall and I agreed on an assignment for the week ahead. He was to go to his local snooker club and play a couple of frames of snooker on his own as a focused meditation on the topic of luck. More specifically, he was to approach the game as a metaphor for how he had been playing his career game to date.

He came back the next week with that *eureka* – or should I say *voilà?* – look on his face. The snooker frames had brought home to him a simple fact: he had been approaching his career like a man who takes the snooker cue and whacks the white ball with his eyes shut, *hoping that the sheer desire for something to be potted will be enough to secure the pot.* When trying to achieve something professionally, Niall had fallen victim to a three-way coalition of error:

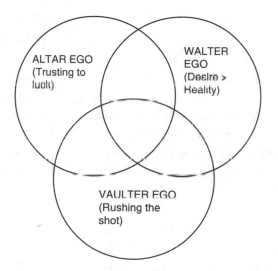

ALTAR EGO
(Trusting to
luck)

WALTER
EGO
(Desire >
Reality)

VAULTER EGO
(Rushing the
shot)

In going for a job or a scholarship, he would fail to take his time by judiciously going through the options before him, considering positioning a couple of shots ahead and making a decisive shot selection. He had allowed some early experiences of 'bad luck' infect his anticipation of every subsequent shot in life. And a series of disappointing results had thrown him into a mighty Salter Ego sulk with the world. On the snooker table, by contrast, he was intelligent and methodical, and more than able to live with the marginal effects of 'bad luck' on the occasional shot.

Clearly, this proficient snooker player needed to apply some of his natural methodical proficiency at the snooker table to his extra-cue-ricular activities.*

§

A couple of quiet games of snooker proved a paradigm-shifting meditation for Niall. It restored his faith in the *rightness* of a given outcome. As he wrote for a short exercise I gave him:

> If I pot the red, it is usually because I have looked at the geometry before cueing. If I want to score bigger points, I need to get the red first before I can go for a colour. This is a handy lesson for someone who wants to aim high but shies away from the idea of going through an intermediary process of training, qualification or work experience first. The notion of building a break in snooker captures perfectly the soft skills I'm going to need to build the career I want: foresight, ability to size up a complex situation, readiness to make allowance for the unexpected.

I told you he was eloquent!

Hearing Niall speak about snooker in this way reminded me of the unforgettable opening passage in the late M. Scott Peck's *The Road Less Traveled*, a book that has influenced me more than I can begin to tell you:

---

* Very sorry.

Life is difficult.

This is a great truth, one of the greatest truths. It is a great truth because once we truly see this truth, we transcend it. Once we truly know that life is difficult – once we truly understand and accept it – then life is no longer difficult. Because once it is accepted, the fact that life is difficult no longer matters.*

Snooker is difficult. It has tough rules. It must be played within the strictest of limits: table size, pocket size, rules for point allocation, number of pockets, number of balls, sequence in which balls must be potted, rules governing fouls, laws of geometry, laws of momentum, laws of gravity, et cetera. *These limits do not spoil the game, they give it definition.* A serious player will not waste energy wishing those limits could be suspended or renegotiated. No, the serious player will see that these limits are what grant the game its very meaning and beauty. Working with and within these limits, the great player will learn to turn them to his advantage.

Thinking about his approach to problems in terms of snooker helped Niall to relate to the idea of *process* in a different way. He began to see the task of career building as a fascinatingly dynamic mixture of predictable and almost randomly unpredictable outcomes.† The player's own role in creating the current state of play is key:

---

* M. Scott Peck, *The Road Less Traveled* (New York: Simon and Schuster, 1978), p.15.
† Here's a nice experiment: take a triangle of snooker or pool balls and smash the white into the top ball as hard as you can ten times, each time striking the white from the exact same spot. Take a photo of each result and compare.

- If I find myself snookered, there's no use cursing the table, the rules or even my opponent. At some level, the possibility of this snooker coming about *happened from me.*
- If I go out of position on the next ball, there's no use blaming the laws of geometry. The skew *happened from me.*
- If I miss the pot, there's no use blaming the size of the pockets. The miss *happened from me.*
- If a mobile phone goes off just as I'm about to take a shot and I see red instead of *the* red, then I have responded unintelligently to the situation. The reaction *happens from me.*

If I am not getting the results I want, there is a more than fair to middling chance that I need to change my cue action or my mental attitude – or both. Either that, or this simply isn't the game for me and I need to stop tormenting myself by trying to convince myself otherwise.

Niall learned to use snooker as a way of *reframing his frustrating experiences* in a more constructive and less fatalistic fashion. It helped him take back personal responsibility for those things over which he did have control, the better to cope with those things which lay beyond his immediate control. The snooker table was for him a wonderful antidote to his Altar Ego tendency. *It took the mystification out of a result.* It showed how absurd it can be to take failure personally. Who am I going to resent if I keep missing? The table? The pockets?? The balls??? Gravity???? Snooker simply won't let me off the hook with easy excuses or short cuts. It will not reward a lazy strategy of hit'n'hope. It will not suspend its laws according to the dictates of my mood or the intensity of my desire.

§

Now let's be careful *not* to take the next step and push the snooker analogy to an unhealthy extreme. This is what Niall did in a subsequent exercise for me. So delighted was he with his new-found understanding of the dynamics of 'luck', that he wrote the following:

> Life will sometimes yield maddening results, but you will not be able to blame the heavenly powers above or 'society' or your childhood for them. No, the game of life is perfectly fair, even when it involves a seemingly 'unlucky' run of the balls.

Have you spotted what has happened here? Niall has allowed his Altar Ego spin-doctor to creep in again by the back door. A commonsense insight has been inflated into an absurd and dangerous overstatement. The game of life is perfectly fair? Tell that to the victims of the Christmas 2004 Asian tsunami. Was it just one of those kicks on the cue ball of life? Easy for us to speak. I don't know about you, but I was thousands of miles away in Dublin, happily making inroads into my selection box while I watched *The Wizard of Oz* for the nineteenth time. Life is *not* fair. Bad things happen to good people every day of the week, and good things to bad. Perhaps we should be open to the idea that there is, underlying the visible surface of life, a deeper providence and justice whose logic we can barely glimpse. Perhaps. But who in their right minds could not be plunged into horror by the wrongful suffering undergone by so many people – and animals – on this planet?

Niall's life-is-as-fair-as-a-game-of-snooker remark is an example of how easy it is to blithely overstep the mark from useful analogy to facile argument. Snooker had proved a pretty powerful metaphor for Niall as he pondered his unhappy career situation. He had, so to speak, 'snookered' himself. So far so good. We then went a step further and surmised that snooker might be a pretty smart metaphor for how he had been approaching practical problems in life more generally. Sounds reasonable enough. But Niall was in danger of getting *hopelessly muddled* if he were to deploy snooker as a metaphor for how we grapple with relationships, friendships, personal authenticity, happiness or (gasp) *love.* Yet this is precisely what the Altar Ego, with a whole New Age industry of 'prosperity gospel' cheerleaders behind it, wants us to do.

§

At its heart, the Altar Ego is a tendency to simplify, simplify, simplify. Life is a game of snooker. Life is a round of poker. Life is a box of chocolates. What's going on here is itself very simple: my Altar Ego recognises that I find life complicated and challenging, and it gives me a compellingly simple explanation. It doesn't really matter what that explanation is as long as it is intellect-numbingly simple. *The only way I will ever defeat Altar Ego thinking is if I stop fearing complexity and uncertainty.* And here's the paradox: once I take it as read that life is not a simple closed system, and that it will not always go to plan, *it starts getting simpler.* This is because I have not confused local action (how to go for *this* job, how to secure *this* flat) with ultimate meaning (what is the *hidden significance* of this incident? what clues is *the universe* sending me about this flat?).

The Altar Ego hates complexity and loves to spin us a facile story. It matters not a whit whether the story is 'positive' (God is on your side, etc.) or 'negative' (you're cursed with bad luck). Both are grand narratives that suck the complexity and uncertainty out of life.

You don't need them.

§

Some Typical Altar Ego Traps

- Substituting the intricacies of daily living with vacuous pseudo-mystical slogans
- Seeing providential patterns where there are none
- Rationalising your fears about standing up for yourself as love for your neighbour
- Susceptibility to the codswallop of astrologists, radio psychics and co.
- Replacing 'God helps those who help themselves' with 'God helps those who make themselves helpless'
- Sending out unspoken 'vibes' to people instead of just asking them for help
- Resenting anyone who voices scepticism about your Spirituality Lite. (Worse still – deciding to 'pray' for them)
- Confusing fact with value, i.e. if something happens then it must be the right outcome
- Refusing to be honest with yourself about how unhappy and anxious you really are
- Being ashamed of your ordinary human egotism and ambition and dressing it up in pseudo-spiritual language
- Confusing failure to get something with renunciation of the desire for it

5

The Vaulter Ego

'It's now or never'

The Vaulter Ego is characterised not by impatience but by *misplaced* impatience. The distinction is far from minor. Impatience, like fire, can either warm you up nicely or give you a nasty burn.

Andrew worked in public relations, a notoriously stressful industry that demands persistence, a thick skin and a constant stream of immediate and visible results. He had a flair for the job and, on a good day, got a real buzz out of it. Unfortunately the ratio of good days to not-so-good days had become uncomfortably low of late, with the result that Andrew was now thinking the hitherto unthinkable: a move not just away from his current PR company but out of the PR sector altogether. His frustration did not centre on any one aspect of the job. Rather he complained of a general feeling of alienation from the goals of the company. He didn't find what they did ethically dodgy or anything, just pretty meaningless in the last analysis. Crashing on the couch at home of an evening, he would find himself wondering whether the latest product or event he was pushing really merited the intensive investment of personal energy required to get it onto the media hotlist. Coupled with this sense of value poverty was a creeping resentment at the fact that he did not seem to be ascending the promotions ladder in the company; this despite over four years of high-yield service. Although no one ever verbalised any dissatisfaction with him to his face, he could not shake the feeling that he was somehow out of the loop in terms of office politics. For some reason that he couldn't quite work out, he didn't seem to be a 'player' in the way a number of (in his view) less talented colleagues were. This perplexed and worried him in equal measure, leading him to wonder whether he should cut his losses and leave while the going was still relatively good. He was after all still only 29.

This was the state of play when Andrew came to me for coaching. It quickly became apparent, however, that the very Vaulter Ego virtues that had made him such an effective PR man – impatience, results focused, zero tolerance for drift – threatened to turn into classic Vaulter Ego vices as soon as he started addressing the topic of career change. Andrew found it excruciatingly difficult to *stop* and take stock of the here and now. This for him was little more than self-indulgent time-wasting. In our very first session he asked me to draw up a timetable for action. When I handed him the following list, he was not a happy camper:

1. Press pause
2. Assess your current situation in terms of your values, work motivators and skills base
3. Keep your finger on the pause button until we meet next week

The simple exercises I handed him for 'homework' and 'reflection' were immediately brushed aside as frivolous, 'wishy-washy' and irrelevant to the task at hand. What was the earthly point of doing a Wheel of Life or a personal values list when there is a new career to be established? Andrew was a concrete operations man through and through. He wanted a 'solution', and he wanted it now. When I refused to hand him one, and instead made it clear that this review process was going to take at least two further sessions, he accused me of mercenary motives and even threatened to cancel our future appointments. I politely told him he was free to leave but that any career coach out there who would sheepishly accede to his demands would be wasting his time and money for real. After a little more toing and froing, we came to an arrangement: Andrew would commit to two more sessions, to be undertaken on the terms already outlined, after which he would be free to disengage at his discretion.

To give Andrew his due, he took to the deal with energy and integrity. Placing his Vaulter Ego on temporary suspension, he took a long hard look at the here and now. This was something he had not done since leaving school. At first he found it almost embarrassing to go into his feelings about his job. It meant showing a whole side of himself that did not get a look-in at work. What came into view quickly was a picture of a man whose job was disconnected from his values and whose natural talents were being applied in only a very limited way. While PR did tap Andrew's dynamism, efficiency and skills of persuasion, it also forced him to suppress his keen analytical faculty as well as the gentler, more empathetic side of his personality. When success is reduced day-in, day-out to the level of immediate concrete results it becomes hard not to apply similarly short-term logic to just about everything around one. To take just one example of the cognitive shift which PR had brought about in Andrew's head, he had gone from being an avid reader of novels and history books to never reading anything longer than a newspaper article. The same went for his inability to switch off outside of work hours. Where he used to enjoy having friends over for long meals, he now restricted social interaction to the occasional game of squash or a couple of pints with associates at the weekend. Friendship, culture, free time – such things had come to seem weirdly intangible, unreal, unfocused. It was as though Andrew could not go from a working world in which everyone was a 'contact' to a personal world in which people might be enjoyed purely for their company, or activities engaged in for the sheer heck of it. Again and again, Andrew's default mode with people and situations was the Vaulter Ego mode of *irrational impatience*. He was finding it impossible to compartmentalise 'work' and 'life'. This, it was clear to me, was a clear case of the job taking over the man – and being out of joint with him.

As soon as Andrew and I got beyond the crucial stage of assessing the here and now, we started aligning his values and strengths in terms of possible alternative careers. Alas, here too his Vaulter Ego went into full saboteur mode.

So used had Andrew become to getting information at the click of a mouse or by means of a quick phone call that he found basic tasks like making trips to the library, writing away for things by snail mail or waiting to hear back from people to whom his name meant nothing intensely disheartening. Again, the association of 'success' with 'NOW!' was so strong in his mind that even a slight delay, setback or complication caused him untold angst. If something did not come to fruition quickly and 'naturally', then it was either never going to happen or not worth going for in the first place.

Likewise Andrew's approach to job applications. When he failed to get called for interview for the first two positions he applied for, his Vaulter Ego was only too happy to draw a hasty, black-and-white conclusion for him: *you're failing … this is getting ridiculous … you're on the wrong track altogether … give up.* It took quite some work to get Andrew to overrule these Vaulter Ego promptings and *hold his nerve*. And it's a good thing he did.

When he finally got called for interview, it was with a leading publishing house whose reputation for quality was almost peerless. They were looking for a market researcher/PR campaign manager for book releases willing to travel regularly and work on a project-by-project basis. Andrew got the job, but not without one last attempted sabotage from his Vaulter Ego.

During the interview, it was indicated that, somewhat contrary to the impression given in the advertisement, the successful candidate would not be taking up the role until the new year. It being now only July, Andrew was shocked – and furious. How could he possibly wait that long? He was, as he told me in our session later that afternoon, 'this close' to telling the interview panel to stick their job 'where the sun don't shine'. Thankfully, however, he resisted this Vaulter Ego temptation, took the news in his stride and made it to the end of the interview in one piece. When the job was offered to him the next day, he enthusiastically accepted it, having put together a careful transition plan with me first. Contrary to every Vaulter Ego instinct in his body, he employed patient step-by-step thinking to get himself from July to Christmas. Amongst other things, this planning enabled him to manage his exit from the PR firm with maximum grace, goodwill – and remuneration.

The point in Andrew's story is not that his career reorientation took some sort of high-level analysis or planning. On the contrary, the solution to his situation turned out to be pretty elementary, as it so often does. The point is that *Andrew's Vaulter Ego was the only real complicating factor in the mix*. Like all the Disappointers, it tried to play havoc by *getting in the way of straightforward, constructive and commonsense action*. And, as usual, the dis-appointing of an over-dominant Disappointer involved the *appointment* of a neglected tendency – in this case, Andrew's Halter Ego:

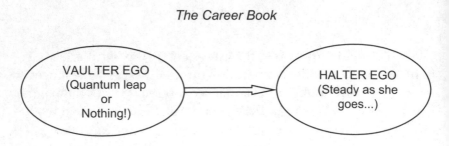

Andrew needed to stop running all the time and learn the very practical benefits that can come from taking baby steps.

§

One of the most common Vaulter Ego errors is to look at people you deem successful and draw simplistic conclusions about how they got there. I want my band to be the next U2 but have no appreciation of the long, hard and often thankless slog it took them and their manager Paul McGuinness to get there. I want to be a great novelist but don't realise just how much sheer *stamina* a great writer like Charles Dickens displayed in taking himself from an unknown parliamentary reporter to the most popular writer in the English-speaking world. I want to be Taoiseach but vastly underestimate the amount of work it took at local and cumann level to get someone like Bertie Ahern onto people's collective radar. I want my boss's job but don't have anything close to the full background story on how he got to the top. I want to 'have it all' like some high-profile 'supermom' who has excelled in both her personal and professional careers, but haven't asked myself just what personal price she (or her loved ones) may have paid for that to happen. You will no doubt be able to find examples of your own here. While it can be tremendously motivating to have role models whose success you find inspiring and worthy of emulation, and while envy can sometimes be a powerful goad, it is important not to make too

many naïve assumptions about their own road to 'extremistan'*
success.

Furthermore, looking at the techniques that brought a Hilary
Clinton or a Michael O'Leary to the top of their respective fields
can be deeply misleading. Why? Because it involves a retrospec-
tive view that gives the plot ending away in advance. Gone is
all the uncertainty that accompanied these people's routes to
success. Forgotten are all their contemporaries who did much
the same thing as them yet didn't make it. Your exclusion of *the
non-winners* from your study of success is giving your analysis a
fatal bias, leaving you working off a very partial picture of how
the world works. The Vaulter Ego, with its taste for quick fixes
and simple stories, wants you to ignore such complicating considerations. It wants you to focus on plot endings at the expense
of narrative detail, success stories at the expense of casualties,
direct routes at the expense of long and winding roads. As I'm
sure you have already spotted, this weakness for the 'zero to
hero' myth is also shared by the Walter and Altar Egos, who
also prefer the big dream to the long hard slog that's required
to make it happen.

In his extremely stimulating recent book, *Outliers*, the quirky
American pop sociology writer Malcolm Gladwell shatters the
Vaulter Ego myth about success as something that comes about
quickly or not at all. The reality, claims Gladwell, is that success
comes with a '10,000-Hour Rule' attached. When it comes to
serving one's apprenticeship to a given endeavour, ten thousand
hours is 'the magic number of greatness'.† And no, geniuses are

---

* To borrow one of the key words in Nassim Nicholas Taleb's fascinating
book, *The Black Swan: The Impact of the Highly Improbable* (London: Penguin,
2008).
† Malcolm Gladwell, *Outliers: The Story of Success* (London: Allen Lane, 2008),
p. 41.

not exempt from this rule. Whether we're talking The (not-yet-famous) Beatles playing inhumanly long hours in Hamburg, the young Mozart being forced to practice *ad nauseam* by his father or the teenage Bill Gates putting in an obsessive level of unpaid computer time at Information Sciences Inc. at the University of Washington, the greatest successes seem to come dropping slow. What ultimately drove all these people was love of their craft. Sure, they were ambitious for fame and fortune, which they achieved on a grand scale (although poor Mozart died a pauper). But *they did not watch the clock.* They established clearly that this craft was their priority and got to work by making any sacrifices needed. So completely did they immerse themselves in their work that they entered 'flow time' – that state in which the self becomes deliciously lost in the activity.

This is what the Vaulter Ego doesn't want you to know. It wants you to lose your nerve as soon as you fail to see immediate payback for your efforts. It is particularly adept at getting you to trip yourself up at the baby-step stage of upgrading your career. Mary, for instance, came to me for coaching knowing perfectly well what was wrong with her current job as a sales manager in an out-of-town furniture store: it was stressful and inadequately paid, plus it forced her to leave her two young twin sons for unacceptably long hours in the crèche. She also had a clear idea about what she wanted to do: open up a small restaurant in her town. But she just couldn't get going. Every time she thought of the first steps involved, she would be paralysed by anxiety on all fronts. How to finance a transition between careers? How to get her employer to give her time off during the day for research without alerting him to her plans? How to get 'buy-in' from her husband? Each question would trigger a disaster movie in Mary's brain, leading her to put the restaurant idea on the back burner yet again. *One hour of laser-beam analysis in coaching of these relatively minor problems, however, rescued Mary from a Vaulter Ego sabotage of the next decade or two of her life.* And even more to the point: *all of the solutions came from Mary herself.* All I did was see to it that her Vaulter Ego *shut the hell up* for that one hour and give her headspace to think calmly and logically.

Vaulter Ego thinking slows you down in life by making you look for quick fixes to everything. It makes you allergic to *short-term sacrifice* and *delayed gratification*, telling you that *they aren't worth it.* You still haven't lost weight after a week of dieting? The diet's a waste of time! You're suffering nasty headaches as a result of caffeine withdrawal? Go back on the coffee! You've spent the afternoon reading a Shakespeare play for tomorrow's English lecture but are still only at Act II? Put down the book and get a plot summary on Wikipedia! When this kind of now-or-never thinking gets applied to the fine art of career management, you end up going nowhere, fast.

§

The old fable of the Hare and the Tortoise teaches young children a really dangerous lesson — that the only alternative to Vaulter Ego impatience is the plodding reliability of the Halter Ego. On the contrary, it is desperately important that we learn to *bide our time when time needs biding* and *run when run we must.* As I stated at the start of this chapter, the Vaulter Ego acts as a Disappointer when it makes us inappropriately impatient. By the same token, however, it can play a benign Appointer role by urging an *appropriate impatience* on us. Sometimes, for example, we need to be opportunistic in order to score career victories. One client of mine, a painter, was in the middle of fine-tuning a tailored CV with me in my office late one afternoon when he got a text message. It was tipping him off about a dinner at an acquaintance's house that evening at which a *very* influential player in the art world was going to be putting in an appearance. I told the client to drop the CV, ring the friend IMMEDI-ATELY and wangle an invitation. After this I told him to go home and get dressed up for dinner. This was pure Vaulter Ego thinking at work, and by gum it got results. My client charmed the socks off the 'player' that evening and got a foot in the door of an arts scene he had been trying clumsily to break into for over two years. Although it took some nine months for tangible success to percolate through from this encounter, percolate through it did. My client was invited to show at a key exhibition in one of London's hippest galleries. The sales he made off the back of this one exhibition put enough money in his pocket to fund the rent on a beautiful and spacious studio in Wicklow. Even more importantly, his name was now seriously on people's radar in the art world. He hasn't looked back since.

Sometimes, then, you *do* have to be pushy and take Vaulter Ego shortcuts – as long as you have the talent, stamina and wit to back it up.

§

Some Typical Vaulter Ego Traps

- Allowing short-term sacrifices deter you from drawing up long-term plans
- Half-doing ten things rather than doing three things well
- Failing to see that not all "short cuts" are true short cuts
- Susceptibility to the soundbite culture and inability to devote sustained attention to any one thing
- Short-termism with money: seeing every investment that doesn't bring an immediate return (e.g. the cost of a college course) as a clean waste of money

---

- Giving up on a goal halfway through because success hasn't yet appeared on the horizon or because the buzz has started wearing off
- Flitting from one decision or plan to the next
- Lack of loyalty towards people

My own values + motivators

6

The Alterior Ego

'I just can't get you out of my head'

The Alterior Ego sets you up for across-the-board disappointment by getting you to base your life not on your own values and motivators but on those of other people – be they family, partner, peers, colleagues, employers, neighbours or even 'society' at large. Instead of being an autonomous, self-directing individual happy to leave your own mark on the world, you become a puppet of other people's expectations.*

Liam had worked within professional multinational operations for most of his career. He was a business consultant/IT man with a client-focused role. He felt that he had become two different people rolled into one: at work the corporate executive and outside of work the happy-go-lucky, health-conscious foody whose friends were what he himself described as 'militantly hippy and alternative'. He could not reconcile the two aspects of his life and was terrified of being 'found out' as a phoney by each side.

---

* Before we go any further I really must mention Tony Humphreys' book *Whose Life Are You Living?* (Dublin: Gill & Macmillan, 2003), which anatomises this Alterior Ego trap with impressive acuity.

This led him to overplay both roles in a desparate ploy for approval. At work, he was putting in excessive hours in order to impress colleagues who would otherwise 'see right through' him. He felt sure they suspected him of not being a true 'team player' aligned to company culture. Perhaps, he had reasoned to himself, putting in long hours might compensate for this lack of spontaneous connection? Liam's over-dedication to his job, however, didn't just exhaust him. It also made him feel embarrassed in his social circle outside of work. His greatest dread was that his friends, whose high regard he valued hugely, would think that he had 'sold out' and become a 'suit'. This led him to over-compensate in the other direction: hanging out until three in the morning rather than admitting that he was wrecked and needed to grab some sleep before an 8 a.m. conference call, smoking joints even though he no longer enjoyed it, going to yoga classes for no other reason than that a couple of mates had joined him up without even asking him first. Liam's bachelor pad in the city centre had become something of an open house for his friends, who would turn up unannounced at all hours and assume he was only too delighted to chill with them for a few hours. Liam, in short, was burning the candle at both ends, overdoing things to a sometimes ridiculous extent both at work and at play. Indeed, as he put it to me at one point, work had become a form of play-acting, play a form of work! Both were 'head-wrecking' and dispiriting. The only regular 'me time' Liam ever seemed to have was his twenty-minute walk to and from work. This at least allowed him to do something *on his own and for its own sake*: listening to his iPod.

As Liam and I started exploring alternative career options, he kept putting up road blocks. Any new idea was immediately vetoed on the basis that Person X, Y or Z would disapprove. This Alterior Ego obsession with what other people would think was reducing his room for manoeuvre to zero. He was boxing himself in, *but convincing himself that the boxing-in was actually being done by others.* He reminded me of the beleaguered citizens of George Orwell's totalitarian state in *Nineteen Eighty-Four*: scared silly of what Big Brother will think. Liam talked as if his life was being lived entirely for the benefit and pleasure of others. Worse than exhaustion, dissatisfaction and stress combined was the thought of other people's disapproval. It took several sessions for Liam to work through his fear of exposure and to build his self-esteem to a point where the self-limiting beliefs sponsored by his Alterior Ego no longer dominated the horizon to the exclusion of all else.

After going into his values, work motivators and skills base, Liam came to the somewhat surprising conclusion that he needed a new job rather than a new career as such. He decided to go freelance as an IT consultant. This involved a number of painful choices, not least of which was a sharp short-term drop in income and a corresponding move to a smaller and less central apartment. To Liam's astonishment, however, not one of the Alterior Ego scenarios he had feared regarding the reactions of others came to pass. His employers and colleagues reacted to the news of his departure with disappointment but also with expressions of support. Indeed, three different colleagues intimated to him 'off the record' that they envied him his courage in taking the plunge. As for his social circle, Liam used his transition to self-employed status as an opportunity to establish some new boundaries. Without making a big deal of it, he made it absolutely clear to each of his friends that he simply wouldn't have the same amount of free time as before. He didn't go into the role they had recently played in bringing him perilously close to burnout. There was no need – it hadn't been their fault that he had failed utterly to assert his own needs. But from here on in things would change. Never again would he say 'yes' to something unless he really wanted to do it. Never again would he allow himself to be held hostage by his fear of other people's negative judgements. And the result of this hitherto unthinkable level of self-assertion? His friends were incredibly supportive and congratulatory. Not a single one accused him of selling out. Not a single one thought any less of him for having asserted his own needs.

The result of Liam's successful realignment of his professional and social worlds was that he thrived in both as never before. Work become enjoyable, challenging and ultimately *very* lucrative financially. Being self-employed suited Liam to a T. Instead of getting distracted by office politics or other such nonsense, he was now able to focus 100 per cent on meeting the needs of clients directly. This freed him up no end, allowing him to take responsibility whenever a job got well done, but also compelling him to take responsibility whenever a job didn't. This newfound autonomy proved invigorating rather than frightening. As for Liam's social circle, the fact that he maintained close ties with his friends lent crucial balance to his new-found happiness at work. In fact, by his own admission, it was what now kept him from falling into the Halter Ego trap of workaholism. And now that he could face the working day *and* the non-working evening without being oppressed by speculations about other people's judgements, he started enjoying his own company for the first time in ages without the old feelings of unease or guilt coming up. In short, his life had become balanced, self-directing and *unapologetic.*

§

Liam's story shows how an Alterior Ego fixation on the opinion of others can work its way right down the line:

• Wrecking one's peace of mind at work

- Forcing one into phoney behaviour with family and friends outside of work
- Scaring one off from even contemplating change

The person who is dominated by Alterior Ego thinking becomes a Pleaser. Ironically, such a person more often than not ends up never really pleasing anyone. I can think of many examples of this phenomenon in the workplace. The employee who puts so much work into their presentations that their employer starts suspecting that they must be hiding a lack of substance. The interview candidate who is so given to flattery that the panel immediately puts her out of contention as insincere and weak. The fawning restaurant owner who makes his clientele feel uncomfortable. The middle manager whose attempts to court popularity amongst his staff backfire completely, earning him the nickname David Brent. The secondary school teacher who loses control of her class by making embarrassingly cack-handed attempts to be 'cool' in the first few lessons in September. The fact is, people *sense* when we are being inauthentic in an alter/ulterior way. Instead of winning respect, our Pleaser behaviour has precisely the opposite effect. People pick up the fact that that *we are not our own centre of gravity* and that we lack the courage of our own convictions and the honesty to be open with our real needs and opinions.

In a workplace culture where advancement up the career ladder often depends upon the almost feudal patronage of the boss, Alterior Ego behaviour becomes particularly prevalent. Instead of being myself, I start second-guessing everything I do, vetting it in terms of how it will be perceived by those above me. This is a secularised form of religious guilt: instead of the sinner obsessing over the thought that God is watching their every move, the Alterior Ego employee puts all their energy into placating the all-seeing company Big Brother. A kind of second spontaneity takes root. The employee says and does all the right things, but something seems to be missing. The Alterior Ego business personality is that bit too polished, too sleek and too conscious of being looked at and assessed. This degree of self-consciousness is corrosive, not just at a psychological level *but also at a professional one.* A person who takes action intelligently and unselfconsciously for the simple reason that it is the correct thing to do is a whole lot more effective than the person who asks at every turn, 'What will X think if I take this action?' Such Alterior Ego thinking can lead to bad decision making and, over time, a reputation for window-dressing superficiality.

§

Our IT friend Liam was lucky in three regards:

1. He was in a field that suited him.
2. His employers did not hit the roof when he announced his departure.
3. His friends did not react adversely to his redrawing of personal boundaries.

Things don't always go so smoothly.

I once had a client, we shall call him Killian, who was in his third year at medical college. His father was a GP, having shared the practice with Killian's now-deceased grandfather. Almost from the day of his birth, Killian had been groomed to take over the family practice. He had no real *grá* for the profession, but had gone along with what was expected of him.

When he came to me for coaching, Killian was in very low spirits. Medical college took the soul out of him. He just didn't want to go into the profession. He hadn't even been all that academic at school – only an intensive two years at an expensive grinds school had gotten him the points required for medicine. He felt out of his league – and out of his element. What he really wanted was to be a primary school teacher. When he had shared this fact with his family over Christmas dinner, holy war had broken out. His father had resorted to the 'over-my-dead-body' cliché, while his mother had burst into tears at his betrayal of his family's plans for him. This familial guilt trip was traumatic enough for Killian, but the reaction of his friends was even more shocking. With only one or two exceptions, they had all told him he was 'mad' to consider dropping out of medical college. This lack of support was not, as he had initially hoped, a matter of their getting used to the idea gradually. It became even more glaring as the months had worn on. Pretty soon Killian had come to the appalled conclusion that his friends' affection for him had been based on one particular picture of him and his future. Put simply, there was more than a little upper-crust social snobbery at work here. To hang out with a prospective doctor was one thing, to hang out with a primary school teacher quite another. Killian could hardly believe the crassness of some of the responses he got from so-called 'friends' when he gave them the news of his intentions to move out of medicine. When one had patronisingly assured him he was just 'going through a phase', Killian had responded sharply: 'Yeah, the phase of thinking you were a friend. F*** off.'

Killian felt like his world was crumbling around him. The only thing that steadied his nerve was the moral, emotional and indeed financial support of his boyfriend, Marc. (Tellingly, Killian's family did know of Marc's existence. In fact, they did not even know that Killian was gay.) Without Marc's unconditional love, Killian would have found it extremely difficult to 'go out on his own' and follow *his* dream rather than that imposed upon him by others. With coaching, I was able to help Killian take a deep breath, extricate himself from medical college gracefully and strategically and make a successful application to a teacher training college. He now works in the primary school sector and is specialising in working with autistic children. I wish I could report that relations with his family and friends were restored bit by bit, but I'm afraid I cannot. Three years down the line he reported to me that things were still extremely brittle at home. Some of the friendships that had come under strain as a result of Killian's change of career had died a quiet death. Others had survived, though Killian felt that things were never quite the same afterwards.

The point here is that his Alterior Ego *had not been lying to him* when it told him that other people's opinion of him would take a nosedive if he became self-directing in terms of his career. *The Alterior Ego lie lay elsewhere*: that life would become unbearable if the approval of these people were withdrawn. Killian showed immense personal courage in facing down this lie. While the price for his new-found autonomy was indeed high, it was far from unbearably so. Did he regret having rocked the boat and thrown his Alterior Ego overboard? Absolutely not, he assured me. He felt as if an albatross had been prised from around his neck. He was, for the first time in his life, a free man.

§

I have seen a number of curious cases where the Alterior Ego gets a person to do something they don't really want to do, not because others *want* them to do it but because others *don't* want them to do it. We might call this the defiant mode of Alterior Ego behaviour. It may appear at first glance to involve a rebellion against the judgement of others. In reality, however, it shares a common root with ultra-conformist behaviour: fixation on *what others think*.

Julie had been a successful graphic designer. After seven years in this field, however, she had decided that it did not satisfy her at a deeper level. What she really wanted was to become (like Killian, as it happens) a primary school teacher. She went back and studied for her Irish Leaving Cert at night and got the honour she needed. She then applied for teacher training and put all the measures possible in place to ensure that she was as equipped as she could be to do a good interview for the college course place. When she came to me for coaching four years later, Julie had succeeded handsomely in her goal of becoming a primary school teacher. But – she was deeply unhappy. The job just didn't suit her personality. She found the routine oppressive and felt she had little in common with her colleagues. At first the actual classroom teaching part of the job had been stimulating and enjoyable, but she had gradually found herself getting more and more frustrated in the job. She found it hard to keep discipline, particularly with such a large group, and was upset at what she saw as the tut-tut response of her older colleagues to her difficulties.

It had all gone horribly wrong. Julie's route to school every morning happened to take her past her old graphic design company. She now found herself looking at the building with nostalgia and regret, feeling envious of the people she saw walking in and out. Their lives seemed so much *freer* than hers!

The more Julie probed her situation with me, the clearer it became that she had made a bad call in going into teaching. This just didn't feel to me like one of those temporary blips that can hit a person when they switch career. No, we seemed to be talking about a straightforward lack of match between person and job. It was also becoming increasingly evident that the work Julie was best suited to was indeed the very area she had marched out of four years previously – graphic design. Looking back at the feelings of discontent that had caused her to leave in the first place, she came to a surprising realisation: she hadn't left the job, she had left one particular colleague whom she had found obnoxious. It just so happened that this colleague had himself recently moved on from the company. There was in principle nothing to stop Julie from making overtures to the company to have her back. From what she had picked up from a former colleague with whom she had kept in touch, there was good reason to believe that the firm would welcome her back with open arms.

This was a no-brainer, right? Sound out the graphic design people and, if the light's green, give fair notice to the school.

But something was making Julie reluctant to take these simple steps. It wasn't any lingering loyalty to the idea of being a primary school teacher. Nor was it any fear that she wouldn't enjoy being back at graphic design. It was something else entirely – and something that only came out almost by accident during one of our sessions:

Julie's mother had warned her that this would happen.

There you have it. Julie could not bear the thought of fulfilling the pessimistic prophecy that her mother had made around the time of Julie's career switch. She had really resented her mother's lack of 'buy-in' at the time. Indeed, when the going had been getting tough with her Irish studies, Julie had been sustained by the thought that she was going to *prove her mother wrong*. Now she was faced with the humiliating prospect of proving her mother right.

Hence her reluctance to go back to Plan A (graphic design). The irony here was that Julie's determination to defy her mother's opinion meant that her mother's opinion was controlling Julie to an unconscionable degree. This was win–win for Julie's Alterior Ego. Had she copped out of going for primary school teaching four years ago, her Alterior Ego would have scored a significant victory by getting her to value her mother's fears over her own judgement. Were she now to cop out of leaving primary school teaching, her Alterior Ego would merely be scoring an ever greater victory by getting her to fear her mother's judgement over her own need for a happy career. Julie was seriously proposing to stick with a job she hated for the next ten-plus years in order to avoid the temporary unpleasantness of an I-told-you-so look on her mother's face.

Through coaching, Julie came to see the absurdity of this state of affairs. In the end, she managed her return to graphic design with grace and grit. How did she deal with her mother? She sat her down and said with a self-deprecating smile on her face, 'Mammy, I never thought I'd say this but you were right about the teaching. Go easy on me!' Her mother was relieved; and, to Julie's relief, didn't rub her daughter's nose in it at all. In fact, she congratulated her on having had the courage to reassess things. Where the Alterior Ego had made this scene appear truly mortifying in Julie's imagination, the reality was gentle and benign. Julie is now back in graphic design and loving it like never before. True, the recession has meant that business has taken quite a hit, but she has every confidence the company will ride out the storm. Her exit from the primary school has had a similarly happy ending. Julie pays frequent return visits there, not out of nostalgia or guilt but because she has pioneered an art scheme for the pupils. This has earned her huge appreciation from her former teaching colleagues. As for Julie's relationship with her mother, it is stronger than ever before.

As is so often the case, an Alterior Ego monster had turned out to be a huggy bear.

§

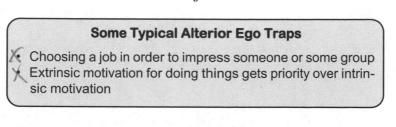

Some Typical Alterior Ego Traps

✗ Choosing a job in order to impress someone or some group
✗ Extrinsic motivation for doing things gets priority over intrinsic motivation

- Indecision
- Obsession with personal appearance and the impression you are making
- Susceptibility to celebrity culture
- Tendency to idealise others, especially those perceived as successful
- Conformism, following the crowd, chasing peer validation
- Having the courage of other people's convictions
- Being a little too quick to change your mind about something
- Flattering people

7

The Salter Ego

'Poor me'

The Salter Ego wants you to feel sorry for yourself. Like the Faulter Ego, it likes getting you to focus on the negative. Like the Altar Ego, it encourages belief in 'bad luck' as a way of life. But it takes a distinctive pleasure in having grievances.

Emmett had been a convenience store franchisee for the past two years. He got to run his own shop, but under the banner of a well-known trade name. This gave him relative autonomy while allowing him to enjoy the appreciable benefits of name recognition. The margin of profit was tight but just about high enough to justify the hard work involved in running the business.

Emmett was at the end of his tether, however. He found the work stressful and unrewarding. The arrangement with the franchise company was not working out as he had projected. He felt they were constantly after their pound of flesh. Relations with staff were also fraught, as were those with customers, many of whom Emmett found demanding and downright rude. There were also youngsters hanging around in groups outside the shop. Emmett was convinced they were keeping potential customers away. The local Gardaí seemed to have no interest in helping Emmett deal with this problem. To complete the perfect storm, a rival convenience store was scheduled to open just around the corner in a few weeks time.

I didn't doubt that Emmett had some genuine grievances and pressures here. Being a small businessman can be incredibly stressful. Being a small businessman in the retail sector can be bloody murder. So I did sympathise. However, it quickly became apparent to me that Emmett seemed to take absolutely everything as a personal slight (at best) or a full-blooded insult (at worst). I listened as he wove episode after episode into a long-running narrative of Emmett Versus the World. He would let the merest incident stress him out no end. In addition, he never ever seemed to take time out to consider the other person's point of view. Thus, to take just one example, one of the ladies working for him behind the counter had been showing strong reluctance to work Sundays. Even when Emmett offered her time-and-three-quarters, she still dug in her heels, claiming she wanted to spend Sundays with her husband. (She was in her late fifties.) Emmett flat out disbelieved her, even accusing her to her face of lying to him. When she reacted badly to this accusation, he levelled a fresh allegation at her – that she was being 'selfish and inconsiderate'. Personnel Management 101! Emmett's face would flush with resentment every time he narrated incidents like this. Wholly absent from his version of events was any notion that he might have been at least partially to blame for the loss of goodwill between him and the other person. It was as if the faculty of self-criticism was missing from his personal repertoire.

It finally reached the stage where I couldn't bite my tongue any longer. 'Emmett, can I ask you a simple question? Why on earth did you go into running a convenience store if you hate every aspect of the job?' He was furious at the question. I hadn't been listening to a bloody word he'd been saying, he thundered. I had no idea of the stresses and strains of running a shop. I was blaming the victim. Immediately turning this around, I asked Emmett why he seemed to spend his time *playing* the victim. Once again, he took the question in high dudgeon.

Emmett's starting assumption in life seemed to be that people had it in for him. No gesture was uncomplicatedly friendly, no comment free of insinuating subtext. This, of course, set in motion a self-fulfilling dynamic:

HARMLESS INPUT IN ——— OFFENCE TAKEN ———TENSION

HOSTILE INPUT IN ——— OFFENCE TAKEN ——— TENSION

Without realising it, Emmett had allowed his Salter Ego to get him hooked on self-pity, righteous indignation and defensiveness. Something in his psyche told him that the other person's default attitude towards him was one of unkindness and under-the-surface hostility. Now let's be clear here. This wasn't a case of clinical paranoia or anything. Despite the impression I may have given in the sketch above, Emmett was not disconnected from reality. Nor was he an aggressive man. What was happening was that he was allowing himself in my presence to verbalise the tacit conclusions he had habitually been drawing about other people's attitude towards him. In all other respects, Emmett appeared to be a well-adjusted, intelligent and likeable man. Only in his business life did his Salter Ego seem to take over and make a misery of things.

Something was not right here. In the second coaching session, we managed to tease that something out: Emmett had been full of enthusiasm when he first opened the shop. It had always been a dream of his to run his own little place. Within a few short weeks, however, he had come to a horrifying realisation – he just didn't enjoy it at all. In his heart of hearts, Emmett just wanted to walk away from the project. He just *knew* it wasn't for him.

But it was too late. Significant money had been invested in the franchise, not to mention the strict contractual commitment he had made. Caught in this impossible trap, he had resorted to Salter Ego tactics to sabotage the whole operation. This involved projecting his own dislike of the business onto everyone else: business partners, staff, customers. Anyone but Emmett himself. It became the world's fault that he hated his job. His anger with himself for having walked into this mess was projected outwards.

In the end, and through a careful seven-step plan formulated with me, Emmett managed to extricate himself from the convenience store over a period of sixteen months. Having smoked out his Salter Ego, we were able to address the logistical and tactical challenge (and, believe me, it was a *big* challenge) without getting distracted by the proxy Salter Ego problem. While the problem was being sorted out, Emmett learned to take a more benevolent view of the people he was dealing with. There was no conspiracy of ill-will against him. He had just made a poor decision, that was all. And now it was up to him to put things right – minus the chip on the shoulder. *Once a plan for the future was in place*, he had more energy for his current job. The emotional resistance was gone. By the time of his very last day in the shop, he had become an emotionally intelligent and well-liked employer, not to mention a man well-versed in the difficult art of customer relations. He was still clear on the fact that this was not the life for him, but could look back with pride at having brought the plane in for safe landing.

Emmett was primed for the next phase of his professional life. He decided to take a year out as a stay-at-home husband looking after his newborn daughter. He was lucky enough to be able to afford to do this in the short term and was willing to make any life changes necessary for it. He would use this time to upskill in business management and attend evening classes, with the intention ultimately of finding a job that suited his personality and met his priority needs in a way that retailing hadn't. We continued working together intermittently over the next twelve months, at the end of which Emmett found a job working as a clinic manager for a chain of medical clinics who were seeking a strong business manager not necessarily from a medical background. It turned out to be a much better fit.

§

I must confess that, when it comes to coaching, the Salter Ego is the trickiest Disappointer of all. The reason is simple. Some people really *do* have extremely difficult lives. Some people really *do* get treated like dirt out there in the real world. Some people really *are* victims. So how do you tell the difference between a legitimate narrative of real-life suffering and a Salter Ego sob story?

I can't answer that in a soundbite. It can be horribly difficult to get this discrimination right. Sometimes all I have to go on is the client's use of language. Do they have a predilection for self-pitying turns of phrase? Do they seem almost to enjoy being the narrator of unhappy tales involving themselves? Do they seem to lack a self-critical vocabulary? Do they habitually seem to downplay the possibility that they may have been at fault somewhere along the line? If the answer to any of these questions is yes, then the Salter Ego may be at work. This is *not* to say that the client has been inventing his or her experiences out of whole cloth. I would *never* accuse a client of doing that. What the Salter Ego does is more subtle. *It gets us to frame our real-life experiences, whether positive, negative or ambiguous, in terms of a suspiciously coherent narrative of victimhood and unfairness.*

§

Ruth was an academic in her mid-thirties. Her specialist field was sociology. Her view of the world was engaged and radical, being informed by an interesting blend of feminist and Marxist theory. We spent a few minutes breaking the ice in our first session by talking about Ruth's subject area. She was an absolute joy to listen to – incredibly well read, intellectually provocative and deeply, deeply passionate about great themes like justice and equality.

And yet, and yet … she was not in a good place career-wise. She had spent the past two years lecturing at a UK university, an experience that had left her feeling restless and underappreciated. Her contract there had one more year to run. Prior to this stint she had spent nearly a decade moving around from one Irish or British third-level institution to the next feeling … well, restless and underappreciated. Not one had made her feel at home. Not one had shown the slightest interest in holding on to her.

The reason? Ruth was in absolutely no doubt on that score: it was her gender. At several points along the line she had gotten into bitter rows with male colleagues. Although gender had never been brought up, even obliquely, Ruth believed the real cause of each row had been covert sexism.

Now I had no idea at first whether or not Ruth's assessment was a sound one. God knows, plenty of women have been kept down by the infamous glass ceiling of institutionalised conservatism. What bothered me here, however, was the dogmatic neatness of Ruth's explanation for her lack of professional progress. Some of the institutions she named were not exactly a byword for male chauvinism. And besides, Ruth herself had already admitted to me that she knew of plenty of fellow female academics who had not had her difficulties in advancing up the career ladder either in Ireland or the UK.

At the risk of giving offence, I put it to Ruth that she might be open to the charge of playing the feminist card. Could she really put her hand on her heart and tell me that her gender was the *only conceivable* variable that might account for her lack of traction in one academic department after another? Was she *absolutely sure* that other factors might not have impacted on her relations with colleagues? Had she, for instance, been an easy person to get on with? What message did she give out to people? What was her publishing track record like, as compared with that of other, more successful peers? Had she played an enthusiastic and committed role in the broader life of the departments she had worked in? When Ruth started batting off these questions with unvarying reference to her gender, I started getting really uneasy. Sure, she could be a little abrasive with people, but that was purely because she had had to defend herself against the conservative culture. Sure, her publications had tapered off significantly in recent years, but that was because she kept getting blacklisted for her radical reputation. Sure, she had opted out of key aspects of college life, but that was because she didn't feel welcome in a heavily masculinist environment ....

It all sounded terribly pat, a convenient catch-all excuse for a stalled career founded on underachievement. That Ruth bore absolutely no responsibility for having failed to get her name on the academic map I found hard to credit. It sounded like a textbook Salter Ego over-simplification.

I invited Ruth to do a Put the Case exercise. This involved activating a simple hypothesis and tracing its consequences. In Ruth's case, the hypothesis was: *Put the case that the reason for my stalled career is not my gender.* I made it clear to Ruth in advance that this exercise was a *thought experiment.* It did *not* require that she commit herself to the premise, merely that she enter its subjunctive space.

The results were startling. Forced for the sake of the exercise to identify home-made culprits for her lack of advancement, Ruth came up with the following:

1. Poor publication record over the past few years; this due to a combination of low submission rate and poor feedback by peer reviewers
2. Lack of a single published monograph to my name*
3. Fairly high absenteeism, including a tendency to cancel classes at short notice
4. Dogmatic and agenda-driven style of teaching students; intolerance of alternative viewpoints
5. Overly confrontational style with fellow academics, both at administrative meetings and seminars/conferences; always playing devil's advocate

Without relinquishing her 'gender discrimination' narrative, Ruth agreed to do an experiment. She would spend the final year of her UK contract systematically addressing items 1–5 to the very best of her ability. Publication would become a priority. She would commit a certain amount of time each week to the large project of getting a monograph underway. She would get her act together on the teaching efficiency front, becoming more reliable and student friendly. She would tone things down in academic discussions (*without* in the least compromising her own radical views). She would try to see colleagues 'in 3D' – i.e. as people rather than rivals. This would involve, amongst other things, making an effort to get to know them socially.

Ruth was happy to sign off on this experiment because it was win–win. If she addressed her own shortcomings, as itemised with commendable frankness in the five points on the list, and still found herself being treated as a second-class citizen, then her gender discrimination theory would have received some pretty powerful supporting evidence. In which case she would have to consider her options in a sober and serious way. If, on

---

* Monograph: a book-length study of a particular topic.

the other hand, her changed approach had the effect of opening up doors for her in the academic world, then she would be free of her Salter Ego *exaggeration* of any role that gender discrimination might have played in damaging her career. The deal was that Ruth would come back to me for a refresher coaching session in nine months time.

When I next saw her she was in sparkling form: intellectually on fire; three articles published already this year; book project beginning to take shape; student attendance at classes much improved due to more reliability and efficiency on Ruth's part as well as a more congenial atmosphere; two solid friendships nurtured with departmental colleagues, one of whom Ruth had previously detested.

There were still problems, to be sure. Foremost of these was the fact that Ruth's contract was fast running out without any sign of its being renewed. However Ruth was less quick than she would have been in the past to interpret this through a Salter Ego prism. A few discreet enquiries had established that it might not actually be in the gift of the department to offer Ruth a renewal of her contract. Funding issues, coupled with some tedious interdepartmental politics, might be to blame. While this was extremely annoying, it was not *personal*. It would also have been quite a stretch to connect these factors with Ruth's gender.

The task now was not to revert to Salter Ego lamentation but to stay ahead of the curve by figuring out what she was to do once this current job was up. Here I challenged Ruth's assumption that she had to seek yet another academic teaching post. Why not change tack and make her book an absolute priority for a year or two? Obviously this would have to be made financially viable. How about being cheeky and trying to source some serious research funding? Despite initial scepticism, Ruth put out feelers both in Ireland and back in the UK. Within a few weeks she had hit bullseye. A prestigious academic establishment in the USA was taking applications for a generous two-year research scholarship in her field. Ruth went for it – *and got it.* The end of her teaching post and the beginning of the scholarship did not dovetail too well, but Ruth wasn't about to let a gap of a few months hold her back now. She came back to Dublin, moved in with an old friend on a low-rent basis and took out a modest credit union loan to tide her over until her trip across the Atlantic. Things really had turned around.

§

Some Typical Salter Ego Traps

- A constant sense of grievance and resentment over perceived slights or injustices to yourself – everything becomes an I'm-ringing-Joe-Duffy-about-this incident
- Taking all rejection or criticism personally
- Envy of others' success – uncoupled from any halfway objective assessment of whether it is deserved or not
- Whining rather than doing
- Seeking out the company of fellow whiners
- Bitching behind other people's backs
- Rejecting solutions even when they are offered
- Misinterpreting data in order to feed an unhappy narrative
- Failing to assert yourself at work, instead rerunning your defeats as a home movie over and over again in your head – though this time with a happy ending in which you devastate the other party with your wit and quick thinking
- Refusing to see any connection between your performance and negative feedback from others
- Setting higher standards for those around you than for yourself
- Loving humanity but not being a big fan of human beings
- Inability to plan for success
- Reducing everything to politics

8

The Exalter Ego

'Baby I can drive my car'

The most common manifestation of the Exalter Ego tendency is to be found in people who want the world to know that they are Mr Alpha Male or Ms Superwoman: high-octane performers who work hard, play hard and live out every cliché in the book. Usually taking their metaphors from the world of sports, Exalter Ego people reduce life to a zero-sum game between antagonists or teams. The Exalter Ego produces obnoxious winners and bad losers. Because it runs on the high-achiever notion that you are what you do, it treats 'success' in the professional and social sphere as the sole source of self-esteem and psychological wellbeing. When the Exalter Ego person is 'winning', this is a disaster – the person becomes intolerably full of themselves. When the Exalter Ego person is 'losing', it's no less of a disaster – the insecurities which made that person take refuge in Exalter Ego ideology in the first place come shooting to the surface.

§

Paul worked in Dublin's International Financial Services Centre as a senior lender. He was 33 and impeccably groomed. A deep tan testified to frequent sunshine holidays, while a polished mid-Atlantic baritone gave off signals that this guy was an accomplished and self-assured networker.

Paul had booked some career coaching sessions with me. Usually this means that the client is looking for intensive prep work for a particular position which they have in their sights. The procedure for this is standard enough:

Research + Application Preparation + Interview Coaching

– all meticulously tailored to the specific echelon.

Something, however, told me that all was not well with Paul. The surface smoothness was contradicted by a marked tendency to avoid eye contact. Paul's face looked a little thin, and it was hard not to get the impression that his small talk was a bit too auto-pilot for comfort. After a gentle introductory Wheel of Life exercise, Paul started letting his defences down. He had recently been diagnosed with a stomach ulcer, and had no doubt that work-related stress was the culprit. While he was superb at his stockbroking job, and had never had any trouble working his way up the ladder and accumulating serious money along the way, he was finding the eternal round of networking and socialising increasingly hollow. He had long since discovered that such add-ons were anything but incidental to life in his sector. In order to remain well connected, you simply *had* to play the game with 100 per cent commitment. At work and at play, no weakness could be shown to others. No bad days were allowed.

This was classic Exalter Ego territory:

* Alpha male behaviour
* Subordination of everything to a bottom line
* Indifference to ethical concerns
* Reduction of the person to a synthetically sleek persona

What made Paul unusual was the fact that he was finding it increasingly difficult to play the game. It was not so much that he was bored. Rather he found himself increasingly *allergic* to the phoney BS that went with the job. While he was perfectly adept at playing the role required of him, he had found himself wondering of late whether he really *wanted* to keep playing this role. The idea of going for a higher position in the firm had stemmed from this soul-searching; perhaps if he moved up the ladder he might enjoy a bit more freedom to be himself? As we talked, however, it became increasingly clear that a vertical move within the organisation would be unlikely to give him such freedom. If anything, it would probably make things worse.

We soon established that Paul was actually at the mercy of *three* Disappointers, of which the Exalter Ego was merely the most symptomatic:

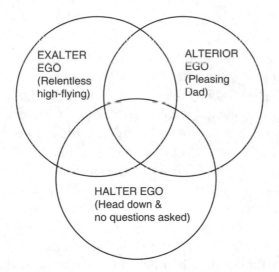

Looking back at the things that had driven his entry into the field of senior lending, Paul came to see that his Exalter Ego drive to be dazzlingly successful had taught him the Halter Ego tactics of keeping the head down, asking no awkward questions and devoting body and soul to the job. Going back to what had originally fuelled Paul's *need* for Exalter Ego affirmation, he immediately identified his Alterior Ego need to be thought highly of. Specifically, he suspected that this need stemmed from the impossibly high expectations of his hard-to-please father, who had himself been a successful figure in the financial services field.

For all the aplomb with which Paul had been playing the role of Self-Made Man, he had been hiding from himself the true reason why he wanted to be a self-made man in the first place: insecurity about his ultimate self-worth. Behind all Paul's long hours working and networking lay one simple goal: *to impress his father*. The Self-Made Man was in reality the Man Made in Someone Else's Image. All these years he had been going about not his own work but his father's. And the cruel thing about this project in self-exaltation was that it was self-defeating. No matter how many promotions Paul got, how many deals he swung or how much money he made, he would never be doing anything other than chasing his own shadow. There would never come a point when he would be able to look himself in the mirror and say, 'There, I've done it, I'm OK.' Why would this never happen? *Because Paul had been looking for self-esteem in all the wrong places.*

I have not mentioned yet that Paul was married. He and his wife, Isobel, had a young son with special needs. Apart from the fact that this circumstance contrasted sharply with the ultra-Darwinian culture of Paul's workplace, it also presented Paul and Isobel with huge practical and emotional challenges. Because of Paul's high-earner status, however, those challenges did not extend to the financial. When Paul's first two coaching sessions with me threw up his growing dissatisfaction with his job, he was understandably alarmed. Could he really contemplate changing career direction at this delicate time for his family?

Over the next few weeks we probed this question carefully, not assuming that the answer was a self-evident yes. I cautioned Paul against over-reacting to his current dislike of the business culture. The fact was, he liked making money. It motivated him. He liked clinching deals. They motivated him. He liked the buzz of a new challenge. Plus – he was damned good at all these things. Instead of leaving the business world as such, might it not be an idea to make a horizontal move out of his current field and into another, more palatable, business enterprise? This idea excited him a lot, and before long sparks started flying in his head. Bit by bit a plan took shape: Paul would ease his way out of stockbroking and start a venture capital firm with an old school friend who had recently made noises in this direction. This friend was someone Paul trusted and, no less importantly, could be himself around. Their friendship went back to third class in school. They had been in a band together. Even after the band had broken up, they had often dreamed of going into cahoots on some grand adventure together. Well here it was. Bringing their astuteness and project-managing skills together, Paul and his friend set up the venture capital firm. From the outset they were clear that not a cent would be invested in any enterprise with which either of them felt less than 100 per cent comfortable. Paul was up for the game, but to all intents and purposes he was out of the Exalter Ego game.

§

An important lesson to take from Paul's story is that being wary of Exalter Ego behaviour does *not* mean being wary of dynamic, enterprising or high-flying behaviour. On the contrary, I have had clients who have been stuck in a Faulter Ego syndrome of under-achievement. These people have *needed* a bit of Exalter Ego get-up-and-go to shake them out of their lethargy. They

161

have *needed* to stand a little taller and aim a lot higher. For some people, the only thing that can give that extra push when it comes to realising vocational potential is Exalter Ego determination and doggedness. Sometimes it's OK to be on an ego trip. Sometimes it's OK to be immodest. And yes, sometimes it's OK to be fiercely competitive. The key question in each case is this: *What makes the person be most true to themselves?*

We might sum this up as follows. An Exalter Ego-*dominated* individual is someone who has fallen prey to an *overly* egotistical way of being. In which case a bit of Faulter Ego self-criticism is called for. A Faulter Ego-dominated person, on the other hand, has fallen prey to an overly self-critical way of being. In which case a bit of Exalter Ego egotism is called for. It's all down to the individual case.

§

Sometimes the Exalter Ego can pick a victim who, unlike Paul, is *incapable of playing the high-achiever's game* with any measure of success. We might call this the Wannabe mode of Exalter Ego behaviour. The Wannabe is a person who tries to get themselves promoted beyond their talents in a given field. They are too slick, too pushy, too crassly go-getting, too eager to make you aware of their opinion that lunch is for wimps. Such a person, in short, makes a fool of themselves by continuously *trying too hard.* No one admires a person like this, for their veneer of self-assurance fails to hide their desperate need to be admired. No one trusts a person like this, for they give off endless signals of disloyalty, calculation and insincerity. These blatant attempts at Exalter–Alterior strategising kid no one – certainly not in the long run.

§

Exalter Ego behaviour can sometimes be pretty subtle. Charles, a 31-year-old, had spent the guts of the past year on the dole. He had previously been a music teacher in a secondary school. But a row with the principal had upset him deeply, leading him to resign his post at very short notice. This event had triggered feelings of despair in Charles about his career prospects. His twenties had been dominated by the dream of writing music for films. Having entered music college from school, his obvious compositional skills had given him the sense that he was marked out for certain greatness in his chosen field. But somehow he had never made good on this early promise, a fact which left him vulnerable to the dread scenario of temp job after temp job. You did not need to be Sigmund Freud to suspect that his run-in with the school principal the year before had given him the excuse he longed for to leave a job he hated. As he told me himself, every moment spent in the classroom had served only to remind him that he had failed in his dream of writing film scores. Being on the dole was not exactly enjoyable, but at least it had the merit of giving Charles enough 'head space' to stay reasonably unstressed.

At the suggestion of his girlfriend, Charles had agreed try some career coaching. In our early sessions, he kept telling me what a 'waste of space' he was, how much of a failure he was compared to his friends and peers. At our second session he even brought along his old school yearbook in order to show me his class photo. 'Get this, Jane. Out of all those guys there, I'm without doubt the biggest failure. Whenever I bump into any of them around and they ask me what I'm up to, I want to burrow down into the ground out of embarrassment.' This sounded like good old-fashioned Faulter Ego talk. However, when I asked Charles what he thought of the various career paths his old classmates had chosen, a very different attitude came out. 'Oh, they've all sold out. Whenever I meet them, it nauseates me to see how middle-aged and smug they've become with golf umbrellas in their hand and golfballs in their mouth.'

Pretty impressive mental gymnastics, don't you think? On the one hand, Charles was attacking *himself* for being the one conspicuous failure in a class of success stories. On the other, he was anxious to establish how much he despised *their* 'bourgeois' notions of success!

Returning Charles to the question of his original dream of being a famous and brilliant film composer, I gently wondered aloud whether his deepest need might not in fact be to feel special, exceptional, different.

'My intuition tells me that you're afraid to take on a career other than that of composer because it would mean having to drop your all-or-nothing perfectionism and join the dreaded crowd. Is this true?'

'You think I enjoy being on the dole?!'

'Of course not. All I'm suggesting is that you may find it *less intolerable* to be exceptionally unsuccessful than to be averagely successful.'

'But I don't want to do a job I hate for people I despise!'

'That's understandable, Charles, but why do you immediately assume that that is the only type of job out there?'

'Spare me the rhetorical questions. *I am a composer!*'

'Then by all means compose away. My question is, could you ever see your way to forgiving yourself for not being a *rich and famous* composer?'

This opened Charles's mind to an idea which, rather surprisingly, he had never thought of before: that it was perfectly valid to be a composer who happened to earn the bulk of his income from something other than his musical compositions. Once this possibility was on the table, Charles could leave behind his Exalter Ego's all-or-nothing attitude to success – one which all but guaranteed failure – and start relating to his music again *directly*, *as an artist.* Fame, fortune and ego-glorification were no longer seen as paramount criteria of success. If they came along as a by-product of excellence, then well and good. If not, then well and nearly as good.

Charles got himself back on track by disempowering not just his Exalter Ego but also three other Disappointers which it had been feeding off:

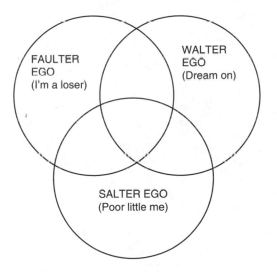

FAULTER EGO (I'm a loser)

WALTER EGO (Dream on)

SALTER EGO (Poor little me)

Once Charles got an overview of the mess he had gotten himself into, he was primed to turn things around. This involved, amongst other things, infusing his new career strategy with neglected Appointer wisdom:

HALTER EGO:
Put the head down and cultivate a
compositional work ethic

VOLTAIRE EGO:
Stop worrying about getting recognised
and start enjoying the task of quietly
cultivating my own artistic garden away
from the eyes of the world

WALTER
EGO
(Dream on)

SALTER EGO
(Poor little me)

FAULTER
EGO
(I'm a loser)

It really was that easy. Within two months, Charles had secured a part-time but very well-remunerated job teaching music at a boarding school. This gave him ample time to work on his composing. Last I heard from him, he was thriving – and, as he mischievously put it to, 'really proud of my new found modesty ;)'.

§

One of the Exalter Ego's favourite and most effective techniques is *comparison*. There is no simpler way to unsettle someone out of a sense of positive self-regard than to teach them to compare themselves unfavourably to others. Jean-Jacques Rousseau, the great French philosopher and social theorist, came up with a theory of where man's unhappiness comes from. He identified the culprit as *amour propre*, a sentiment we might loosely translate as 'envy'. Rousseau's basic contention was that our natural joy in life is shattered as soon as we begin to compare our situation with that of others. I can be living a simple life on a small farm, as happy as the days are long. But give me just a glimpse of someone living in a grand house with a host of wonderful diversions, and suddenly a new thought will creep into my soul: *I have less than that person*. At that moment, *amour propre* has begun to displace *amour de soi*, which is the natural, unreflective contentment an unspoiled person has with themselves. Whereas before I lived with the feeling that my life had its own centre of gravity, now I find myself plagued by the awareness of other, more attractive centres of gravity elsewhere. Inasmuch as I begin to envy others, I start to depreciate myself.

Clearly there is no escape from the logic of comparison once you embark upon it. No matter what you achieve or what your skills are, no matter how brilliantly you do what you do, there will always be criteria by which you will seem to be and have *less than* others. The Exalter Ego exploits this fact with cruel glee. First it encourages you to compare your strengths favourably with other people's weaknesses. Then it encourages you to compare your weaknesses unfavourably with other people's strengths. Then it gets you to compare your strengths unfavourably with other people's *stronger strengths.*

One reason the Exalter Ego finds 'comparisonitis' so delightful is that it often involves *drawing inaccurate conclusions from accurate perceptions.*

Alan, a Canadian IT whizz-kid in his late twenties living and working in London, contacted me for some coaching. He designed interactive computer games for use in an educational context. Word of his talent and flair for original work had obviously started spreading. For the past couple of years corporations and research departments had been flirting with him, dangling ever larger cheques and scholarships in front of his eyes. Yet, he confessed to me, he got absolutely no pleasure out of his growing success in the field. The reason? One of his colleagues on his current research project was 'simply in a different league' to him, a fact which took all the good out of the work for Alan. Not that this other guy was an unfriendly or unsupportive colleague. On the contrary, he was a brilliant person to work alongside. No, it was just that his effortless ability to generate ideas and solutions which Alan could not come up with in his wildest dreams was hitting a raw nerve. Alan was used to being the brains of the class. Indeed, so used was he to having no cognitive or intellectual equal at school or university that he had assumed that this was just one of those happy facts of life. As he noted ruefully, 'Meeting this guy has taught me that I'm not a competitive guy – except when I'm losing.' Working alongside the new genius was poisoning Alan's spirit so much that he knew that even if he were to move to the other side of the world he would still be haunted by the knowledge that there was at least one other human being who made his own best efforts look 'totally lame' by comparison. Alan was like a man who wins a frame of snooker but feels like he has lost because a man on the *next* table has just made a maximum break of 147.

I asked Alan if he had ever seen the film *Amadeus*. Based on Peter Shaffer's play of the same name, it tells the story of a composer named Salieri who becomes consumed with envy at the genius of a certain other composer by the name of Mozart. Alan's smile of recognition told me that he had indeed seen it – three times, as it turned out. He found the point of comparison both amusing and uncomfortable.

I cite Alan's story because it shows that the Faulter Ego and the Exalter Ego are secret buddies. The Faulter Ego does not restrict its prey to what we might think of as low achievers. By any reasonable standards, Alan was a high flyer. His Faulter Ego had teamed up with his Exalter Ego to see to it that, out of all the human beings currently living on planet Earth, it would be the slightly higher-flying colleague working next to him who would get all his attention.

Comparison need not be handed over to the Exalter Ego as a whip with which to scourge you. It need not be a source of unease, resentment or insecurity. Noam Chomsky, the celebrated American linguist and political commentator, has had some fine words to say on the topic:

I am personally quite convinced that no matter what training or education I might have received, I could never have run a four-minute mile, discovered Gödel's theorems, composed a Beethoven quartet, or risen to any of innumerable other heights of human achievement. I feel in no way demeaned by these inadequacies. It is quite enough that I am capable, as I think any person of normal endowments probably is, of appreciating and in part understanding what others have accomplished, while making my own personal contributions in whatever measure and manner I am able to do. Human talents vary considerably, within a fixed framework that is characteristic of the species and that permits ample scope for creative work, including the creative work of appreciating the achievements of others. This should be a matter for delight rather than a condition to be abhorred … My pleasure in life is enhanced by the fact that others can do many things that I cannot ….*

I showed these words to Alan and asked him whether he had ever been envious of people before.

'Not really, I always managed to shine at school and college.'

'I find it interesting that you immediately translate my question in terms of your educational abilities.'

'Isn't that what you meant?'

'Well, no, it was a more general question. Academic performance is only one marker of personal achievement, isn't it?'

'I've always known that being academically gifted was my strongest calling card in life.'

We were on to something here. As we delved further into this topic of academic success, which had been the guiding thread of Alan's story for as long as he could remember, we began to

---

* Noam Chomsky and Carlos Peregrín Otero, *Chomsky on Democracy and Education* (London: RoutledgeFalmer, 2003), p. 116.

discover that he had been unconsciously using studies and later information technology expertise to suppress a whole range of insecurities relating to his social and relational skills. One of Alan's most painful memories was of a sports class in early high school. Two basketball captains were nominated by the teacher to pick teams. To his utter humiliation, Alan was the very last to be picked. 'It's weird', he commented to me when he had finished recounting the experience, 'but it's one of those memories I knew was there but just never allowed myself to replay in full.' His eyes were welling up with tears. 'You know what's freaking me out? I remember really clearly, as if it happened yesterday, that the next class after gym that day was math and how we got our test results back from the day before. The teacher got me to stand up at the front of the class because he wanted everyone to know that I'd scored a record 98 per cent.' A tale of two Alans.

It is not often that you hear a life paradigm being so elegantly captured in one simple anecdote. Alan's Exalter Ego had been working in him at a much more pervasive level than that revealed in his recent demoralisation over his new colleague's genius. A profound sense of inadequacy in social areas had led him to seek compensation in the area of intellectual endeavour. And the gambit had paid off – until, that is, Herr Mozart had come along.

In a sense, Alan's brilliance had been his greatest curse. Without it he would not have been able to distract himself so effectively from his insecurities. Had he not found such solace in his intellectual giftedness, he might have been forced to work on his social insecurity at a much earlier stage.

I have met many people for whom the Exalter Ego opens up a whole nightmare of insecurity and future anxiety. But the cardinal point I take from Alan's story is that his Exalter Ego had been using both negative *and positive* comparison to block his personal growth. His sense of self as he went through school and college was founded on the conscious awareness that he was *brighter than* his peers – and on the unconscious terror that in other departments he was *not as good as* them. Comparison is a dangerous game. If you get too much sustenance from comparing yourself favourably, then do not be surprised if you find yourself getting bitten in the ass by unfavourable comparisons. This is what Alan's distress at working alongside a computer genius was really all about. *He was encountering the downside of the dangerous Exalter Ego law upon which he had built his social identity – the law of comparison.* What comparison gives with one hand it may take with the other. As mentioned earlier, the danger of this law resides precisely in the fact that it uses *accurate* local perceptions –

I am better/worse than person X, Y or Z in this one specific area

– to fuel inaccurate and unhealthy self-esteem ideas –

I shall build my sense of self upon this one aptitude.

Alan *was* brighter than his peers. And, unless he was completely misrepresenting things to me, his new colleague *was* even brighter than him. It would have been useless for me to try to talk him out of these conclusions. The only way for him to build a more sustainable and calmer self-regard would be to accept these local insights but limit their effect on his overall self-image.

I cannot stress this point strongly enough, for it applies with equal force in the opposite direction. If you are one of those people who relentlessly compares themselves negatively with others, then the chances are that you also compare yourself favourably with others in other fields. Self-regard, self-disregard, regard of others, disregard of others: *all have potential to be used as Exalter Ego weapons.*

Alan, instead of fighting the feelings that his new colleague had stirred up in him, began to welcome them as a painful but necessary barometer of where he had been going wrong. We looked closely at the reality that he had designed his life so entirely around his skills that his research work had become a comfort zone in which his superior aptitude granted his insecure self a kind of existential sanctuary from challenging experiences. To put this another way, *Alan's Faulter Ego had gotten his Halter Ego to build a comfort zone for his Exalter Ego.* The new colleague's invasion of this Exalter Ego comfort zone had actually been a gift in disguise, for it had forced Alan to face his Faulter Ego demons.

When Alan had first come to me, he had been very close to throwing in his research position. After we had gotten to the real heart of the problem, he saw what a huge mistake that would have been. The brilliant colleague was not the *source* of his distress but its *trigger*. Alan stayed where he was, but began working on those other areas of his life which he had been neglecting: fun, recreation, socialising and dating. He found these areas really threatening, for they brought up his very deepest fear about himself. The only way he was going to overrule his Faulter Ego — the demon lurking beneath his Exalter Ego attitudes — was by playing to his strengths (i.e. continuing his research, at which he was brilliant) *and refusing to flee those situations which made him feel inadequate.*

Bravely realising that some of the self-esteem issues he had been battling since childhood were deep and painful, Alan decided to follow up our four life coaching sessions by going to see a counsellor I was only too happy to recommend. Alan kept himself fully functional at work while shifting the focus of his life significantly. It was obvious to me that real growth was happening here. *Sometimes the single most important thing I need to do as a coach is to know that I am not a counsellor or therapist.*

§

In recent years I have seen nothing short of an exodus of people from Exalter Ego-associated areas (like business, finance, sports, media, politics and high-end academia) to areas where frenetic competitiveness is prized less (such as teaching, the civil service, consultancy, social work, healthcare). Sometimes the switch is a smart move, a timely recognition of the fact that a gentler work environment suits the person's character and values better. Sometimes, however, the switch proves a mistake, revealing itself to have been an over-reaction to problems in the original job. When this happens, the new job can prove just as frustrating in its own way as the old job had been. This is the tricky thing with the Exalter Ego. Some people are wired for challenges. Some people are high achievers. Some people need the adrenalin rush of competition. Some people *are* truly exceptional. For such people, it can take a bit of Exalter Ego single-mindedness to get them where they need to go. The Exalter Ego stops being a friend, however, when it tries to turn you into Gordon Gecko II.

§

Some Typical Exalter Ego Traps

- Behaving like a shallow, anti-social narcissist who only ever thinks of Numero Uno
- Doing things that are contrary to your deeper ethical values
- Neglecting the emotional needs of loved ones, especially children, by making it obvious you care more about your work than time spent with them
- Trying too hard to be something you are not
- Using people and then dropping them when they are no longer of use to you

- Looking down on people less successful than you and blaming the poor for their poverty
- Being snotty with waiters and waitresses in restaurants
- Defining your self-worth in exclusively professional and/or financial terms

9

The Voltaire Ego

'There's no place like home'

The person who has come under sway of their Voltaire Ego has become trapped in a narrow world of home, neighbourhood and/or family. This is domestic comfort zone living, equivalent to the professional sphere's Halter Ego tendency. The Voltaire Ego gets you to prize predictability over possibility and security over freedom of spirit. Again like the Halter Ego, it is a steady-as-she-goes tendency that keeps you risk averse and unimaginative. Gráinne was in her mid-thirties. She was the mother of three children, aged seven, nine and thirteen. Her husband was a successful salesman. They had spent the past nine years living in a salubrious estate in south Dublin. Gráinne herself didn't work outside the home. Her world revolved around children, home and the local tennis club. When the kids were at school, she would spend long hours down at the club, either playing tennis or helping out with various fundraising or social events.

So far, so idyllic. What had prompted Gráinne to come to me for coaching? Her husband Tom had recently been made redundant. It turned out that, prior to this development, he had been incurring some serious personal debts in order to keep the family's standard of living from sliding. He had done this because business had been slackening somewhat. Hopefully it would pick up sooner rather than later and allow Tom to clear all debts quietly without Gráinne ever having to find out about them. Not alone did business fail to pick up, however, but Tom lost the bloody job! Thanks to the recessionary collapse in house prices, Gráinne and Tom now faced an indefinite period of negative equity. Selling the house to pay off the debts was thus not an option for the foreseeable future. The sector in which Tom had been doing sales was very much a luxury sector. Hence it was hit particularly badly by the downturn. Tom's skills were unusually field specific, and he was now finding it impossible to get his foot in the door anywhere else. His morale was very low − so low in fact that he was finding it hard to get out of bed in the morning and continue his hunt for a job. As if to cap off the catastrophe, he had reacted very badly when his employer had broken the news of the redundancy to him. They had had a blazing row, with the outrageous result that his ex-boss was now refusing to give him a decent reference for prospective future employers.

All of this had come out of the proverbial blue for Gráinne. The safe little ecosystem she had been inhabiting for the previous few years was suddenly thrown into complete disequilibrium. It was becoming harder and harder to keep up appearances with the neighbours and with the ladies down at the tennis club. Gráinne was too ashamed to share with *anyone* apart from her own parents and siblings what had happened. The strain was becoming unbearable. Previously small things like a renewal of her tennis club fees or even putting petrol in the family 4×4 so that she could pick up the kids from school were now proving major challenges.

Thankfully, Gráinne was not without a sense of humour to help her put some perspective on matters. 'I'm like some cliché that's walked straight out of a David McWilliams book!' she remarked in our first session. And indeed she and Tom had ticked every box for a particular type of Celtic Tiger suburbanite couple: property-owning, upper-middle-class, almost achingly proud of their newfound wealth, etc. It had taken real guts for Gráinne to book an appointment with a career coach in order to make a priority of finding paid work for herself. Just a couple of months ago, such an idea would have been off the agenda altogether.

What struck me most about Gráinne's attitude to the world she and Tom were being forced to leave behind was her new-found clarity about it. It was a measure of her maturity and character that she was determined to treat the current crisis as an opportunity to *leave her comfort zone* and *build up muscles that had been neglected* during what she herself described as 'the Yummy Mummy years'. One muscle that needed particular work was the muscle of empathy. It was, she said, very difficult to feel empathetic towards people when you yourself have things so easy. Genteel poverty had opened her eyes to things she had never before noticed – the tiredness on the face of the lady who served her at the deli counter in her local supermarket, the self-consciousness in the body language of the guy dressed in luminous orange who sold *Evening Herald*s at a traffic light junction near her home. In addition, Gráinne was becoming more sensitised to all the ways in which her needs had been met by *other people's hard work*. And yes, she included Tom in this category. His obvious distress at being made redundant, and his failure to land a new job, did not leave Gráinne feeling let down or disappointed. On the contrary, she felt desperately sorry for Tom and could see the toll all this was taking on his self-esteem. She realised with no small feeling of guilt just how much she had been taking his hard work for granted over the years. He had provided, she had consumed. He had worked his backside off, she had flitted around the tennis club. He had incurred debts in order to protect her from the realities of their financial situation, she had carried on happily oblivious to such petty concerns.

I hasten to make it clear that the above critique of Gráinne's behaviour came not from me but from Gráinne herself. If anything, I told her she was being a little *too* hard on herself in all this. After all, hadn't Tom bought into the same value system as she had? Was it really fair to lay all the blame for this fiasco on her shoulders? And what about all the time and energy she had put into caring for the three kids? When I put these points to Gráinne, she acknowledged them but insisted that they were almost academic at this stage. What counted now was that she do everything humanly possible to help get the family out of the current mess.

Making a list of her transferable skills, she soon hit on a resourceful idea. She would launch herself as a children's tennis coach once she had put all the measures in place to do this (such as getting a coaching certificate, sorting out liability insurance, etc.). At first her friends down at the club were taken aback that she would even consider taking money for such an endeavour. But she pressed on regardless, having warned herself in advance against the Alterior Ego trap of letting herself be held back by fears over what others might think. Bit by bit, Gráinne started letting word get out that she and Tom were going through a rough patch financially. She informed people of this in a no-nonsense, matter-of-fact way. She had come to a firm decision beforehand: anyone who gives me grief or shuts me out as a result of this information will get the verbal equivalent of a slap in the face. Their number will be deleted from my phone and they will be crossed off my friends list. Let the chips fall where they may.

Gráinne, as you can see, was well capable of being a tough cookie. In our final session together, she made a remarkable confession to me: 'Jane, I can't believe I'm saying this, but I haven't felt so alive in years. I've dropped the BS with people and the mad thing is this has given them permission to drop the BS with me. I've gone from being a lady of leisure always on my best behaviour to being *myself.* The sense of freedom is incredible.' One of the most interesting side effects of Gráinne's newfound authenticity, as indicated in her words above, was the fact that other neighbours and friends had started to become more open about the various ways in which *they too* were feeling the effects of the recession. Even as Gráinne learned to let down her own defences, she found herself being shown a whole different side to these people.

Gráinne's tennis coaching enterprise took off. The income it started bringing into the family home was modest but critically important. It took some of the immediate pressure off Tom to be the sole earner. It also enabled Gráinne to approach her bank and secure a loan that would tide the family over for the next few months. Energised by this stabilising of the family finances, Tom resumed his own job search in a much more positive frame of mind. He eventually found some part-time work with an advertising agency. Although the pay was far lower than what he was used to, he received some encouraging signals from the agency as to the possibility of putting his employment on a firmer and more remunerative footing down the line. And then something truly remarkable happened. One of Gráinne's sisters made a quiet gesture of extraordinary generosity. She offered Gráinne a sizeable sum of money to tide the family over. Gráinne was stunned by the offer, but insisted that she would only take the money on one condition: that it be considered a loan not a gift, and that it would be paid back in full if and when she and Tom were in a position to do so. Her sister agreed and the money was used to pay off all of Tom's outstanding debts. No longer having that particular wolf scratching at the front door was a tremendous relief.

Last time we communicated, Gráinne was continuing with her tennis coaching lessons. She had also started doing a couple of nights volunteer work for an organisation dedicated to helping the homeless. She was finding this work a real eye-opener. All in all, she felt her life entering a new, and richer, phase. Her form, she declared, was 'never better'.

Not everyone has a well-off family member who can get them out of a financial hole, of course. Gráinne was unusually fortunate to receive the help she received. It is worth pointing out, however, that the momentum towards recovery came not from this near-miracle but from Gráinne's prior seizing of the initiative. She had risen to the challenge of the family's straitened circumstances by booking a series of career coaching sessions. She came to the first session firmly committed to the principle that she needed to pull her weight by bringing in some real income of her own. Personally I found Gráinne's handling of the whole crisis extraordinarily inspiring. Here was a woman whose whole existence had been governed by the twin concerns of Voltaire Ego and Alterior Ego:

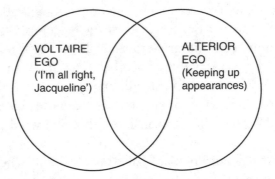

Tom's redundancy had rudely catapulted Gráinne out of her Voltaire Ego comfort zone. Without having had any practice in the fine art of coping against the odds, she had taken to the task of reordering her priorities and values with guts and gusto. The results of her courage went way beyond the financial. The crisis – or rather Gráinne's very post-Voltaire Ego response to the crisis – opened her up as a person. Her worldview became more realistic and generous. Her friendships become more authentic. Her marriage had deepened. Her self-esteem rose. A remarkable woman!

§

Many, many women come to me for help with entering (or re-entering) the world of paid work. It can be a daunting prospect to break out of one's Voltaire Ego nest.

When Julia came to me, she had been separated from her husband for nearly ten months. He had walked out on her after admitting to having met another woman. The marriage had lasted nineteen years, during which time Julia had been a housewife. Although she had trained as a nurse before getting married, she had come to an agreement with her new husband that they would opt for a more traditional division of labour: he goes out to work, she stays at home. Although she didn't explicitly say she regretted this move, which she felt had genuinely benefitted the couple's two children in their formative years, Julia now felt that it was time to start broadening her horizons. She mentioned to me that she had been through a counselling process to try to accept what had happened within her marriage and now felt ready to move forward. She found the day-in day-out home environment increasingly oppressive and dull. Despite regular contact with some of the other women in their housing estate, the social round had become increasingly repetitive. With two children – a boy of seventeen and a girl of fifteen – growing up fast, Julia dreaded the proverbial empty nest syndrome. Would the kids' absence from home expose a terrible vacuum in her life?

It was with these fears in mind that Julia came to me. Without yet having any concrete idea of what she wanted to do, she had decided to explore the possibility of entering the world of work for the first time in her life. This was a big move. She had, after all, gone straight from school to nursing college to married life. Not surprisingly, she was wracked with self-doubt, her speech peppered with self-deprecating Faulter Ego comments like 'Typical me', 'I'm a bit clueless about …' and 'Knowing me, I'd probably make a mess of it'. The more she felt free to assess her situation, however, the more she began to voice her resentment of what she saw as her husband's patronising attitude towards her. It was as if he had forgotten that she had ever had career plans of her own. The intervening nineteen years had all but knocked the stuffing out of her.

It was clear to me that Julia needed to flush out the beliefs of her Voltaire and Faulter Egos by *playing their negative tapes at full volume* for me. She gladly itemised the reasons why she would have a 'nightmare' trying to enter the workplace:

- She couldn't drive (a *very* common topic of anxiety and embarrassment among clients who feel they don't make the grade in life).
- She was computer illiterate.
- If her awkwardness in the company of the other housewives on the estate was anything to go by, she would be a disaster with any prospective colleagues.
- She had suffered anxiety attacks the last time she had done something significant on her own initiative – a visit to her sister in London four years previously, undertaken against her husband's wishes. His response when she had to cut the visit short? A brutally hurtful *I-told-you-so*.

Any projection of independent activity for Julia gave rise to deeply embedded feelings of insecurity and low self-esteem.

Over the years she had internalised her husband's chauvinistic belief that a woman had nothing constructive to offer outside the home. This internalised belief, with all its attendant self-doubt and self-sabotage, had come under the guardianship of her Voltaire Ego, which would kick in any time she tried to project a more stimulating, self-directing and open future. The tiny world to which her husband had consigned her was *safe*. Any attempt to venture beyond it was *dangerous*.

I asked Julia to cast back to the time before her wedding when she was still training to be a nurse. How self-confident had she been back then? She told me that her decision to go into nursing had caused nothing short of consternation back home in Leitrim. The second youngest of five girls, she had been born into a family that was staunchly conservative when it came to the role of women in society. None of her sisters worked. Three had become housewives while the other had become a nun (an unusual vocation for a girl of her generation, though Julia described her as a woman of genuine piety). Nursing college had thus been a huge milestone in Julia's journey of self-determination. Looking back, she was struck by the fact that she had become attracted to a man whose value system represented a regression to that of her parents. Astonishingly, this fact had never struck her before. It was as if her acquiescence to her husband's chauvinistic assumptions represented an unconscious retreat to a familiar pattern.

With vicious ingenuity, Julia's Voltaire Ego had been teaming up with her Faulter Ego to exploit these circumstances. First her Faulter Ego had fed on Julia's anger with herself for having sold herself short as a married woman: she was an 'eejit' to have made such a total concession to her husband. Next her Voltaire Ego stepped in and helped the Faulter Ego twist the knife of paradox by telling Julia that it was a *good* thing she had given up any dreams of her own career: sure wouldn't she have made a mess of it anyway, not being fit for anything outside the home?

Having been caught by this classic Faulter–Voltaire joint manoeuvre, Julia was now coping with the added trauma of marriage breakdown too. That the separation had been instigated by her husband and not herself only reinforced her feeling of being a humiliatingly passive onlooker in her own life.

The closer we explored Julia's situation, the clearer it became that she had in fact fallen prey to a devastating coalition of not just two but three Disappointers:

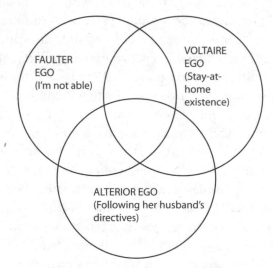

The Voltaire Ego contraction of Julia's world to home and neighbourhood had been the result of her Alterior Ego error of allowing her husband dictate the terms of their marriage. Robbed thus of her sense of self, she had then taken the Faulter Ego step of internalising her husband's chauvinistic evaluation of her abilities.

It took quite a bit of work for Julia to plot a way out of her housebound existence. The results, however, were impressive. Harnessing the Vaulter Ego virtues of impatience and risk-taking, she enrolled in a massage therapy course. Within a year, she had set up her own small practice in her home, with a client base that was growing by the month. Within two years, she had learned to drive. This allowed her to expand her practice to include visits to clients in their own homes. She still loves the work and is brilliant at it. She has also developed quite a taste for foreign travel, using her hard-earned surplus income to see a bit of the 'big bad world' that had been closed to her for so many years.

§

By definition, the people who come to me for help with getting out of a Voltaire Ego rut realise the need for change. Something – be it an alteration in financial circumstances (Gráinne) or boredom with a constricted domestic world (Julia) – has impelled them to come to coaching for a new start in life. The people I most worry about, however, are the silent majority of Voltaire Ego victims who don't even realise how limited or bored they are by their current situation. When a person's circle of concerns never goes beyond housekeeping, the latest afternoon magazine telly programme, what the neighbours are saying or whether hubby would prefer chops or stew for dinner, I worry. Is this person really enjoying life or are they merely in retreat from it? It is of course up to each individual to decide, and I in no way wish to denigrate women who make a principled decision to stay at home. All I am saying is that we need to be wary of the Voltaire Ego. Like its professional first cousin, the Halter Ego, it disappoints people by tranquilising them. It turns life into a game of avoiding pain at all costs. How to avoid pain? Avoid novel situations and encounters. How to feel in control over your life? Reduce your sphere of influence to a tiny little space. Nervous about breaking your routine? Hover the carpet. Anxious about getting into unfamiliar situations? Listen to your favourite radio programme. Finding the big bad world frighteningly complicated? Make sure the neighbours think you are respectable.

§

Apart from women who are pressurised into a traditional housewife role, the two groups most vulnerable to the curse of the Voltaire Ego are retirees and the unemployed.

Many working people spend years looking forward to the day of their retirement. They tell themselves that it will truly be the first day of the rest of their lives. The guilt-free lie-ins! The leisurely coffee and newspaper! The books they never got round to reading! The hobbies they can devote serious time to! For some strange reason, however, a large number of retirees soon find themselves feeling depressed and listless, as though their life has had the purpose sucked out of it. They have been sucked into a Voltaire Ego fool's paradise. Just as *too much work* can be a pain in the backside, so too can *too little work* be a complete head-wrecker.

Fergus, for example, was a recently retired CIE bus driver, with nearly twenty-five years' experience in the company. The happiest day of his life, he told me, had been his last ever day at work. The worst had been the day after that. He had awoken with a feeling of unprecedented dread. What was his life for? What had he ahead of him now only death? How on earth was he going to fill up his days? He was hit by a wave of panic – something he had not seen coming at all. So much had he looked forward to the unaccustomed freedom which retirement would offer him that he had given absolutely no thought to what he would actually *do* with all this free time. His wife was still working as a nurse. The kids had long since grown up and left the nest. Fergus found this new Voltaire Ego existence frighteningly empty. He quickly came to associate retirement with *cold feet* – literally, the feeling of coldness in his feet that came from sitting around doing nothing. He would try to stave off the boredom by walking into the local village and pottering around the shops and cafés. But he quickly grew self-conscious doing this. He felt like the stereotypical 'auld fella', a role which galled him. People seemed to treat him differently, holding doors open for him and offering up their seats to him on the bus. For the first time, he was feeling his age – and it depressed him thoroughly.

Feeling trapped, Fergus retreated into full-blown Voltaire Ego mode. On a typical day he would sit indoors reading biographies for hours on end, breaking the monotony only to catch the news headlines or make himself a sandwich. He could feel his feet get colder by the day as his energy levels waned further. He didn't even enjoy the books, for God's sake! *The only reason he was reading them was to fill up the long hours as painlessly as possible.* He was behaving, in effect, like a patient in a hospital bed. His mood was deteriorating, as was his interest in the world around him. He felt used-up, useless and horribly, horribly bored. No wonder his wife was worried enough to persuade him to get some coaching.

Some forty years younger than Fergus, but no less prone to Voltaire Ego habits of lethargy and aimlessness, was Derek, a young man who had been out of work for the past thirteen months. Since dropping out of college, Derek had held down a string of jobs in music retail. Since being let go from his last job, he had gone into total Voltaire Ego mode. His father was now desperately worried about him and set up a coaching session with me. Derek freely admitted that he spent all day lounging around the house, smoking spliffs and watching telly. His social circle had grown very thin. He had not had a girlfriend in ages. What made Derek's situation different to Fergus's was that he did not feel any strong antipathy towards his Voltaire Ego existence. In a certain sense he found it quite cosy, almost like a return to the warmth and safety of the womb. He had absolutely no desire to go out into the world and build up a career for himself. It literally felt like too much work.

There is only one surefire antidote to the narcotic influence of the Voltaire Ego: *excitement*. Both Fergus and Derek needed to get their mojo back by finding something that made them feel passionate, curious and open to new possibilities. It was clear that for both men this something would have to contain a social dimension. It would need, in short, to get them out of the bloody house.

In Fergus's case what did the trick was community work. After a bit of focused research, Fergus decided to volunteer for three afternoons a week at a drug rehabilitation project in the city centre. This simple step proved his salvation. It got him up and out of the house. It got him travelling (on a free bus pass!). Most importantly, it made other people reliant upon him. By helping others he helped himself, and lost the feeling of redundancy that had been haunting him since retirement. He also made some good friends with his co-volunteers. Within a year he was busier and happier than he had ever been as a bus driver. None of this work was paid, of course, but that didn't matter. Thanks to his pension, Fergus had no need for a supplementary income. He had managed to turn his retirement from a disaster into a triumph. His values of service and social concern had solidified into a rewarding full-time occupation. He still had ample time to get through a biography a week, but the fact that he was no longer reading in unsplendid isolation from real life meant that the narratives now came to life for him. Listening to Fergus describe this circumstance, I was reminded of the words of G.K. Chesterton: 'There is a great deal of difference between the eager man who wants to read a book and the tired man who wants a book to read.'

How did young Derek get out of his rut? Again, he found a passion and used that as a springboard to systematic change. In his case it was music. He was an enthusiastic guitarist who had been in a couple of rock bands as a teenager. I persuaded him to put an ad up on Boards.ie looking for some like-minded musicians. After meeting some frustratingly unsuitable messers in some grotty rehearsal rooms, Derek finally hooked up with an already formed band that happened to be looking for a second guitarist. He was over the moon with this development, so much so that I had to warn him not to slip into Walter Ego dreams of overnight fame and fortune! To his credit, though, he went in with his eyes open and made a real connection with the other guys in the band. Meanwhile, he gave up the spliffs and started jogging. He also acknowledged the need to earn some cash both for himself and for his dad. After much searching around, he finally got a job at an Xtravision store. Within a few months he had moved on to a cinema multiplex. This was a start, and a good one. His enthusiasm for the band gave him a *context* in which going out to earn a few bob became meaningful and empowering. Instead of seeing his work hours as a curb on his freedom, he saw them as a way of helping his plans along. Those plans involved enrolling in a multimedia course. Thanks to some careful research, he managed to get a decent grant towards his studies.

Although Derek's long-term career prospects are still a little uncertain, I am confident that he has 'the wind beneath his wings'. It seems to me highly unlikely that he will ever slip back into Voltaire Ego mode again. The world out there is just too damned interesting!

§

Some Typical Voltaire Ego Traps

- Obsessing over order in your home space
- Obsessing over what the neighbours think
- Allowing your horizons to shrink to your particular neck of the woods
- Lack of curiosity about the world and life in general
- Addiction to daytime TV, DVDs, etc.
- Lack of physical exercise
- Living through your kids and/or partner
- Risk-averse behaviour
- Social conservatism

PART II

APPOINTMENT

STOP!

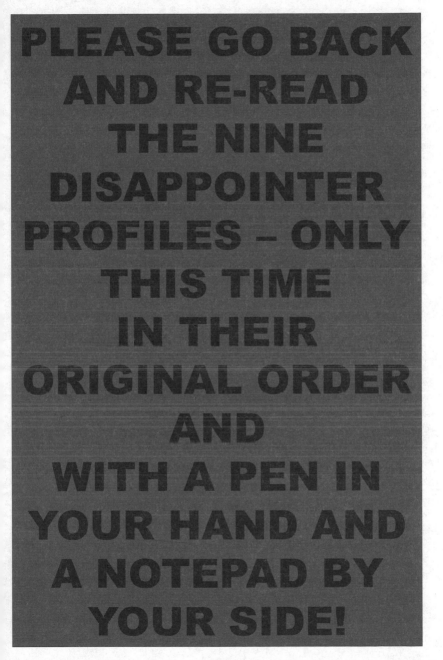

PLEASE GO BACK AND RE-READ THE NINE DISAPPOINTER PROFILES – ONLY THIS TIME IN THEIR ORIGINAL ORDER AND WITH A PEN IN YOUR HAND AND A NOTEPAD BY YOUR SIDE!

Yep, reading is re-reading, my friend.

Your first reading of the Disappointer profiles has familiarised you with the various Disappointers.
Your second reading will be an exercise in self-analysis and self-recognition.
What is the pen for? To mark, underline or annotate anything – *anything* – that strikes a chord with you.
What is the notepad for? To jot down *any* idea or observation that strikes you in passing. It may relate directly to what you have just read or it may be a tangential notion that came into your head as you were reading. *It doesn't matter.* It's all good.

In a few moments I'm going to type out three asterisks on the next page. I'm trusting you not to look at them until you have finished your re-reading of the Disappointer profiles ... ;)

***

10

Appointers, Disappointers and *Your* Career

Welcome back!

You have now (hopefully) re-read your way through all nine Disappointer profiles.

You have now (hopefully) developed a very good idea of what each Disappointer represents and of the various ways each has of getting individuals stuck in unproductive attitudes, habits and modes of behaviour.

You have now (hopefully) noted several instances of how things can be turned around when people:

a. Dis-appoint their key Disappointers

b. Appoint hitherto neglected Appointers

You are now in a position to create an overview of your own Disappointer–Appointer relationships.

This self-assessment involves two simple steps:

STEP I.

ON THE DIAGRAM ON THE NEXT PAGE, IDENTIFY YOUR THREE KEY DISAPPOINTERS.

THESE MAY OR MAY NOT BE THE SAME AS THOSE DISAPPOINTERS YOU RANKED 1, 2 AND 3 IN YOUR EARLIER 'WHEEL OF DISAPPOINTMENT' SELF-ASSESSMENT.

USE THE BLANK PARTS OF THE PAGE TO JOT DOWN ANY KEYWORDS THAT YOU ASSOCIATE WITH EACH DISAPPOINTER.

THESE KEYWORDS MAY RELATE TO YOUR CURRENT JOB, GENERAL HABITS, REVEALING INCIDENTS, WORRIES OR ANYTHING ELSE YOU MIGHT DEEM RELEVANT.

YOU SHOULD ALSO USE THIS OPPORUNITY TO WARN YOURSELF IN ADVANCE OF ANY SPECIFIC AREAS WHERE THESE THREE DISAPPOINTERS COULD TRIP YOU UP AS YOU GO ABOUT UPGRADING YOUR CAREER (E.G. AT INTERVIEW STAGE? WHEN YOU ARE UNDERTAKING RESEARCH? WHEN YOU ARE COMING TO DECISION TIME?).

BETTER TO ANTICIPATE THESE RISKS <u>NOW</u> RATHER THAN LET YOUR DISAPPOINTERS CREEP UP ON YOU IN THE WEEKS AND MONTHS AHEAD!

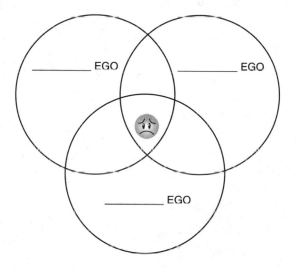

_____ EGO   _____ EGO

_____ EGO

STEP II.

On the next page, re-enter the names of your three key Disappointers.

Then nominate three Appointers whose tendencies you need in order to counterbalance the tendencies of your key Disappointers.

Again make notes on the page itself indicating how these Appointers might bring positive change to your career.

(No need for full sentences here, buzzwords and phrases will do fine. These are your private notes!)

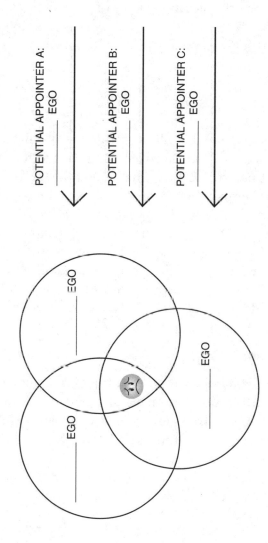

You have just done an absolutely crucial focusing exercise. Mark my words, it will stand you in very good stead as you start moving now into the consecutive phases of:

1. Vocational self-assessment
2. Research
3. Decision
4. Action

As you start getting into the nitty-gritty of upgrading your career, you *must, must, must* keep checking back to the above exercise. Check it before you meet that friend for coffee in order to sound him or her out about a field you're interested in. Check it before you get working on your CV. Check it before your appointment with the recruitment agency. Check it as you are preparing for your interview. Make a photocopy of it and stick it up on your wall! Above all else, keep it visible. It is your best hope of NOT getting lost in the details that lie ahead and NOT reverting to old habits. It is nothing less than your *innoculation against renewed disappointment.*

§

So – what are you going to do with the rest of your life?

I want you to grab your (hopefully half-filled) notepad and get into the habit of drawing *your own* maps and schematic diagrams. There are two reasons why I want you to do this:

1. Maps and drawings are *infinitely* more effective than wordy paragraphs for when it comes to giving yourself an overview

of options and options-within-options. You are literally learning to *draw alternative futures* for yourself.
2. As discussed in the Preface, this is a career coaching book, not a career coaching session. I cannot possibly cover *all* the various permutations of what you might need to examine as you contemplate a career upgrade. You must start drawing up options that make sense *for you*. All I can do on my side is give you the templates, guidelines and high-precision tips you need to get yourself going.

§

So how might a client of mine go about exploring the possibility of upgrading their career? We have of course already seen lots of examples in action in the Disappointer profiles, but let's focus on this phase of career management in its own right.

We are going to take a rather generic example and trace some of the steps involved. Please bear in mind that what follows is a somewhat simplified and abstract account of what you yourself are likely to be doing soon.

§

Meet Sally. She's a young professional who has come to me for career change coaching.

The first thing Sally needs is a basic road-map of the territory ahead. This always makes things a lot less scary and random-seeming:

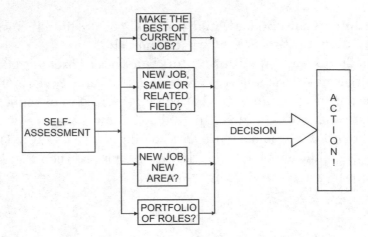

The first phase of Sally's coaching involves a series of thorough self-assessment exercises:

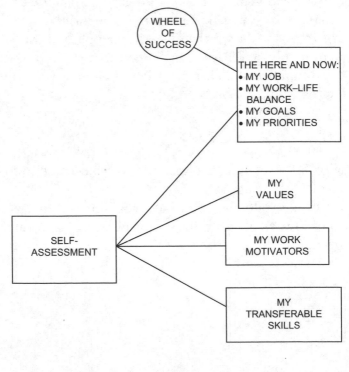

Having:

a. Gained a robust sense of what makes her tick
b. Identified the various strengths, talents and interests that she promises to bring to any new role

Sally takes a first exploratory look at future options.

She is careful NOT to just plump for one 'obvious' solution to her current career dissatisfaction. Mindful of just how momentous these explorations may well turn out to be in terms of their impact on her life for the next decade and beyond, she is happy to brainstorm and give several different possibilities a fair hearing.

Accordingly, Sally looks at each of four *general* options in detail:

First up is the option of staying put and addressing some of the sources of her present discontent within the parameters of her current job:

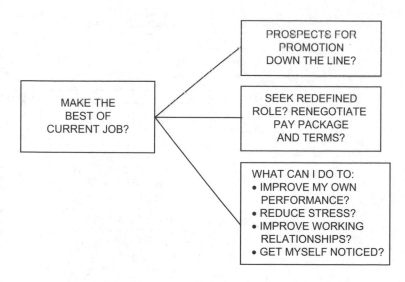

Next, Sally wonders whether this might be a case of Wrong Job, Right Company/Field:

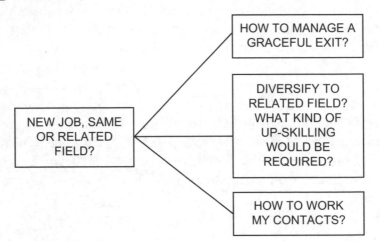

Now Sally considers a bold move out of her current area altogether:

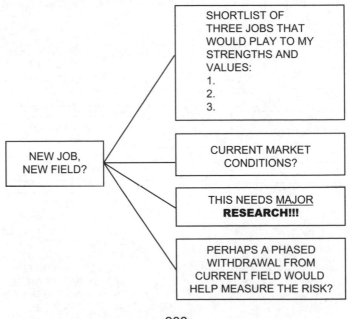

Finally, Sally challenges her own initial assumption of One Person, One Job.

Might not a portfolio approach free her up in so many ways?

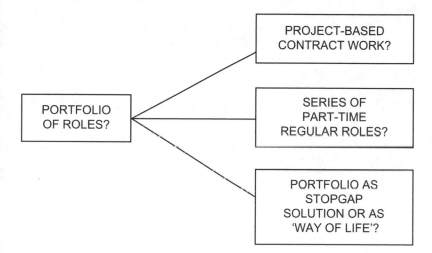

After several *weeks* of intensive research and soul-searching, Sally has narrowed her options down to just one:

> NEW JOB,
> NEW ROLE,
> RELATED FIELD

If Sally decides to go for this option, it will involve a certain amount of risk – something that Sally, whose Halter Ego mentality originally got her into an unhappy situation in the first place, has traditionally fought shy of. Indeed, Sally's initial instinct was to go for the 'Make the Best of Current Job' option. After much debate with herself, however, she has come to the recognition that this would represent a Halter Ego retreat from the kind of challenge and change she really needs.

So ... it's time for a final decision. Will Sally start taking steps out of her current job and into a new one? Will she go back to the drawing board? Or will she stay put, at least for the time being?

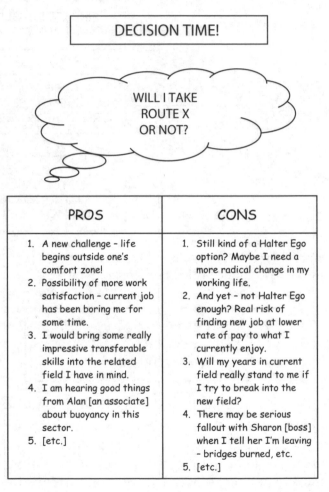

PROS	CONS
1. A new challenge – life begins outside one's comfort zone!	1. Still kind of a Halter Ego option? Maybe I need a more radical change in my working life.
2. Possibility of more work satisfaction – current job has been boring me for some time.	2. And yet – not Halter Ego enough? Real risk of finding new job at lower rate of pay to what I currently enjoy.
3. I would bring some really impressive transferable skills into the related field I have in mind.	3. Will my years in current field really stand to me if I try to break into the new field?
4. I am hearing good things from Alan [an associate] about buoyancy in this sector.	4. There may be serious fallout with Sharon [boss] when I tell her I'm leaving – bridges burned, etc.
5. [etc.]	5. [etc.]

A lengthy period of reflection ensues – though not one so lengthy that Sally will become paralysed by indecision and allow momentum to wane.

She takes note of one key fact: her Cons list is predominantly fear-based. That is to say, it is feeding off the old Halter/Faulter Ego energies. Sally made a promise to herself at the outset that she would not allow her future to be dictated by these Disappointers any longer. At the same time, she does not feel prepared to make a radical switch of career paths.

So she decides that the 'Route X' option is the right one after all:

New Job, New Role, Related Field.

This, she concludes, represents a fair compromise between her Halter Ego desire for security and her Vaulter Ego impatience for a fresh start.

Is she apprehensive? You bet! But she has done some really terrific work on herself since starting this process. This has included warning herself in advance not to let either her Halter Ego risk-aversiveness or her Faulter Ego pessimism sabotage her decision to GO FOR IT. She is determined, and shows great resolve in seeing her plan through from beginning to end.

The plan of attack is perfectly straightforward.

It is in Sally's attention to detail, however, that she really seals the deal.

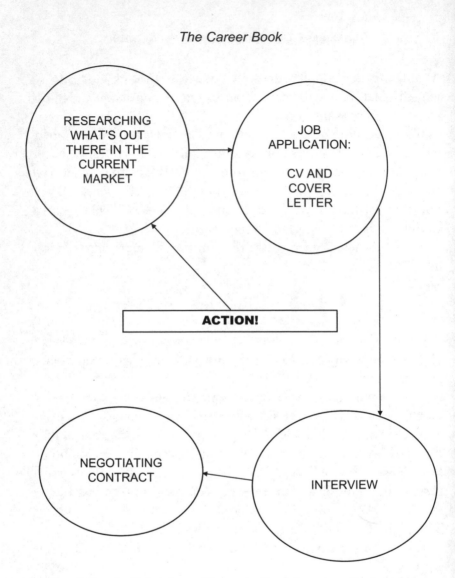

And seal the deal she does. She gets the job, manages her departure from her current employer with real panache and enters a
new phase of her life with excitement and ambition.

How about you?

  Your job is to EMULATE Sally's journey, not to COPY it.

Here is a list of the *general* steps you are going to have to work your way through:

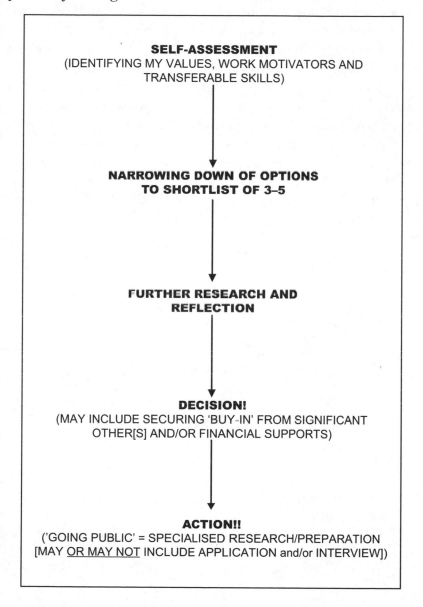

SELF-ASSESSMENT
(IDENTIFYING MY VALUES, WORK MOTIVATORS AND TRANSFERABLE SKILLS)

↓

NARROWING DOWN OF OPTIONS TO SHORTLIST OF 3–5

↓

FURTHER RESEARCH AND REFLECTION

↓

DECISION!
(MAY INCLUDE SECURING 'BUY-IN' FROM SIGNIFICANT OTHER[S] AND/OR FINANCIAL SUPPORTS)

↓

ACTION!!
('GOING PUBLIC' = SPECIALISED RESEARCH/PREPARATION [MAY OR MAY NOT INCLUDE APPLICATION and/or INTERVIEW])

The pages that follow have been carefully put together to help
you plot your route from the here and now to a more compelling
career future. Some sections will inevitably have more relevance
to your situation and priorities than others.

One last plea before you get going: keep watching out for any
reflex Disappointer reactions you may experience as you read
through the following pages. *Try to name the Disappointer that is
putting the unconstructive or sabotaging thought in your head.* Thus,
for instance, you may be reading through some tips relating to
executive business interviews and find yourself feeling left out
and put down because you are not a high-earning professional
yourself. Relax – you're having a Faulter Ego or Salter Ego
moment! *Name it and tell yourself you will NOT let it block your
ability to keep going in a positive and can-do frame of mind.* In the
present instance, this will mean simply skipping over the points
that are irrelevant to you. No trip, no self-condemnation, no
problem.

11

Designing a Career or Career Change that Works for *You*

As a career coach I work on the premise that in the past we found work based on what we could *do*. I now believe that drastically changed economic conditions (even in this recession) and greater access to education for most mean that people need to move to a model of choosing work based on what they can do *combined with who they are*. Who you are is a crucial element in the key to finding a career you love. *If you are committed to the challenge*, you really can find work that energises you.

Not that we should be utopian about this. Every job will have its rough days – or weeks, or months. If, however, you are in the job that's right for you, you will be able to handle this. You will not lose sight of the benefits of your job – a fact that will prevent you from giving way to the kind of resentment and unhappiness which short-term stresses can create.

As a qualified career coach assessor and practicing career coach, I once again urge you not to explore new career options and paths without first exploring some deeper questions about yourself.

215

There are six Golden Steps in this process of discovery:

> STEP 1: Examine your current situation and what needs to change
>
> ***
>
> STEP 2: Identify your purpose and your values
>
> ***
>
> STEP 3: Know what motivates *you* in your work
>
> ***
>
> STEP 4: Define what 'success' means to *you*
>
> ***
>
> STEP 5: Identify your transferable skills, signature strengths and work experience to date
>
> ***
>
> STEP 6: Match your purpose, skills, experience and career goals to the business reality and design a plan for achieving your career goals

Steps 1–4 involve SUBJECTIVE analysis (of what makes YOU tick).

Step 5 requires an OBJECTIVE analysis of what you have to offer.

Step 6 seals the deal by integrating these results into an OBJECTIVE analysis of current market conditions.

Let's take a closer look at each step.

Step 1: Examine Your Current Situation and What Needs to Change

Looking at the here and now (your current career) will offer a lot of insight in what isn't working for you and what you will need from your next career in order to feel happy and successful. Spend some time on this.

A word of caution: Ensure you look at your life as a whole,

not just your job. What happens outside the workplace has a huge influence on the energy we bring into the workplace. You may of course find, after taking an honest and full look at your non-working life, that it is sufficiently developed to allow you to lay the blame for your unhappiness at work squarely at the door of the job itself. Fair enough – in which case it is definitely time for a career change.

§

Step 2: Identify Your Purpose and Your Values

We each have a purpose in life. Some of us have always known what it is – it is nothing less than a vocation. Others fall upon their purpose. Still others have to go through a rigorous process of self-discovery and learning in order to unleash theirs. The bulk of my coaching clients have fallen into this latter category. What many don't realise is that its OK to be in this place, but *only* if you take the time to self-discover and act. Otherwise you will more than likely go through life feeling deeply unfulfilled in your career. 'Something' will be missing, but you won't be able to put your finger on what it is.

The concept of honoring your personal values in your day-to-day work is something I have become unapolegetically evangelical about as a career coach.

Be crystal clear on your top five values.

Oftentimes a client will discover it is not the job itself that is wrong for him/her but the culture and environment. Therefore when you are clear on what your values are you can decide if the changes you want are a case of 'Right Job, Wrong Company' or 'Wrong Job, New Career Please'.

§

Step 3: Know What Motivates *You* in Your Work

Identifying your work motivators will put you on the royal road to successful career transition. Take some time out to draw up your own personal priority list of work motivators – the things that would get you out of bed in the morning with a feeling of excitement and energy. What we are looking for here are the conscious and unconscious drivers that make work fulfilling for you. Knowing these will help you tailor your next career move. Probably for the first time in your life, authentic job satisfaction will be on the agenda.

§

Step 4: Define What 'Success' Means to *You*

Everyone's definition is different, so what's yours? Don't *assume* you already have an easy answer to this question. Your answer must do *justice* to the complexity of your character!

In assessing this, you might consider the focusing questions below:

1. *What is your life really about?*
2. *What do you want it to be about?*
3. *Do you live to work or work to live?*
4. *What are you willing to do to achieve your dream career?*
5. *What, to you, is the purpose of work in your life?*
6. *What do status and power mean to you?*
7. *What limits you in your work?*
8. *What gives you a sense of passion, challenge and/or accomplishment in your work?*
9. *What do you need to stop/start doing to arrive in a career that you would enjoy facing each morning?*
10. *What are your three most important goals in life right now? (You will want to make sure your life goals are in someway congruent*

with your career goals. For example, if you have a young family, are seeking a better work–life balance and wish to become a doctor, you will want to consider the practicalities of this ambition. I would never say it cannot be done, but you must be clear-eyed as to its long-term viability.)

§

Step 5: Identify Your Transferable Skills, Signature Strengths and Work Experience to Date

Transferable Skills

By really drilling down and brainstorming this topic, you can quite easily come up with a powerful list. The key here is to remain open-minded and positive and not to shoot down a transferable skill because you feel its relevance is not immediately apparent. Do NOT underestimate the skills you have gathered to date in your career. Knowing your transferable skills will also embolden you at interview stage, enhancing your prospects of getting a position you want.

Signature Strengths

Martin Seligman, in his book *Authentic Happiness*, argues convincingly that a career that plays to your 'signature strengths' is a fulfilling career.

Do you know what your top ten signature strengths are?* Think about this and look for evidence to back it up. Perhaps you have received feedback from work colleagues, management or friends? Such feedback can give you an excellent insight into your own personal signature strengths inventory.

---

* Do a free online test at http://www.authentichappiness.sas.upenn.edu/
Default.aspx.

219

Work Experience

There are two aspects to this:
[Work done] + [Skills developed and demonstrated]

§

Step 6: Match Your Purpose, Skills, Experience and Career Goals to the Business Reality and Design a Plan for Achieving Your Career Goals

You have 'researched' yourself. You have used this to develop a strong 'work theme' for yourself. Now you must take the crucial step of familiarising yourself with the market.

This will involve three methods for researching the business reality out there:

- Basic information gathering (including online resources)
- Acquaintance with the literature and lingo of the field (a really, really important one, this)
- Networking (friends, acquaintances, friends of friends, friends of acquaintances, acquaintances of acquaintances – you NEVER KNOW who might end up giving you the insight, suggestion or indeed inside track that gives you the edge)

§

12

Work–Life Balance

It's about time...

Put simply, work–life balance is about having enough time to work AND to have outside interests AND to cater for your family and personal responsibilities.

We are all too aware that life is a complicated business these days. Many people are trying to juggle work, home and leisure commitments but are often left feeling they are not getting the best out of any of them. The reason? Work is taking over their lives.

As a practicing coach I see an alarming number of clients who cannot understand why they feel so unhappy when they have the trappings of what is perceived by many as success – good job, nice car, house, family.

Why is there still a void? Because *poverty comes in different guises*: time poverty, emotional poverty, authenticity poverty, value poverty, motivation poverty, and more. Often the culprit is work–life *im*balance.

Once a client becomes aware that they are living to work rather than working to live, they can begin to take back their personal control.

Do NOT fall into the trap of treating work–life balance as a luxury that you cannot afford at this juncture in your life.

By placing the focus firmly back onto your authentic values, goals and needs, you can find resourceful ways of making your work accommodate your life rather than the other way round. Do this, and the world suddenly opens up for you.

Top Tips for Achieving Work–Life Balance

1. Slow down
2. Know what is causing you stress
3. Don't compare yourself to others
4. Learn better time management; avoid procrastination
5. Put your job in perspective
6. Take charge and set priorities
7. Be proactive rather than reactive
8. Ask for assistance
9. Simplify and de-clutter
10. Master your *own* motivation
11. Consider getting some coaching
12. Put a value on yourself and your abilities

Tip 1: Slow Down

Life is simply too short, so don't let things pass you in a blur. Take steps to stop and enjoy the things and the people around you. Schedule more time between meetings. Don't make plans for every evening or weekend.

§

Tip 2: Know What Is Causing You Stress

Once you recognise these stress sources, you can start scheming to distance yourself from them.

§

Tip 3: Don't Compare Yourself to Others

Don't try to be superhuman. Everyone has different energy levels. Plus, you just never know what might be going on behind the scenes with another person.

§

Tip 4: Learn Better Time Management; Avoid Procrastination

For many people, most of the stress they feel comes from simply being disorganised and prone to habits of procrastination and task avoidance. Learn to set more realistic goals and deadlines – and then stick to them. You'll find not only that you are less stressed but that your work is better.

§

Tip 5: Put Your Job in Perspective

Easier said than done, this, but learn to let things go once in a while. So what if you didn't file that paperwork away last Friday or make that unimportant phone call? Learn to recognise the things that don't really have much ultimate impact on your life. Don't beat yourself up for letting them go occasionally. Adopt a 'nobody has died' attitude to such matters.

§

Tip 6: Take Charge and Set Priorities

Ask yourself continually, what is the benefit of me getting this done? What will this give me? Sometimes it's easier for us to allow ourselves to feel overwhelmed rather than take charge with a prioritised list of things that really need to get done.

§

Tip 7: Be Proactive Rather Than Reactive

Move out of 'fire-fighting' mode. Add a planning element to your day, week, month and year. This is the key to effective time management.

§

Tip 8: Ask for Assistance

Don't be afraid to do this. If you do not have time for a given task, or if it doesn't fit in with your current priorities, you have two choices: delegate it or knock it off your 'to do' list.

§

Tip 9: Simplify and De-Clutter

It seems human nature for just about everyone to take on too many tasks and responsibilities – and to own too much. Find a way to simplify your life. Change your lifestyle. Learn to say 'no' to requests for help. Get rid of the clutter and baggage in your house, and in your life. Become your own centre of gravity rather than letting yourself get dispersed every which way.

§

Tip 10: Master Your *Own* Motivation

Don't always rely on material or financial incentives to do things. Don't always wait for your manager or other key players to offer praise and motivation. The most effective approach is for the employee to motivate themselves by putting their own personal key strategies in place. The old advice to employees to act 'as if you were self-employed' is pertinent in this context.

§

Tip 11: Consider Getting Some Coaching

If you are feeling overwhelmed by your work responsibilities, please consider getting help by seeking life and/or career coaching for yourself. In most cases you will find hitherto unrecognised options for easing the pressure.

§

Tip 12: Put a Value on Yourself and Your Abilities

Make yourself indispensable by creating a pact with yourself to work *smart*. This means constantly prioritising the work that needs to get done and that will serve *you*. It does *not* mean choosing to work excessively long hours on a regular basis. That, believe me, is a mug's game. If you feel you need to do it to impress your boss, then something's wrong.

§

13

Motivation

Yes, times are tough.

Yes, they're scary.

Yes, we are in the dark as to when the economy is going to pick up.

But no, everything is *not* out of *your* control.

Even in this market, you *can* control *your* attitude and *your* approach to *your* career.

Top 10 Motivation Tips

1. Recognise that motivation is the key
2. Develop your life outside of work – and be careful not to scapegoat your job as the cause of all your unhappiness
3. Put things in perspective
4. Raise your game
5. Know your own unique work motivator combination
6. Focus on your negative tapes so you can turn these around
7. Define success for yourself
8. Put your emotional intelligence skills to use

> 9. Celebrate your successes
> 10. If, even after implementing the above strategies, you still find yourself chronically unmotivated in your job, consider a job or career move

Tip 1: Recognise that Motivation Is the Key

There are several aspects to this:

Be Honest With Yourself

Admit that you feel despondent and are working in autopilot. Be aware of this feeling rather than trying to deny or change it. It is what it is. Clear your energy drains/'to do' lists. Let people know that you have a backlog to clear and that you will deal with their issues when this has been done.

Make the Change

When you take stock and begin to see more clearly *you will know* what changes are needed.

Break it down into manageable steps. Identify one small step you can take today to begin implementing that change. Take another step tomorrow.

Improve Your Self-Care

What are the ways in which you can begin to take better care of yourself within work? Staying away from toxic people? Drinking more water? (Take it from me, this can make a BIG difference in terms of energy levels.) Saying 'no' more often in order to say 'yes' to other opportunities that serve you better?

Develop Relationships

Research shows that people don't usually leave jobs, they leave managers. Is there anyone in your office that you need to build a better relationship with? If so, could you swallow your pride and begin building a better relationship with them? This will greatly lessen your energy drains in work and create a more congenial work environment for *you*.

If You Choose to Stay in Your Current Job

Then the key to motivation will be to know the benefits of what this job gives you. Remember your motivation for taking this role in the first place. Be very clear on the advantages this job has right now and focus on these, not the things that are out of your control.

§

Tip 2: Develop Your Life Outside of Work – And Be Careful Not to Scapegoat Your Job as the Cause of All Your Unhappiness

It's unrealistic to expect your job to grant you sole and ultimate satisfaction in life. You are more than just your career. If you don't develop the totality of your life, you may fall into the trap of granting exaggerated importance to your job.

A healthy work–life balance will of itself bring renewed energy and increased happiness into work with you. This will improve your positivity, optimism and happiness levels – and hence your overall performance, including at work.

Make a pact with yourself to work on your life outside of work *today*. Ask yourself how much time you are putting into fun and recreation in your life. Fitness? Developing relationships with friends, family and romantic partners? Stimulating your mind with intellectual and cultural interests? When is the last time you took a night class?

These things do not involve a large cash investment, so won't make a large dent in your budget.

§

Tip 3: Put Things in Perspective

If you have a job at present, then give serious consideration to the notion that you should celebrate this fact. Given the current market, you are in a more fortunate position than a lot of people.

Put your job in perspective. Realise you are more than your job. Focus on what you can do within your work as opposed to what you feel you can't.

Know what is working for you in your life and what you are thankful for.

Such positivity may rekindle a romance with your current job. Alternatively it may keep you sane while you plot your escape route.

§

Tip 4: Raise Your Game
Become Positive

Bosses, companies, colleagues and society gravitate towards positive-minded people and shy away from low-energy individuals. Avoid always playing devil's advocate. Study the tact and emotional intelligence with which enthusiastic people raise difficulties or objections during meetings. Watch how people react to them.

Motivation

Become Known in the Workplace

Volunteer for a high-risk or high-profile project. Don't fade into the background.

Clarify Expectations

Get clear about your boss's expectations of you, and start to drip feed your own expectations to your boss now. Lock it down and schedule regular meetings.

Gain Credibility and Respect

Do not over-promise. Do not go overboard in trying to impress. Be mindful at all times of your long-term reputation.

§

Tip 5: Know Your Own Unique Work Motivator Combination

We all have work motivators that are unique to us. These are the unconscious and conscious drivers that make work fulfilling for us. What is your distinctive combination? Try drawing up a shortlist of five to ten top work motivators.

§

Tip 6: Focus on Your Negative Tapes So You Can Turn These Around

One of the ways you can learn to make accountability a way of life is to get rid of the Faulter Ego conversations you hold with and about yourself every day. Such conversations – or negative tapes – are ones you play over and over in your thoughts. They have the power to keep you from making better choices or developing new behaviour patterns.

When you catch yourself in Faulter Ego mode, ask yourself, *Does this thought serve me well? Do I have sufficient evidence to back this up?*

Train yourself to come up with more positive tapes.

Example:
Faulter Ego: 'This company is going downhill.'
Positive Tape: 'I will take control of *my* role and perform to the best of *my* ability as *my* way of helping this company get back on track.'

§

Tip 7: Define Success for Yourself

As you face into the future with your current role, ask yourself, *How would I define 'success' in this role?* What five things are needed in order for me to feel more successful? How can I start working towards these *today*?

§

Tip 8: Put Your Emotional Intelligence Skills to Use

Emotional intelligence involves the ability to understand and manage your emotions. In particular, an individual's emotional intelligence is a measure of their emotional, personal, professional, social and coping skills.

For example:

- You might believe you are sharp and copped on, but if you can't convey what you know or mean to other people, it's no use.
- You might be skillful, but if you behave impulsively or inconsistently, no one will stay around long enough to admire your skill and creativity.
- You may be an intellectual high-flyer, but intellect minus EQ will seriously reduce your ability to make an impact with people and in organisations.

It is vital to understand the part *you* are playing in how others treat you and respond to you.

In employment terms, therefore, EQ defines your ability to work with colleagues, bosses and subordinates, helping you to understand what is motivating them and therefore how to manage situations better.

Not for nothing is it sometimes said that while IQ can get you a job, EQ will get you promoted.

§

Tip 9: Celebrate Your Successes

Come up for air and take note of what you have already achieved. Don't be so caught up in the present and the future that you omit to celebrate these things. Avoid being too hard on yourself. Set realistic goals, and give yourself kudos when you deliver on them.

§

Tip 10: If, Even After Implementing the Above Strategies, You Still Find Yourself Chronically Unmotivated in Your Job, Consider a Job or Career Move

There are no medals in this life for being a martyr to your job. Change, even in the current climate, may well be a serious option – *as long as* it is negotiated carefully, realistically and strategically.

§

14

Transferable Skills

'In terms of the options open to you, you are your transferable skills.'

I say this to my clients time and time again.

Transferable skills are those skills that you have picked up in your current role or in previous roles, and that you can actually 'take away' for deployment in future roles.

Looked at in this way, your past becomes mere prologue to a future full of possibilities.

Everything you did in the past remains with you, for it has been added to your transferable skills bank. *Nothing was wasted!*

Transferable skills help you:

- Clarify what it is you have to offer
- Target the right roles
- Tailormake the role you want
- Make your own unique sales pitch
- Tell people what you are about
- Summarise your career to date to a recruitment agent or job interviewer
- Maximise the impact of the profile at the top of your CV

- Highlight any skills gaps that may require up-skilling on your part

When I cover transferable skills in my coaching sessions or career workshops I notice that clients tend to perk up and almost get excited. They have moved from a deficit model of themselves to a surplus model. They now know what they have to offer, what they have learned to date and the logic for each role they worked within. *They now know why they could seriously be considered for a job they deem desirable.*

An Example of Transferable Skills in Action

Simon was a very successful mortgage broker. In fact, he was director of a mortgage broking business. This being a particularly exposed sector in the economy, the downturn forced Simon to take stock and make a career change plan. It was obvious that he would soon be redundant.

We set about listing the transferable skills Simon had gained in his career to date. We had also decided in a previous session that he would really like to work in the area of credit control within the mortgage lending section of a bank.

Simon already had all of the essential ingredients:

- Had worked within financial services, so knew their systems and practices for the most part
- Understood mortgages extremely well
- Had excellent client relationship skills
- Was comfortable with figures

He also felt there was scope for development in a role like this – due to the rather unfortunate fact that credit was a fast-growing area.

One piece of the jigsaw that was missing, however, was a credit management qualification. Instead of getting stuck on this gap and exaggerating its importance, we set about

---

assessing the fastest and best path available for Simon to plug it. As I write, he is working through year one of a two-year part-time Diploma in Credit Management. This is going to give him the following benefits:

- Upskilling him for the area of credit control
- Sending the right message to a future employer that he really was taking this move into credit management very seriously and would be a committed employee
- Adding to Simon's feelings of pro-activeness, credibility and self-esteem

Simon is now in the process of constructing a CV that can be impressively tailored to his area of choice. I am generally wary about making bold predictions, but in Simon's case I can confidently forecast that he will soon walk into the job he wants – and will do it brilliantly.

So how do you itemise your transferable skills?

Start by breaking them down under the following headings:

1. Technical and area-specific
2. General
3. Educational
4. Soft skills

1. Technical and Area-Specific

These skills relate to the actual technical skills needed to do a job. They might include, for example:

- Using a SAP IT system on a daily basis to process business information
- As a legal secretary knowing how to audiotype
- As a doctor specialising in cardiovascular disease
- As an accountant having strong skills in the area of ABC cost accounting

- As a salesperson selling office equipment and all that entails
- As a product salesperson working within an FMCG area
- As a publishing editor being skilled in copyediting

Perhaps you work in what you think of as a non-technical area, such as, say, as an executive assistant or PA? I would still argue that this role has gained you very relevant technical and area-specific skills, including perhaps knowledge of banking systems/processes or diary management using a certain IT system, etc.
Don't sell yourself short!

2. General

Under general skills you need to consider the following type of competencies:

- Client relationship management
- Administration
- Coordination of office
- Receptionist skills using a busy switch
- Management of a team
- Recruiting staff
- Presenting at or chairing meetings
- Sales
- Marketing
- General management
- Use of MS Office Suite

3. Educational

- Degree?
- Diploma?
- Certificate?
- In-house training courses?
- Refresher courses?
- One-day intensive courses?

NOTE: If you have completed short courses, it can be important to note them on your CV — *but only if relevant* to the role you are applying to.

4. Soft Skills

AHA! My favourite subject when it comes to transferable skills. Your soft skills are those skills which determine:

• How you react in the workplace
• How you handle yourself
• Your experience in dealing with difficult clients, colleagues, managers and negotiators
• Your skills of social functioning (a.k.a. emotional intelligence)

For more on soft skills, see Chapter 15.

15

Soft Skills

Soft skills are our set of skills which influence how we interact with others. They can also include such abilities as creativity, analytical thinking, diplomacy, change-readiness, leadership and team-building. Soft skills are ultimately those personality traits which make us unique in the workplace.

All other things being equal, it is your soft skills that will determine whether you get picked over another candidate at interview.

It is therefore imperative that you make some reference to them in your CV, as well of course as displaying them with aplomb at interview.

Having identified *your* top ten soft skills, you might ask yourself the following questions:

- Is there a gap between where my soft skills are now and the field/area of interest I want to move into?
- Is there a gap between my soft skills and my current area of work where I intend to stay?

- What can I do to develop these?
- What are the soft skills needed to perform successfully in the role whose job specifications I am examining?

P.S. You should always prepare for interview by coming up with (true!) situations that demonstrate how you displayed particular soft skills in the past.

To give yourself a better understanding of what exactly soft skills involve, check out some examples of soft skills profiles below.

Sample Case 1 – Solicitor

Key soft skills associated with being an effective solicitor:
- <u>Negotiation skills</u> → negotiating agreements on behalf of clients
- <u>Influencing</u> → getting your point across clearly and winning the argument if needed
- <u>Assertiveness</u> → standing one's ground and letting needs be known (one's own and those of the client)
- <u>Problem-solving</u> → acknowleding a problem and creating a workable solution
- <u>Decision-making</u> → knowing when a decision needs to be made and not procrastinating
- <u>Multi-tasking</u> → managing several case loads at any one time
- <u>Time management</u> → adhering to deadlines and ensuring punctual court attendance
- <u>Confident/skilled communication</u> → in court and with clients

---

Sample Case 2 – Career Coach (!)

- <u>Passion for helping others</u> → a genuine interest and skill in helping
- <u>Goal-setting and goal-achieving</u> → to ensure that clients get results

- <u>Drive and energy</u> → to make things happen for clients
- <u>Problem-solving</u> → taking a problem, assessing it and generating a realistic solution
- <u>Risk-taking</u> → encouraging clients to take measured risks to improve their career
- <u>Optimism</u> → an educated conviction that things will get better
- <u>Empathy skills</u> → being able to step into a client's shoes
- <u>Strong communication skills</u> → to give a correct and consistent message to clients
- <u>'Stickability'</u> → seeing projects through to completion
- <u>Strong emotional health</u> → to handle clients to the best of one's ability
- <u>Assertiveness</u> → to be able to stand one's ground when necessary
- <u>Self-esteem</u> → to avoid second-guessing oneself as a coach
- <u>Time management</u> → to multi-task effectively in order to see things through

Sample Case 3 – Doctor

- <u>Independence</u> → to be able to make decisions without needing to depend on others
- <u>Stress management</u> → to be able to avoid caving in under stressful situations with patients
- <u>Empathy</u> → to have a genuine interest in doing good for others and stepping into patients' shoes
- <u>Flexibility</u> → to changing situations and demands
- <u>Time management</u> → to manage your diary effectively and be available for out-of-hours calls
- <u>Problem-solving</u> → to assess the needs of a patient
- <u>Communication skills</u> → to win the trust and respect of patients or colleagues
- <u>Listening skills</u> → to be able to read between the lines and use intuition

16

Redundancy

Were you recently made redundant? Did you see this coming but still found it hit you like a ton of bricks? Are you still in shock and disbelief? Are you feeling negative and despondent? Are you tormented by defeatist questions? *How do I even begin to remotivate myself to get back on my career track? How will I explain this at future interviews?*

If you haven't been laid off, do you see the writing on the wall? Are you wondering how to handle things when the day of reckoning does come?

I want the tips below to give you some very practical pointers for coping with what can be a really, really traumatic and frightening experience.

No matter how down you may feel about being made redundant, you *must* somehow use this 'negative' experience to deepen your self-awareness and *act on* this deepened self-awareness. You may have been dealt a serious blow by the recession, but it has not robbed you of your core competencies, your qualifications, your experience or your transferable skills. Show yourself that it has not robbed you of your resilience either.

Top Tips for Managing Redundancy

1. The reflect and act formula
2. Accept and move on
3. Embrace short-term sacrifice
4. See risk as 'measured' risk
5. Manage your short-term financial commitments
6. Manage others' worry about the situation
7. Manage your negative tapes/self-esteem
8. Get clear about the challenge ahead
9. Face things head on
10. Stay on track
11. Network with old colleagues/friends

Tip 1: The Reflect and Act Formula

Reflection + Action = Response to Career Trouble

This double response model applies not just to coping with redundancy but also to dealing with job dissatisfaction. Both redundancy and job dissatisfaction can be viewed under the banner of *Career Transition* rather than the banner of *Career Disaster.*

Without reflection and action, you will more than likely sleepwalk through your days feeling horribly unfulfilled and anxious, haunted by the feeling that 'there is no way out' or indeed 'no way back into the workplace'.

Lose either item from the left-hand side of the double response equation, and the result will be your own personal purgatory of stagnation, frustration and helplessness.

§

Tip 2: Accept and Move On

Taking redundancy personally will not serve you well. I have noticed that clients who accept what has happened and put their energy into a new job-search plan fare much better. If they can you can too.

§

Tip 3: Embrace Short-Term Sacrifice

What am I willing to *sacrifice* in the short term in order to get to where I want to be? It may sound like a dirty word, but *sacrifice is usually an intrinsic part of finding career success.* In looking at 'winners' in various career fields, it is easy to overlook this fact. If you are not willing to tolerate any measure of sacrifice, you may struggle to find or hold onto a job. Sacrifice is intimately related to the anti-Vaulter Ego virtues of *commitment, resoluteness* and *patience.* Short-term sacrifice may come in the form of monetary tightening, reduced time with loved ones and friends, reduced recreational time, fewer luxuries, putting up with dull stop-gap jobs, change of status, evenings spent studying, etc. Teach yourself to expect and accept that some or all of these things will come into your life as you bring your plan for career success into the realm of concrete action. *Do NOT let your Vaulter Ego trick you into thinking that these things are an index of failure!*

§

Tip 4: See Risk as 'Measured' Risk

The concept of taking a measured risk is one I discuss regularly with my clients. We all have responsibilities, be they financial commitments, family to support or lives to live. I am NOT encouraging you to be irresponsible or slip into 'anything goes' mode. Take measured risks, not gambles or wild shots in the dark. A measured risk avoids the extremes of Vaulter Ego impulsiveness and Halter Ego risk aversion. A measured risk may take time but, once you have done your homework and are clear on all eventualities, including benefits and short-term sacrifices, you won't lose your nerve or your good judgement.

§

Tip 5: Manage Your Short-Term Financial Commitments

Oftentimes clients who come to me for post-redundancy career coaching have one major energy drain which they feel is going to hold them back from making a successful career transition – MONEY!

If at all possible you should try to secure an interim stop-gap role. This will bring a host of benefits. First off it will take away some of the financial pressure. Secondly, it may give you new skills. Thirdly, knowing that this job is merely a stop-gap will remove the negative energy you might otherwise be investing in it – 'dull job', 'humiliating', 'way below my qualifications', 'dead-end work', etc. See this job for what it is, and you will be able to conserve your energy for your *real* job or career search. No doubt there will be mornings (and afternoons and evenings and possibly even nights) when you will find it hard not to believe that you are disappearing into this job. It will be then that you *must* remind yourself that this job is merely a means to an end – useful in the short term but devoid of long-range significance.

If you simply cannot find *any* stop-gap work, then you will have to hunker down for a period of living on the dole. I am not playing word games when I say that you must try to see this as a period of between-job regrouping rather than 'unemployment' as such. You *must* hold your nerve and see your dole-drawing status as a *transitional* and *temporary* 'blip'.*

§

Tip 6: Manage Others' Worry About the Situation

The key here is to select your personal golden circle. These are the people with whom you can be yourself and talk things out. Know when to have fun with these key supports too, though. Don't do a Salter Ego and play the victim constantly.

Watch out also for the acute Alterior Ego discomfort that can be associated with redundancy. So often (and I believe it to be an Irish phenomenon) I have clients tormenting themselves over comments made by neighbours, friends of friends and suchlike: 'I heard you were made redundant, is it true?', 'You must be beside yourself', 'What are you going to do?'

I'm sure (most of) these people mean well, but you need to learn to manage their perception. This involves refining what I call your 'meet and greets'. The most effective action here is to have one phrase you can use, such as, 'Yeah, I'm busy getting a new plan together. I'll be grand.' This will fob the feckers off! Meanwhile you can share your concerns and insecurities with your golden circle.

Above all else, you must conserve your energy in order to tackle the job search with maximum vigour.

§

---

* For some terrifically helpful advice on coping with the nitty-gritty financial pressures of redundancy, see Chapter 7 of Caroline Madden and Laura Slattery's *The Money Book: Everything you ever wanted to know about your finances (but were afraid to ask)* (Dublin: Blackhall Publishing, 2009).

Tip 7: Manage Your Negative Tapes/Self-Esteem

Redundancy is one of those occasions when you *must* hold your Faulter Ego and/or Salter Ego on the tightest possible leash. Indulging in daily or even hourly conversations with yourself on defeatist themes – 'I am never going to get a job', 'I'm a loser', 'If only I had' – may give you a Faulter–Salter narrative buzz, but how will it advance the goal of finding a new role? Choose a more empowering line of thought: 'This is a blip, but I'm going to get through it', 'Maybe this has happened for a reason', 'Things will come good'. Choose your own positive tape, one that will trigger a more constructive attitude, and practise this tape. You may feel I am committing the cardinal sin of over-simplifying the situation, but believe me I have seen the benefits of positive auto-suggestion in action. It takes practice but will be worth it – *as long as your linguistic fightback is accompanied by planned practical fightback.*

§

Tip 8: Get Clear About the Challenge Ahead

Know what challenges are ahead for you.

Once you are clear on exactly what the challenges are you can take constructive and targeted action.

Perhaps you are not sure what type of role you now want:

→ Spend some time determining your values, work motivators and transferable skills by doing a self-assessment in each.

Perhaps it has been quite a while since you last had to go out and look for a job. Perhaps you feel your CV, sales pitch and interviewing skills need serious polishing up:

→ Brush up on your facing the market skills.

§

Tip 9: Face Things Head On

Do NOT, whatever you do, retreat into Voltaire Ego, make-the-world-go-away mode – hanging around your home all day, sleeping late, watching TV or DVDs for hours on end, etc. When you sink into this mode, the outside world can become a very threatening place in your head.

Nor should you treat redundancy as a holiday. It is a transitional phase in your career that will allow you to make a career upgrade. So discipline yourself into a regular routine.

Use this time to plot your re-entry into the world of work *and* to work on skills and interests that your last job kept you from cultivating as much as you would have liked.

Your next task will then be to get:

1. Inspired (about what you want)
2. Informed (about the market you have decided to focus on)
3. Planning (to make your move on the jobs market with impeccable CV and interview skills)

Time and again I have seen clients who start out severely demoralised by redundancy discover hidden reserves of resilience in themselves. What turns things around is a switch:

* Reaction → proactivity
* Worry → research
* Self-doubt → an attitude that *I am not some sort of professional basket case, I am someone who really can add value to a company or organisation*

Once you get inspired through putting in research and time, you will find yourself spotting options that hadn't struck you before. You will go from a model based on fear of the future to one based on excitement. A nice feeling, and an incomparably effective catalyst in bringing about positive change.

§

Tip 10: Stay on Track

Take regular pit stops, come up for air, manage your planning like a project. Take headspace time out too. Avoid jumping headfirst into something. Better to get a stop-gap role. Use this redundancy as an opportunity to develop your life outside of work and get to those things you didn't get an opportunity to do when working. The logic here is to take a balanced approach to your job search and planning so it doesn't consume your every waking moment. This is all about keeping a healthy perspective on things, and being able to see the wood for the trees.

§

Tip 11: Network with Old Colleagues/Friends

Email or call past colleagues and friends to let them know you are actively looking for a new role, having been made redundant; if anyone knows anybody in a particular industry or area of interest could they please let you know?

Even if you feel that you don't have an extensive network of plugged-in associates, *start from where you're at.* You just never know, someone somewhere could provide that missing link between you and your ideal job. I have seen this phenomenon happen – a lot. The reason? You are more than a non-descript series of black marks on a CV profile page to people who know you. You are already individualised. Even their word of mouth to others regarding you gives you a reality in people's minds that could make all the difference.

§

17

The 'Stay at Home' Mother Planning to Return to Work

Many women in the home feel like they are juggling their life away. 'What about *my* career?' they ask. As a coach I would say life is about balance – balancing all areas of your life so they work well for *you*.

Running a home is a full-time job at the best of times. However, you may decide you want to return to paid work for any number of reasons. Perhaps you need the money. Perhaps you seek increased adult interaction, a greater sense of wellbeing or more intellectual stimulation. Perhaps the kids are now at school.

Whatever your motivation, it is essential that you put the right steps in place to manage this transition back into the marketplace.

Tips for Returning to Work

1. Take time to assess what you have to offer – what are your transferable skills?
2. What up-skilling is needed to freshen up your skills base?

How can you go about finding relevant courses?

3. What do you now *want* to do? You will need to firmly establish your priorities around your answer to this question, and recognise the sacrifices involved too. If this is a change of career direction, then time and investment of energy will be required to plan it right.

4. 'My CV – how do I explain the gap?' Just put the date you stepped out of the workforce and put something in like, 'Full-time mother' or 'Manager of a small family empire!'

5. What message are you going to give to the market? Avoid apologising for being out so long but come across as confident that you still have a lot to offer (which in all likelihood you DO).

6. Gather two strong references so you have these ready to vouch for you.

7. How are you going to handle the juggle? What plans do you need to put in place regarding childcare? How many hours of work are you looking for? Full-time? Part-time? Job share?

8. 'How do I put it to a potential employer that I only want a part-time job?' By talking up the benefits of this to the employer themselves. For example: they will get someone very capable and committed and only need to pay a part-time salary. Create a solution for the company around hours which will span the week but which will be short, making you visible and present almost daily (a win/win situation). This recession could work to your benefit. Employers need to cost-cut so might actually be very open to a reduced working hours agreement.

9. Do you know anyone with a very similar skills set to you? Could you apply in unison and suggest a job share?

10. Lock down your interview skills to ensure that you impress if invited for interview.

11. Allocate time to your career planning – even if it's when the kids go to bed in the evening. You gotta do what you gotta do!

12. If called for interview do your utmost to get there at the time slot suggested by your potential employer. Punctuality

gives the message, 'I am available.' Lateness gives the message, 'I am snowed under with kids' stuff. Hire me at your own risk.'

13. Remember – being a stay-at-home mother is a serious job and it has not robbed you of your core competencies, experience or transferable skills, let alone your qualifications. You need to get real because every day you spend feeling down-hearted and in Faulter/Salter Ego victim mode is a day that does not serve you well. In fact it holds you back and damages you and those close to you.

14. Set clear goals and stay focused on the motivation behind them. Keep reminding yourself what returning to work with give *you*. Not the kids *you*.

15. Finally UP-SKILL all the way. Go to www.fas.ie for free courses which will really show your commitment to returning to work, as well of course as giving you some fresh, up-to-date up-skilling on your CV.

Above all else, DON'T ADOPT A DEFENSIVE ATTITUDE. When I worked in the world of recruitment I remember frequently getting calls from companies specifically mentioning that they would love 'a mother returning to work'. This for them meant someone with maturity, motivation, interest, emotional intelligence and commitment. Most recruiters would tell you this. Maturity counts!

Good luck!

§

18

Facing the Irish Marketplace

The recruiting landscape has changed significantly as a result of the recent economic downturn. Many organisations have undergone hiring freezes and headcount reduction – a move that has also hit a number of internal HR resources who were responsible for recruitment. Recent business articles are suggesting that annual turnover may double in the upcoming years as people start to change jobs post-recession. This will inevitably sharpen the focus on recruiting all over again. Companies are already starting to forecast an increase in hiring over the next twelve months or so and are looking at ways of managing the volume without having to fund additional in-house resources.

The strategy you adopt when facing the market, or what I call 'going public', will determine how well you succeed in becoming visible to employers who are recruiting.

Your strategy can be broken down into two distinct groups:

- Traditional methods
- Non-traditional methods

Traditional Methods

Traditional methods for facing the market include recruitment agencies, job sites, job exhibitions or fairs and newspaper advertisements

Agencies
*Please refer to separate section on recruitment agencies (Chapter 20).

Job Sites
Job websites serve a real purpose for the job hunter. Be careful though not to base your entire search strategy on job sites. They are effective *when used in conjunction with other job search methods*. Get to know the sites relevant to your specific area. Ask friends/colleagues in your field which one they would recommend. One tip I always give job hunters is to go to the employers' section if possible – bypassing agencies to see who is looking for direct applications. Job sites can also be helpful for learning about various companies out there and what they do. When applying through a job site remember it is vital to summarise very effectively what you have to offer to the role. Another option here is to attach a cover letter with your CV, if the system allows you do this. Also remember, however, to *answer any screening questions they may have posted*.

Job Exhibitions/Fairs
Job exhibitions are beneficial in two ways:

• They sometimes help the job hunter to meet face-to-face with the company decision-makers – a real opportunity to impress.
• They also help the job hunter to build a profile of the companies that are proactively recruiting at the moment.

Facing the Irish Marketplace

How do you get the most out of jobs fairs?

- Make absolutely sure you know what you are about before you engage with any of the people on the stands.
- Have a clear sales pitch about yourself and what you now want.
- Ensure your CV is 100 per cent up to scratch before you attend.
- Also a good idea is to have one set of generic CVs (for unplanned encounters) and a number of targeted CVs (tailored to companies you know in advance will be there).

Negatives of job fairs:

- Don't get disheartened if the bulk of positions do not relate to your area or if you feel you are being pushed by good sales recruiters into areas you do not want. Try to target the correct job fair for your industry as against general job fairs.

Newspaper Advertisements
Do not discount this as a route to securing a role. This strategy is still sometimes used by organisations. The Sunday papers can be good here too. Dublin's *Evening Herald* is effective for more junior roles. So too are the local newspapers: *Northside* and *Southside People*, *Cork Independent*, *Connaught Tribune*, *The Kerryman* and the *Leinster Leader*, etc.

Non-Traditional Methods

Networking
Whatever the role or level you are at, it makes sense to select the top ten companies you would like to work for. Once you select them you can put in the groundwork building up a profile and portfolio for each. This may seem like hard work but trust me, it pays off.
Stop hiding behind your computer – There are excellent online strategies for sourcing a new job, such as job boards and

259

social media networking. However, real world human inter-action should not be ignored. When you are meeting people and talking to people you are opening yourself to ideas, leads and powerful information. Remember to *be alert* as you inter-act with people everyday.

Phone ten people daily – Target easy calls initially, including ex-work colleagues, friends and relatives. Your goal is to get a job but any conversation can deliver information to maintain momentum. Remember if people don't know you are looking they can't help you.

Join LinkedIn – This is a popular tool for professionals to net-work. Once you join you can create a profile, connect with contacts, develop your connections and join online network groups. The important point is to make yourself visible online. Help employers find you.

Creating Your Own Job Specification
Depending on your level it can often serve you really well to define and create your own job spec based on your skills, ex-perience and strengths. This you can then use as a blueprint when approaching the market. Of course you may not get a role which ticks all of these boxes but it will help with your search.

Email Friends to Advise Them You are Available
Clients are often very surprised at the results this can yield. People do talk and people do like to help others. Networking with friends and previous colleagues or business contacts is a very clever and proactive way of thinking 'outside the box' when it comes to your job search strategies.

19

You and Your CV

There are only two types of CV in all the world:

- A CV that gets you called for an interview
- A CV that doesn't get you called for an interview

$$\approx$$

Claims About What You Are Capable Of + Evidence + Λ Strong Narrative = Effective CV

$$\approx$$

In 2009 a Dublin recruitment firm sampled 500 CVs they had received.
How many passed the basic CV quality test?
8 per cent.

$$\approx$$

The researchers also estimated the average time a prospective employer spends reading each CV they get.
Their estimate?
30 seconds.

≈

The high number of applications per vacancy in the current climate means that the person whose job it is to screen CVs will go through a process of de-selection before finalising a shortlist.
What is the most popular technique for sorting out the wheat from the chaff?
Dismissing poorly constructed CVs.

≈

Also gaining momentum within Human Resources functions is what is called optical recognition technology.
It scans your CV for required skills, experience and relevant qualifications needed for the position.
Therefore at a basic level your CV must contain key phrases and keywords relevant to the skills being sought for the job in question. Otherwise you will miss out.

> **Top Ten CV Tips**
> 1. Include a profile on the top of the first page of your CV summarising your skills set and experience, and stating exactly what you now want.
> 2. Offer a key skills summary on the first page of your CV under your personal profile.
> 3. Give website links for each company or organisation you have worked within, followed by a couple of lines explain-

ing concisely and to the point what the company or organisation did.

4. Use lots of action verbs and ownership statements when listing each role's responsibilities.
5. Make sure to mention any IT skills you have.
6. Include a references section with something like, 'Delighted to supply references upon request.' Nothing more is required.
7. Perform a full spelling and grammar health check.
8. Deploy lingo and phrases relevant to your area of interest.
9. Strategically tailor your CV to the specific role you are applying for.
10. Give a consistent message (AKA a strong narrative).

Tip 1: Include a Profile on the Top of the First Page of Your CV Summarising Your Skills Set and Experience, and Stating Exactly What You Now Want

Remember, the first page of your CV has the greatest impact and sets the tone in terms of what you are about in relation to the role being applied for.

Be aware that page one of your CV will ultimately decide whether or not you are put in the 'Yes' pile.

Think of it this way – if the other pages of your CV were to get mislaid, would your first page be strong enough to get you selected for interview?

Any key information or summary of skills relevant to the role being applied for must go on page one straight under your personal details. (See Sample CV template below.)

Your statement of exactly what you want now must be tailored (made relevant) to each role you are applying for. It is wise to have a generic profile that you tweak and amend depending on the particular position being applied for.

Your profile should be no longer than four concise sentences. It should not be a short story!

Sample 1 – General Profile

Motivated graduate of business studies with a demonstrated proficiency in listening to my manager's needs and formulating a tactical action plan to achieve results. Honest with a genuine passion for achieving goals for self and others. Possessor of superior interpersonal dynamics, interfacing seamlessly with others from all levels, backgrounds and cultures. I am now keen to move into the area of ... in which I feel I could add real value and bring very relevant transferable skills.

Sample 2 – Specific/Targeted Profile: General Manager

Financially astute general manager conversant with accounting systems and principles with significant experience within the telecoms and distribution industries. Well-developed attention to detail and proven success in the implementation of best practice work methods along with a strong attention to the bottom line of a business. I am now seeking a management role in which I can utilise these transferable skills to add real value to a business.

Sample 3 – Specific Profile: IT Sales Consultant

Senior software services and solutions sales executive with successful selling experience in enterprise software solutions across Europe. Now seeking to bring these strong transferable skills into a similar fast-paced business arena.

§

Tip 2: Offer a Key Skills Summary on the First Page of Your CV Under Your Personal Profile

Under your profile you will want to provide a summary of your key relevant skills for the particular role/area you are targeting. This should be in bullet-point format along the following lines:

Sample Key Skills Summary for PR/Event Director

Key Skills Summary:

- **Key Qualifications** – Degree in Business (UCD) and a Masters in Public Relations (NCIR)
- **PR Consultancy** – Brand name clients within drinks, software and online gaming industry
- **Event Management** – 'From cradle to grave' for brand name clients
- **Business Operations** – Heavily involved in the business operation itself as a company director
- **Leadership** – Directly managed a team of six PR account managers, including HR procedure implementation
- **Client Relationship Management** – Attained customer loyalty as a leader in the PR industry
- **Stakeholder Management** – Worked with groups of stakeholders at all levels
- **IT Skills** – Highly computer literate with experience of statistical packages, spreadsheets, mail merges, desktop publishing and e-mail/internet.

Sample Key Skills Summary for Social Care Worker

Key Skills Summary:

- Diploma in Social Care (UCD)

- Management/support of people and coordination of client services
- Monitoring of improvement programmes and delivery of training programmes
- Well-developed empathy skills with a real compassion for people
- Listening skills in order to engage well with people
- Voluntary work experience – with homeless people, including conflict management/crisis prevention and disciplinary issues when needed (discipline book) and team meetings
- Team player with a sense of humour

§

Tip 3: Give Website Links for Each Company or Organisation You Have Worked Within, Followed by a Couple of Lines Explaining Concisely and to the Point What the Company or Organisation Did

This is something of an innovation in CV protocol, and it makes good sense. Almost every company or organisation has a website. Make reference to it so that potential employers can check your past company out. It also gives the subliminal impression that you have nothing to hide about your past work there.

Put this information next to the company name (please refer to sample CV below).

§

Tip 4: Use Lots of Action Verbs and Ownership Statements When Listing Each Role's Responsibilities

Your CV needs to be full of action verbs and statements showing that you take ownership and responsibility and that you are proactive.

A simple method for doing this is starting with an action verb when describing each role in bullet-point:

Sample Role Responsibility Summary for a Sales Manager

2004–present: Head of Sales – Suishi Ireland www.suishiireland.com

- Direct line reporting to MD
- Achieved and met rigourous monthly sales targets
- Designed, introduced and maintained a complex CRM database to improve the customer experience
- Demonstrated strong creative skills in liaising with the marketing department to come up with new revenue generation ideas
- Created and implemented weekly sales meetings to increase ownership and responsibility within the team
- Effectively coached and managed the sales team to success
- Displayed financial acumen in forecasting, controlling and monitoring significant budgets for the sales department on an annual basis

A general rule of thumb: when detailing your experience, give more detail for your three most recent roles and less for your previous roles.

§

Tip 5: Make Sure to Mention Any IT Skills You Have

IT skills count in almost every job. Therefore it is wise to make reference to these skills on your CV. Better still, rate your skills, e.g basic/intermediate/advanced.

Note any relevant large database knowledge you may also

have (e.g. SAP/Oracle). This is always important as it's a real transferable skill.

§

Tip 6: Include a References Section and Simply Have One Sentence Like: 'Delighted to Supply References Upon Request'. Nothing More is Required

No need to put names in as these may be contacted without your permission, which would prevent you from giving the referees the 'heads up' to expect a call.

Remember, you want to control the reference time as much as possible.

§

Tip 7: Perform a Full Spelling and Grammar Health Check

Sorry to state the obvious but you would not believe the number of typo-infested CVs that companies and recruiters receive.

No excuse here. Use the spell check function on your computer. However be aware that it is not wise to rely solely on your computer spell check. There are two reasons for this:

1. Most computers are defaulted to American English and not British/Irish English
2. Spell checks don't recognise when you use homonyms or creative misspellings that actually spell another word in the dictionary, e.g 'their' or 'they're' instead of 'there'

Therefore I would strongly urge that you have someone else proofread your CV, as a writer is often blind to errors, reading what (s)he remembers wanting to write, not what is actually written. A real, live human being will also be able to spot the kinds of stylistic and grammar booboos that no computer program can spot.

§

Tip 8: Deploy Lingo and Phrases Relevant to Your Area of Interest

This is one of the most important tips I can give. It will add no end to your credibility factor when your CV is being assessed. Every industry has certain phrases, a certain insider lingo. Use them! You want to convey the message that you are fully submerged in that industry. An easy way to do this is to build a portfolio of job specifications (perhaps gleaned from job advertisements) for roles in your desired field and pinch phrases you like! Easy peasy, lemon squeezy.

§

Tip 9: Strategically Tailor Your CV to the Specific Role You Are Applying For

Too often when screening CVs as a recruiter I used to come across CVs that were completely irrelevant to the role being applied for. The candidate might as well have stamped the words 'ALL-PURPOSE GENERIC CV!!!' across the page.

So be clear: You DO need to create a generic CV for yourself.

Generally speaking, you will NOT be sending this generic CV out to prospective employers.

The purpose of this *generic* CV is to be kept on file so that it can help you *generate* a *specific, tailored* CV for each job application you make.

The only two times you will actually hand out your generic CV will be the occasional encounter at a jobs fair or if you decide to circulate your name amongst your network of friends and associates in the hope that someone's eye might be caught by your profile.

On the *tailored* CV, make sure the information you give regarding your qualifications and experience is strategically weighted to *this particular* role.

This means not just placing special emphasis on certain skills and achievements, but also nuancing your language in the direction of the role you are going for.

At all times keep things achievement- and results-focused.

The same also applies to your CV profile: tweak this as necessary for the particular role being applied for.

§

Tip 10: Give a Consistent Message (AKA A Strong Narrative)

Your CV needs to 'stack up'. This means that what you say you are and what you say you can do needs to be backed up with evidence on your CV. Inconsistency or mixed messages are a fatal turn-off for employers. They want clarity. They want to feel that you 'stack up' on paper and in person.

§

SAMPLE CV LAYOUT

Please note: This is intended solely to give you an idea of the format/layout needed in a CV. Information will need to be tailored to your field of interest.

Curriculum Vitae

Susan Lynch
1 The House, The Town, The Country.
Email: susanl@gmail.com
Tel: (m) 086 1234567 (h) 043 1234567

PROFILE
A graduate of Management with an Advanced Diploma in Marketing with over eight years' industry experience as a Marketing Executive with exposure to Irish, UK and European markets. I am well experienced in research techniques and have a strong understanding of the FMCG and retail food industries. I am now seeking to bring these transferable skills and add value within a role of ....

KEY SKILLS & EXPERIENCE SUMMARY
- Marketing Executive in a subsidiary of one of Ireland's largest companies with exposure to UK and European markets (XXX Group Plc).
- Creative and innovative thinker with a successful record of achievement in implementing marketing concepts.
- Solid exposure to e-marketing strategy implementation along with web optimisation.
- Computer literate with experience of word processing, statistical packages, spreadsheets, mail merges, sales ordering/ invoicing system, desktop publishing and e-mail/internet/ world wide web.
- Experience of quality control and the successful preparation and implementation of ISO 9000 certification.

EDUCATION & QUALIFICATIONS
- 2006   The University College, The City – Bachelor of

Science in Management Degree (Hons). B.Sc. Mgmt
• 2003   College of Marketing and Design – Advanced Diploma in Marketing Techniques
  2006   Dissertation/Thesis – 'The Future for the Irish Private Supermarket Industry'

CAREER HISTORY
Sept 2003–present Stellar Management Ltd <u>www.stellarmgmt.com</u>

Marketing Executive/Quality Manager
Reporting to the chief executive with responsibility for both the town and the country plants.
• Marketed the company's products throughout Ireland, the UK and Europe in addition to maintaining quality control standards for two plants.
• Researched and successfully developed a new added-value product currently on sale throughout the UK.
• Researched, analysed, presented and circulated information on market size, trends, prices, transport costs, contacts and added-value products.
• Monitored and analysed customer sales volumes and prices and provided customer service and competitor analysis.
• Organised, managed and attended trade promotions, arranged PR activities, subscriptions, sponsorships and advertising through radio, press and trade publications.
• Liaised with The City University language centre to develop a corporate video on the industry for German industrialists.
• Researched the potential for business opportunities in Germany and eastern European states and set up contacts for trading.
• Successfully managed the preparation and implementation of ISO 9000 certification, including preparing manuals for on-going maintenance of the system.

- Maintained the quality system within both plants.

Nov 2000–Aug 2003 The Small Company www.company. com

Sales Manager
- Reported to the managing director on daily operations for two of the group's five retail outlets, including stock and cash control.
- Successfully opened new city centre unit, trained staff and managed its launch.
- Built good customer relations and maintained high standard of service.
- Carried out promotional activity such as product displays and customer support.
- Conducted market research for the company's range of products in Ireland and secured sales contracts with major companies.

Apr 1997–Nov 2000 The Company Limited www.company. com

Marketing Executive
- Client relations – targeting and contacting potential clients, responding to queries and requests, developing an ongoing business relationship.
- Market research on new products.
- Prototype development – computer systems and support service.
- Analysis of export market potential.
- Planned and coordinated all aspects of international trade fairs, including follow-up activities.
- Marketed strategic decisions regarding trade fairs from

setting objectives and budgeting to negotiating with potential clients.

- Liaised with the Irish Trade Board.
- Organised grant applications from EU and national funding programmes, successfully obtaining many grants for the company.
- Occasionally translated letters and other documents from German into English.

Feb 1996 –Mar 1997 Company Marketing Services www. company.com

<u>Marketing Consultant</u>
Responsible for carrying out research on the Irish supermarket industry.

- Quantified market and carried out a competitive analysis.
- As a result of work carried out, the client successfully obtained a grant for the development of a new company.

Aug 1995–Jan 1996 Master Supplies Ltd www.master.ie

<u>Project Manager</u>
- Responsible for monitoring the work of four graduates, including telemarketing, consumer surveys and analysis of market potential. This was a fixed term project.
- Successfully formulated questionnaires.
- Conducted extensive market research (telemarketing).
- Proactive compiling of research data.
- Completion of reports.

Apr 1994–Jul 1995 Bishop Food Supplies <u>www.bishopfood.</u>
<u>com</u>

Telemarketing Executive

- Conducted extensive telemarketing research.
- Rigourous calling to attract new customers.
- Implementation of relevant data into in-house database.
- Attended and gave input at sales meetings.
- Successfully met hourly/daily calls targets.

FURTHER RELEVANT INDUSTRY TRAINING

- 2004   Goethe Institute, Dublin – Advanced Business German.
- 2002   FAS Employment and Training Authority – Introduction to Desktop Publishing (Corel Ventura).
- 2000   Irish Quality Association – Lead Assessor Training Certificate (ISO 9000).
- 1999   Irish Marketing Institute – The Marketing Audit Workshop (Auditing Business).
- 1998   Irish Marketing Institute – New Media Marketing Seminar (Multimedia).
- 1995   The Training Group – Sales Training Conference.

PROFESSIONAL MEMBERSHIPS

Member of the Marketing Institute of Ireland (MII).

IT SKILLS
Computer literate with experience of word processing, statistical packages, spreadsheets, mail merges, sales ordering/invoicing system, desktop publishing and e-mail/internet/world wide web.

LANGUAGES

- German – Intermediate/Advanced
- Spanish – Intermediate
- Italian – Intermediate

REFERENCES
Delighted to supply upon request.

NB! NB!! NB!!!

COVER YOURSELF WITH YOUR CV COVER LETTER

In the current market, HR experts and recruiters are being inundated with CVs. The cover letter to write with your CV is therefore of utmost importance.

Key Points

- Keep it brief and relevant
- Stick firmly to the actual role being applied for
- Stand out from the rest with your ability to summarise
- If using email, be less formal
- Try to find out the hiring or recruitment manager's name before sending in
- Use positive language
- Do NOT beg!

≈

Rules for writing an EFFECTIVE Cover Letter

Structuring the letter
The covering letter needs to be short and to the point. It should have three paragraphs: opening, middle and closing paragraph.

A good opening paragraph:

• Grabs the attention of the reader
• Explains why you are writing
• Quotes the reference number (if there is one) along with the job title

A good middle paragraph:

• Is factual and doesn't simply give your opinions
• Always keeps the employer in mind and aims to demonstrate that your skills and attributes are what they are looking for
• Uses bullet points to summarise your key relevant skills

A good closing paragraph:

• Says 'I would like meet with you to discuss further'
• Personalises things by saying why this particular organisation or company appeals to you
• Always says 'Thank you for your time' before signing off

Dos & Don'ts Checklist

• **Do** use three main paragraphs
• **Do** say where you saw the advertisement
• **Do** specify selected skills and achievements that will interest the employer
• **Do** have your homework done by (if possible) researching the company that is advertising the job

- **Do** proofread your letter before sending it (ask someone to check it for you)

- **Don't** address it to a 'Dear Sir' or a 'Dear Madam', use the name of the hiring manager/recruitment manager instead
- **Don't** end 'Yours faithfully', use 'Many thanks for your time'
- **Don't** be too pushy by stating you will contact them, give them the option of contacting you too
- **Don't** state how you would expect the job to benefit you
- **Don't** write the same generic letter for each application
- **Don't** use generalisations such as 'I enjoy challenging work'
- **Don't** state your current salary unless specifically requested to do so

---

Sample HR Cover Letter

Dear John

Re: Position of X as advertised on Y

I am delighted to attach my CV for the above position.

In short, I have six years' experience in Human Resources: four years in telecoms and more recently two years as a HR consultant. I am a graduate member of CIPD and am looking for a move back into operational HR. I am especially keen on this position as it is in the telecoms sector, in which the bulk of my experience lies.

Key experience relevant for this role is as follows:

- CIPD qualified
- Adept communicator at all levels of the organisation
- In-depth knowledge of adhering to best HR practice methods
- HR procedures and policies interpretation

- Training design and delivery management
- SAP HR/data management
- Recruitment and contract creation
- People management
- Performance management

[Company name], as an operation, appeals to me as it to the forefront of the telecoms industry and, from my research, I believe the culture fits well with my personality and style of working.
I am required to provide four weeks' notice to my current employer and am available for interview at your convenience.

Looking forward to hearing from you,

Many thanks for your time.

Warmest Regards,

Paul Smyth
E-mail: paulsmyth@12345.ie
Mob: 086 1234567

20

Using Recruitment Agencies

Recruitment agencies can be of real help to the job hunter *once you are clear on what their job is – and isn't.*
There are several rules for getting the best out of them.

> **Top Tips for Using Recruitment Agencies**
> 1. Treat your first encounter as a first round interview.
> 2. Ask impactful questions.
> 3. Don't rant or moan.
> 4. Don't skimp on prep time.
> 5. Select no more than three key agencies.
> 6. Keep in regular contact with your three golden circle agencies.
> 7. Be in control of where your CV details are being sent.
> 8. Do your own independent research into companies that interest you.

Tip 1: Treat Your First Encounter As a First Round Interview

Often candidates at all levels fail to realise that when they meet with an agency consultant this consultant is representing *the client who has the job.* This means that their first mission is to ascertain *your* suitability. If you fail to impress a recruitment consultant, the likelihood is you won't hear from them again.

It is therefore important to use the time with a recruitment consultant to impress, build rapport and *let them interview.* At the same time you must be clear with them about your own 'checklist' regarding what you want or don't want from your next role.

§

Tip 2: Ask Impactful Questions

At the end of the agency interview, always ask any questions which may benefit you, e.g.:

- Is there anything you would change or amend on my CV?
- What is the market like?
- Do you feel my salary expectations are realistic?
- How would you rate me?
- What is your recruiting approach – i.e. are you reactive to roles coming in or strategic and targeted?

Obviously you don't want to 'interrogate' the recruitment agent here, you just want to ask questions.

§

Tip 3: Don't Rant or Moan

The market's bad? Not the recruitment consultant's fault.

You've been having struggles? Not the recruitment consultant's fault.

They are not your counsellor, nor even your friend. They are professionals working on a commission basis to supply employers with optimal candidates for vacant positions.

Their diplomatically sympathetic response to a Faulter/Salter Ego rant should *not* be taken at face value. Rest assured that it will *not* have done you any favours.

§

Tip 4: Don't Skimp on Prep Time

You should be clear as to what you are seeking *before* you go to a recruitment agent. These professionals for the most part are not career coaches or career guidance experts but highly qualified experts in the fine art of 'selling' appropriate candidates to companies. They have great knowledge of the current market, but it is not their job to tell you what you want to do with your life!

§

Tip 5: Select No More Than Three Key Agencies

It is important to explore all channels open to you in this market, but be moderate. You should identify three key agencies who you feel:

• Are working hard on your behalf and showing enthusiasm about your skills and experience level
• Have jobs on their database
• And/or are willing to take a strategic approach to finding you a job

Oftentimes what happens to job hunters is they apply to a lot of agencies directly in response to an ad campaign in which they saw a job they like. If this job doesn't suit and they are not put forward they may find they are suddenly registered with ten agencies. The key is to retract your CV nicely if the position which you originally went for is no longer available and if you already have established solid relationships with other recruiters. You will be taken more seriously by the agencies you have selected.

§

Tip 6: Keep in Regular Contact With Your Three Golden Circle Agencies

Build a close relationship with your consultant via phone or email at least twice a week, letting them know you have selected them as one of your niche agencies. No matter what your level as a job hunter, this will impress as it shows your skills in being strategic and focused.

§

Tip 7: Be in Control of Where Your CV Details Are Being Sent

Keep a notebook. Be aware that another agent cannot go back to that company for at least twelve months based on agency regulations and ethics. So if Recruitment Agency A has sent your CV to Company Y then Recruitment Agency B can't contact them for twelve months. Most recruitment agencies are members of the National Recruitment Federation (NRF), which makes these rules.

§

Tip 8: Do Your Own Independent Research into Companies that Interest You

Although a good idea at all levels, this can be especially beneficial at a more senior level. It gives you a chance to impress a key consultant enough that they will drop everything for one hour and 'do the sell on your behalf' to these companies. That's quite an ask, though, so it's up to you to do the impressing!

§

21

Interviews

Here are some simple yet highly effective tips based on my experience in the world of interviewing and interview coaching.

Interview Prepartion

You don't have to be super-extroverted to ooze confidence. Preparation is the key. You must know as much as you can about the company *and* about yourself before you go into that interview.

Basic pointers for successful interview preparation:

RFL – Get Clear!

Your Reason For Leaving each role gives the interviewer a very good insight into how you function and ultimately manage your career. So Step 1 is *get clear* about your reasons for leaving each role and ensure the message you are getting across is that it was a strategic decision. Should you use this question as a chance to rant about your negative experiences in the role? NO!

Know What You Learned From Each Job

The ability to summarise each role effectively will automatically impress the interviewer. It will display your ability to get a message across without rambling or going into too much unnecessary detail. SO many job hunters fall into the trap of overtalking on this one. When preparing a summary of each role make sure you *keep it relevant* to the role you are interviewing for!

Sample Summaries in Action

a) I spent five years with X. The rationale for that was I was continuously learning. These guys were in growth mode so a lot was happening, which gave me an opportunity to segment my skills in the following areas .... I chose to leave in order to not get boxed off into one industry type setting. Also, I've always wanted to explore the telecoms industry. That's why I am here today ....

b) My time with X was positive. It was my first real job and it gave me the opportunity of learning key skills in the area of ....
After two years I was promoted, which gave me a further challenge .... I made an executive decision to sound out the market at that point. I felt I needed to build my skills in key account management as that is the route I decided I wished my career to take. Key account management was a limited area within X so it meant that for my career to develop I needed to move on. However I really enjoyed my time there and made some great friends too.

Professional Demeanour and Appearance

You need to convey professionalism and to come across as credible so that the interviewer can visualise you in the role.

How you communicate at interview is nearly as important as *what* you communicate.

Ten Top Tips

1. Arrive professionally dressed (even if it's a casual dress environment) and avoid wearing clothes which make too strong a statement. Keep it relatively conservative.
2. Use the names of the interviewers when answering their questions.
3. Watch your body language. Don't fidget. Keep your hands gently clasped on your lap if needs be.
4. LISTEN TO THE QUESTION. Clarify if you are not clear on what is being asked.
5. Reflect and *pause* before answering. Remember – pausing is powerful. It allows you to formulate your answer and show control and calmness.
6. Keep your answers relevant to the question and the job you are interviewing for.
7. Focus on what you can bring to the table and how you can provide a solution.
8. Address the individual who is asking the question but look at the other interviewers too to keep them interested.
9. Keep it brief and check to establish if your answer requires expansion.
10. Keep your reasons for leaving each role positive.

Interview Strategy and Approach

Aim: to create a consistent message and take control so you can show your personality.

Run a Positive Tape in Your Head – Ground Yourself

One good tactic to adopt when about to go to an interview is to make a pact with yourself to have one positive mental tape which you are going to use before and during the interview itself. Those sometimes anxious minutes before going in and when you go in can be eased by a tape running in your head along the lines of:

- I can do this.
- I deserve this role.
- This is my showdown.
- I can handle this. '
- This is my role.
- I am going to enjoy this, I've nothing to hide.
- Bring it on.
- They would be doing well to get me with all of my relevant skills for this role. (Not so catchy, this one, but what the heck, it works.)

Pick one that suits you best. When you enter the room ensure you make eye contact and shake hands well. Take a sip of water before you commence.

Listen to Understand and Speak to Be Understood

Knowing the art of listening when being interviewed will differentiate you from most other candidates. Not listening can make you fail to pick up on the question correctly, engage with the interviewers and read between the lines to gauge their reaction.

When I say listening I mean really listening. I am sure you have experienced what it's like to speak to someone, even in a social situation, and feel they are not listening. Maybe they are busy coming up with an answer to what you are saying. Or maybe they are just not present to you and are looking around. It is very off-putting and creates a negative message.

When you truly are listening to a question, you don't have time to come up with an answer. Better to listen and then pause and show control by saying something like, 'That's a good question, let me have a think for a moment.' Alternatively, take up your glass of water, have a sip and say, 'I am just digesting that question.' Yes, it's OK to do this!

When you are truly listening you can sense if the person(s) interviewing you is/are zoning out and has/have heard enough. Then you know it's time to ZIP IT!

So the simple message here: listen to understand first.

When it comes to your time to speak you will want to make sure you are understood. Think before you open your mouth and keep checking in with yourself as to your response's relevance to the role you are interviewing for.

So often I have interviewed people only to find I don't understand what they are getting at or the relevance of their answer to my question. Better to check in and ask for the question to be repeated if you are not sure. Don't hazard a wild guess or it could go seriously pear-shaped.

Conversely, ensure you are being understood! Even ask the interviewer if you are unsure about this: 'Has that answered your question for you?' This will also allow you to show control and confidence in communication – a double win!

Keep It RELEVANT!

Keeping it relevant is a vital strategy for any interview. It is your job to constantly check in with yourself to ensure what you are saying and discussing is relevant to the job you are interviewing for. There is no point in focusing on details that do nothing to help the interviewer choose you. You will want to make it easy for the interviewer to be impressed by YOU. Be crystal clear on:

- The role you are applying for
- The job specification given to you
- What your transferable skills are for the role

In other words, know the five most important tasks in the job. That way you will ensure you are not derailed. Remember the sole focus of an interview is for you to demonstrate what you can bring to the role and to come across as the solution to their recruiting need.

Show Your Personality

You are your personality. You won't be successful if you just have the 'skills' to perform the job. Personality is the other large part of the jigsaw. The true purpose of a face-to-face interview is to determine whether a job candidate has the personality and so-called 'soft skills' to easily fit in with the culture of the company or organisation. It is important to remember that certain types of behaviour are expected of *all* job candidates during a face-to-face interview.

Research shows that *people make their minds up about someone in the first few seconds of meeting with them.* Scary but true! So it's best to get off to a good start from the outset by showing your personality.

How do you do this?

- By engaging well with interviewer(s) – listening and speaking to be understood so you are in the flow, in control, relaxed and therefore much more capable of being yourself
- By smiling
- By deploying the odd bit of humour (but gauge the situation first)
- By saying something like 'Good question!' and smiling

- By displaying enthusiasm and commitment to the task at hand

Typical Format/Phases of an Interview

Types of Interviews

- Screening interview
- Competency interview
- Board interview
- Phone interview
- Second interview
- Final interview

Screening Interview

A screening interview is conducted to narrow down the candidate field. It can consist of probing questions designed to determine if you can move on to the next stage in the process. Questions can be based on technical knowledge or behavioural characteristics. Typically these interviews are short, lasting 30 minutes, and can be completed over the phone or face to face. Oftentimes recruitment agencies hired by the clients take responsibility for the initial screen so remember, treat this phone screen or face-to-face meeting with an agency seriously! These guys are not your best friend, they are there to filter out the strong from the weak. It really does benefit you to sell your skills at this stage. A good tip is to offer to put down in writing why you feel you strongly fit the role (directly relating it to the job specification).

Competency Interview

With behavioural/competency/scenario-based interviewing, employers are looking at past examples of behaviour as a useful way of predicting future behaviour. They go beyond the basic content requirements of the job and try to identify certain competencies and qualities that you may have demonstrated in previous roles. Some of these could include teamwork, flexibility, initiative, leadership, organising, problem-solving, persuasiveness and work ethic.

With this in mind, it makes sense to consider the competencies involved in the role you are applying for. This way you can prepare some brief SAR (Situation–Action–Result) stories to reflect these competencies.

To prepare for questions like these, you should review any roles and responsibilities you've held and think of examples of situations that illustrate your capabilities. Probe your own motivations and what you learned from the experiences. Your preparation will certainly help the interviewer to see you as a strong 'match' candidate. There is no need to overcomplicate your answers by giving too much information. Keep it simple and relevant – the way you would if you were telling a joke!

The interviewer will look at how you handled situations in the past to assess whether you have the skills and abilities to perform well in this job. They are looking for a *narrative* that will help them imagine you as a *character* in their own *plot*.

You can therefore expect to hear questions that focus on how you coped with stressful activities or project failures. Instead of asking, 'Do you work well under pressure?', the interviewer may ask, 'Describe the most high-pressure situation you have dealt with recently and how you handled it.' Your response will help them see a more realistic picture of how you handled the difficulties and *what you learned from the experience*! Be prepared for the interviewer to follow up with probing questions that will reveal more details of the situation – how you took action, the results, etc. The key to success with competency-based interviewing is to a) have an example bank of SAR stories prepared under various headings relevant to the role you are applying for, and b) mix and match these at interview using SAR to guide you. In order to do this you will need to ascertain what competency they are examining. So, LISTEN TO THE QUESTION!

> • Situation: Think of a situation in which you were involved that would reflect, for example, your ability to prioritise tasks.
> • Action: Specify which actions you took in the particular situation/scenario in order to complete the tasks.
> • Result: What result did you get arising from your actions? This is the crucial bit. So often when interview coaching I notice that clients of all levels and aptitudes forget to seal the deal here.

Board Interview

A board style interview does what it says on the tin: involves a board or panel of interviewers questioning a candidate. The applicant's goal is to establish a rapport with each interviewer by using direct eye contact. Whatever the interview situation or style, you will need to be able to communicate clearly your strengths, relating them directly to the role you are interviewing for. You will usually have one lead interviewer here like a HR expert and another person for the technical questions relating specifically to the job. Others may jump in with ad hoc questions. You may also have one interviewer just taking notes and not asking any questions or engaging with you. Do not be put off by this. It is normal practice.

Phone Interview

Telephone interviews are used for three main purposes:

1. When you send a CV to an employer who is not interviewing on site or wishes to simply screen first.

2. Recruiters often use the telephone for screening interviews although this may not be apparent to you. So always be on guard and answer effectively.

3. Finally, many phone interviews are placed by managers or supervisors who do the actual hiring. After a HR manager/ recruiter interviews you, your CV is often given to the department head who may be interested in employing you. Frequently, these managers will telephone you before extending an invitation to come for a site visit. When it is a line manager interview they will usually focus for the most part on your technical skills. But stay on top of this and create opportunities to show your personality too.

Always treat a telephone interview as seriously as a face-to-face interview and prepare beforehand just like you would for any other type of interview. What you will want to do is build rapport via the phone. If you smile, for example, the interviewer will actually hear it in your voice. Try to show your personality where you can just like you would in a face-to-face interview. Provide concise and relevant answers. Have some key notes in front of you on what you have to offer in that particular role. Also be sure to have the job specification and your CV to hand.

Second Interview

A candidate being seriously considered by a prospective employer is usually invited to visit the organisation for further interviews. One purpose of the site interview is to provide you with an opportunity to meet other staff or plant personnel, and to give additional interviews to help determine whether a good match is developing.

All invitations should be acknowledged promptly even when you are not interested.

The usual course of action at second interview stage is to meet with the line manager and member(s) of the team (if HR were present at the first round). What does this mean to you? It means that in all likelihood it will be a technical interview and a real chance to build rapport and show your relevant transferable skills to someone who knows your job well.

Final Interview

The final interview happens, you will be shocked to hear, in the final round. This is your chance to summarise once again why you are the person for this role. It will usually be with a HR/line manager and possibly a senior manager (depending on the size of the organisation). It is also your opportunity to ask effective questions to further impress.

Salary expectations or negotiation may also come into it so be prepared for a question or two in this direction.

Play to Your Strengths

Key point:

Learn what YOUR transferable skills/strengths are so you can play to these at interview.

The process of building your own unique transferable skills bank and learning to use that information for successful interviewing is essential. Remember:

You are your transferable skills.

Doesn't it make sense to know exactly what these are in the context of the role you are interviewing for?

Get clear on *your* transferable skills and back them up with SAR stories and examples.

Dealing With Difficult Questions

Question Time – The Six Must Knows!
Q1. Tell me a bit about yourself.
Q2. Talk me through your CV.
Q3. Tell me about a key weakness you have.
Q4. Why should we hire you?
Q5. Why do you want to work here?
Q6. What are your salary expectations?

Q1. Tell Me a Bit About Yourself

This can often be one of the two opening questions at interview and allows you the opportunity to impress from the start once you get this right.

It's wise to follow the following format:

Personal → Career summary → Feedback in career to date → Reason why you're here today

Example

So my name is John Cusack and I live in Ranelagh. I am married to Róisín and have two children. In terms of my career to date I have worked in three distinct areas – customer service, account management and sales – within the following industries: FMCG, IT and publishing. My current role title is Sales Manager, managing a team of eight sales consultants. Feedback in my career to date from bosses and colleagues has been as follows: easy to work with, very motivated and focused. The reason I am here today is I want this job. I want this job because it certainly feels like a very logical and worthwhile career step for me and it very much excites me.

Key points:

- Remember this question is not the full interview. It serves only as an introductory question. So do *not* go off on a wild tangent!
- Interviewers will very much value your ability to summarise well a question like this and, establishing the correct tone from the beginning, your answer will set you up to win for the rest of the interview.

Q2. Talk Me Through Your CV

Key point: *Summarise what you took from each role.*

This again is not the full interview. Simply talk through each employment role and summarise briefly why you took it and what you took away from it in terms of skills and experience. Should you start from the beginning or with your most recent role? Your choice. Just let the interviewer(s) know where you plan to start from.

Leave your education piece until the end. Here you will briefly summarise your educational track record relevant to the role.

In terms of roles you have had not in traditional/paid employment, do make reference to these but only if relevant to the role/area you are applying for. This will demonstrate a commitment to learning in your field even where it was unpaid.

Q3. Tell Me About a Key Weakness You Have

Turn a negative into a positive. The main thing is to be comfortable about your weakness and show that you have worked on it and have taken control of it. Remember: we all have weaknesses. It's best to be as honest as possible here as it will enhance your credibility as you speak from experience.

Examples

I tend to want my work done to high standards. This can cause personal frustrations, especially when the reality of business demands or deadlines take over and the job needs to be done at speed. I have worked on this tendency by applying common sense and by improving my ability to make decisions and run with things.

I am sometimes guilty of working long hours, which can affect my work–life balance and energy levels the next day on the job. I have sought to rectify this by making a conscious decision to work 'smarter' and put a real value on my time. This might involve, for example, asserting myself nicely with time wasters or getting on top of my time leaks.

Q4. Why Should We Hire You?

Lovely! Here is YOUR chance to really sell yourself.

You will want to succinctly lay out your relevant qualifications, strengths, transferable skills and ultimately what you can bring to the table in terms of this role. Avoid giving too general an answer. I have often heard people say something along the lines of: 'I am motivated and focused and that's why I believe I should get this role.' You would score about a 4 out of 10 for that. What you need and want to do is to set yourself apart by telling the interviewer about qualities that are unique to you. So tap into the sales pitch you have created for maximum relevancy to this role and – let them have it!

Examples

First off I believe I have very strong transferable skills in the area of strategic sales within a business-to-business setting. Secondly, I believe my educational track record highlights my relevance and commitment to this field. Finally, I have

---

experience using the technology that is used by X so I feel I could hit the ground running, which would be a big benefit to you in the current economic climate.

Although I do not have five years' experience within manufacturing, I do have three solid years in a manufacturing plc and have covered a very similar role to this. I may not yet be fully qualified but I hope I have demonstrated here today that I have provided highly effective support in my most recent role producing accounts to high standards and within compliance frameworks similar to those entailed in this role. I am mature, focused and enthusiastic about this role.

Q5. Why Do You Want to Work Here?

This is the question most interviewers use to ascertain if you have done your homework on their company. What they need from you here is evidence that you know the industry, the competitors and the direction the company seems to be going in. If you have researched this adequately, you will be able to use this question as a peg on which to hang the point that your experience matches the company, adds real value and provides a solution for them.

Example

I believe I should be very much considered for this role as I have already gained experience in a start-up situation like Global Solutions, have worked successfully within an EMEA environment, have strong transferable skills in the areas of SAP and accounts payable within a multi-currency framework, and have worked the French market already. Global Solutions is leading the way within its niche area and I want to work for the best. I also read what your CEO had to say in the feature article in last Sunday's *Sunday Tribune* and, frankly, I liked what he had to say. I believe my approach is aligned to this company's.

Q6. What Are Your Salary Expectations?

This is one of the hardest questions. The first thing to do before going to your interview is to research the salary range in your field to get an idea of what you should be earning. Steer clear of discussing salary specifics before receiving a job offer (if you can). Let the interviewer know that you will be open to discussing a realistic salary when the time comes. If pressed for a more specific answer, *always give a range* rather than a specific number. Alternatively, let them be guided by your current salary plus total package worth. By 'package worth' I mean any benefits and bonuses that make up your full package amount over and above basic annual salary, e.g. health insurance, pension contributions or car allowance.

Another useful tactic is to demonstrate your ability to negotiate by saying something like, 'If you feel I am the right person for the role come back to me with the best you can do and we will take it from there.' What in effect you are saying is: 'Look, I want this job. Don't not come to me if you feel I am right but fear that my salary expectations are too high. Come to me and we can discuss it from there.' You are telegraphing the message: give me an offer!

The Home Run – An Opportunity for You to Question

During your interview (usually at the second or third round), in order for you to determine how well you would fit into the organisation, you may want to ask some questions of your own.

Sample Effective Questions to Ask

1. What would I be expected to have accomplished by the end of my first six months? My first year?
OR

What are the key things I would need to do from your perspective in order to make a real impression within the first six months?

2. If I were employed, and performed above expectations, where would this job lead me?
3. How do you feel this role affects the overall performance of the business from your perspective?
4. How would I be evaluated? By whom? How often?
5. How would you describe the culture of this organisation and what are your most important values?

* At a more senior level it is wise not to wait until the end of the interview to ask questions. Ask your questions throughout the interview and engage with the employer. What are their opinions about the role?

Wheel of Success Interviewing

For a successful interview, you need to attend to ALL of the following aspects:

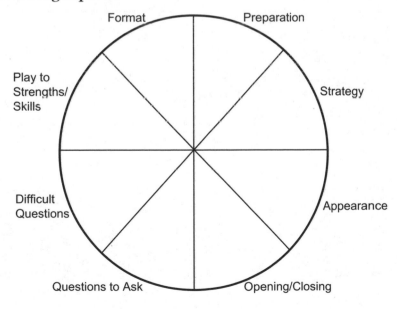

22

Creating a Good Impression in Your New Role

Top Tips for Creating a Good Impression In Your New Role

1. Dust yourself off.
2. Focus on listening to engage.
3. Relax!
4. Avoid the moaners, groaners and bitchers.
5. Get visible.
6. Manage and set expectations with your boss/manager.
7. Create a vision of what you want to achieve in:
   a. The first 12 months
   b. The first 24 months

Tip 1: Dust Yourself Off

Nothing is more calculated to sabotage your effectiveness in a new job than old Faulter Ego habits, as this particular Disappointer mode is likely to be most common during this time. (That is not to say of course that the other Ego habits aren't every bit as dangerous, so do pay attention to them too.) Don't come to this role with lots of limiting beliefs and negative experiences in your mind from your old job. Focus on positives – what you learned from your last role and what you can bring to this one.

§

Tip 2: Focus on Listening to Engage

Each workplace has its own communicative ambience. You should be real in your interactions with your new colleagues, but do try to suss out what is acceptable and what is less so in terms of communicative norms. This will help you create a com-munication strategy for yourself – *without* erasing the unique individuality you bring to the role.

§

Tip 3: Relax!

Remember, you wouldn't have been offered the role unless the company felt you were capable. So go easy on yourself and try not to get into the frame of mind that you have to prove yourself to *everyone* at *once*. Break your role down into manageable steps and enjoy the process of getting familiar with your new brief.

§

Tip 4: Avoid the Moaners, Groaners and Bitchers

Nobody put a gun to your head and forced you to apply for this job. So stay away from energy vampires who try to enlist you into their game. Apart from anything else, such people are particularly prone to quote (or misquote) you to third parties, thereby damaging your reputation.

§

Tip 5: Get Visible

Volunteer for a high-risk or high-profile project and create the message of being a committed employee with a fresh approach. Get known for being a deliverer.

§

Tip 6: Manage and Set Expectations with Your Boss/Manager

Suss out their preferred style of communication. Get clear on their expectations of *you* and start to drip feed your expectations to them now.

Use your emotional intelligence skills to 'read' their needs and expectations.

§

Tip 7: Create a Vision for What You Want to Achieve in

a. The First 12 Months
b. The First 24 Months

It can be all too easy to get swallowed up by the day-to-day minutiae of a new job. Cultivate a double lens through which to look at your job:

LENS I: Short-term (success = efficient delivery of X, Y and Z).

LENS II: Long-term (success = lasting legacy).

If you neglect the former lens, you will raise early doubts about your basic efficiency and productivity.

If you neglect the latter, you will expend all your energy on putting out fires – and none on making a real impact on your company or organisation.

§

In Conclusion

These are not easy times we are living in. A lot of people have had the stuffing knocked out of them by the recession. When things like redundancy, job insecurity, cutbacks and a credit crunch strike, it can feel like everything solid in your life has suddenly melted into air. And I mean *everything*. Self-image; self-esteem; family life; social life; health. You name it. A recession creates a new kind of atmospheric pressure in people's heads. I've *seen* this atmospheric pressure written on people's faces day in, day out – from my career coaching clients right through to friends and family. So this book was not, I assure you, written in a vacuum. It was written in the context of other people's anxieties, stresses and (in some cases) feelings of panic.

Many of the ideas in this book, however, pre-date the economic downturn. They grew out of my experiences in career coaching and recruitment during the so-called boom years. And they were boom years, at least for certain segments of the population. Yet very few people I was meeting were anything close to happy in their work. For many, their level of happiness actually seemed to be in inverse proportion to their level of

309

professional 'success'. These people felt stressed out, time poor and trapped on someone else's treadmill. Others felt they were doing moderately well but still tormented themselves with the idea that they should be doing so much better in what *looked like* a get-rich-quick culture. Making ends meet was no longer admirable, it was boring. Putting food on your family's table was no longer an achievement, it was a given. With everyone around you losing their heads with talk of sudden wealth and seemingly endless and effortless property acquisition, it was easy to think there must be something wrong with *you*. And it was hard not to be sucked into the pathetic game of pretending to be better off than you really were. If anything went viral in the Celtic Tiger years, it was financial pretentiousness.

The recession has called time on a lot of that old nonsense. And a good thing too. But it has created a whole new set of problems, some of which are just downright scary. This book was written for one simple reason: to offer authentic and BS-free guidance on how to make the most of yourself in the career field, whatever your personal circumstances and whatever the current economic climate. It has asked you to consider the notion that the way to start making the most of yourself is, paradoxically, to start making a little less of yourself – or at least those aspects of yourself that make you get in your own way. Your Disappointer/Ego tendencies need to *shrink* before you can *grow*. If you want to make progress in the real world, you must first become a little less unreal yourself.

Your ability to get the most out of the book you have just read will be determined by your ability to connect these two dimensions – the unreal you on one side and the real world out there on the other. As already flagged at a number of points along the way, there are two whopping big mistakes you can make with this book. Each is the contrary of the other:

In Conclusion

- Whopping Big Mistake 1: You jump prematurely into real world considerations, without having grappled with all the things that make you yourself unreal.
- Whopping Big Mistake 2: You get lost in navel-gazing introspection and fail to put yourself out there and actually design a new or better career for yourself.

We are talking here, of course, about your ability to connect Parts I and II of this book. Here, more than anywhere else, the limits of a book compared to a career coaching session are unavoidably encountered. My job with a client will be to not let them get away with either of the two whopping big mistakes above. This book has given you the same tools as my clients, but you yourself are going to have to be the one who lets yourself away with nothing! Always bear in mind that the 'you' in Part II who:

- Sits down and thinks about where to go career-wise
- Goes out and researches a new area or a new job
- Sends in job applications
- Turns up for interview
- Starts a new job

is not some other being altogether from the 'you' we have been meeting in Part I. If you can spot the connections between the two sides of the equation, you will have empowered yourself to fuse restlessness with realism.

I sincerely hope this book has been, or will be, of lasting help to you. If you have any feedback − positive, negative or just downright interesting! − I would love to hear from you. You can send your comments to thecareerbook@gmail.com. While I unfortunately won't be able to reply to messages individually,

311

you may rest assured I will make a point of reading each and every one.

Thanks – and the very best of (non-Altar-Ego!) luck with everything.

Jane

Appendix A:
Self-Assess Your Work Values

Some commonly expressed values are listed below. Rank each
of the listed values as:

1. Not important
2. Moderately important
3. Very important

to you in your choice of career by circling the correct number.

Enjoyment (having fun at what you do)
1   2   3
Helping Other People (in a direct way)
1   2   3
Friendships (developing close relationships with co-workers)
1   2   3
Helping Society (contributing to the betterment of the world)
1   2   3
Freedom (flexible schedule, independence)
1   2   3
Recognition (being acknowledged in a tangible way)
1   2   3

Appendix A

Creativity (having the opportunity to express your ideas and yourself in work; innovation)

1   2   3

Location (being able to live where you choose)

1   2   3

Competition (matching your abilities with others')

1   2   3

Power and Authority (being in a managerial or leadership position; supervising others; having decision-making authority)

1   2   3

Achievement (accomplishing desired objectives; mastery)

1   2   3

Compensation (receiving money and other benefits commensurate with services rendered)

1   2   3

Variety (having a mix of tasks to perform and people to interact with every day)

1   2   3

Security (a feeling of stability; no worries; certainty)

1   2   3

Prestige (being seen as successful; obtaining recognition and status)

1   2   3

Aesthetics (attractiveness of work environment; contributing to the beauty of the world)

1   2   3

Morality and Ethics (working and living according to a code or set of rules; enhancing world ethics)

1   2   3

Intellectual Stimulation (working in an environment that encourages and stimulates thinking)

1   2   3

Public Contact (working directly with others, as opposed to working alone or working with objects only)

1   2   3

Pace (busy versus relaxed atmosphere)

1   2   3

Risk (monetary or other types of risks – e.g. new product development or start-up enterprise)

1   2   3

Any other values that are very important to you but are not on this list?

List your top five work values:

1.

2.

3.

4.

5.

Appendix B:
Self–Assess Your Interests

Interests and Passions Inventory

If you need some extra stimulus, go through this list and tick all the activities in which you've ever been interested. It's not an exhaustive list, and you may want to add more items. Choose three of these which represent those interests you feel most passionate about.

Advising		Gambling	
Art history		Giving parties	
Amateur dramatics		Helping people	
Antiques		History	
Archaeology		Hunting/fishing	
Architecture		Judo/karate	
Attending lectures/workshops		Knitting/sewing	
Campaigning		Meditation	
Bargain-hunting		Mentoring	
Beekeeping		Museums/art galleries	
Belonging to clubs		Networking	
Building models		Photography	
Building things		Playing a musical instrument	

Appendix B

Camping		Politics/current affairs	
Card games		Problem solving/puzzles	
Caring for children		Reading	
Caring for/breeding animals		Reading palms/cards	
Caring for sick or elderly people		Researching	
Car mechanics		Residents' Association	
Chess		Sightseeing	
Church		Singing	
Cinema		Skydiving	
Clubbing		Socialising with friends	
Coaching sports teams		Speaking/debating in public	
Collecting		Spirituality	
Composing music		Sports – specify:	
Committees		Team sports	
Computers		Theatre	
Concerts		Travel/other cultures	
Cooking		Tutoring/teaching	
Counselling		Visiting gardens/houses	
Crafts		Volunteering/community work	
Dancing		Walking/hiking	
Design		Water sports	
DIY		Wildlife	
Dog walking/grooming		Wine tasting	
Doing things outdoors		Woodworking	
Drawing/painting/sculpture		Working out/exercise	
Fashion		Working with your hands	
Food and drink		Writing	
Fundraising		Yoga/pilates/t'ai chi	
Gardening			

My top five interests are:

1.

2.

3.

4.

5.

Appendix C: The Career Disappointers at a Glance

Ego	Choice of Career	Researching a New Job	CV	Interview	At Work	When Faced With a Setback
Faulter Ego	Punching below one's weight, underestimating one's abilities	Defeatist and unsystematic approach; not really believing one stands a chance; too timid or embarrassed to ask others for pointers	Underselling one's achievements and skills; putting very little time into CV prep; slow to approach references for permission	Poor body language and self-presentation; use of self-deprecatory humour; feeling like an imposter	Fear of being 'found out', of making mistakes; poor planning; lack of initiative	Instinctive pessimism about one's ability to solve the problem

(Continued)

(Continued)

Ego	Choice of Career	Researching a New Job	CV	Interview	At Work	When Faced With a Setback
Walter Ego	Haphazard; often one temp job after another; choice of job rarely related directly to 'dream' career; no short- to medium-term criteria for success	Little or no planning or even curiosity	Little care taken due to discomfort and embar- rasssment at lack of substantial professional achievements	Waffly answers; overtalking; poor listening to questions; over- reliance on humour	Poor delivery, efficiency and reliability; easily dis- tractable from task at hand; lack of basic priority-setting	Flight not fight
Halter Ego	Safe option	Restricting one's research to safe bet or familiar options	Efficient but dull; geared to giving impression of 'safe pair of hands'	Scripted answers; lack of spark; focus on being reassuringly charisma-free	Routinised; plodding; often letting colleagues walk all over one	Often clueless, rarely proactive

(Continued)

(Continued)

Ego	Choice of Career	Researching a New Job	CV	Interview	At Work	When Faced With a Setback
Altar Ego	Flitting from one thing to another OR getting trapped in one particular low-satisfaction job	Expectation that 'the right job' will 'come to me' out of the ether; lack of follow-through	Poor attention to detail	Staking all on creating a good 'vibe' with interviewer(s); vague style of answering	Little real interest taken or energy invested in specific tasks; running away from logistical challenges; fear of personal accountability	Quick to resign oneself to defeat
Vaulter Ego	Tendency to go for something that is not aligned with values, work motivators and/or soft skills	Tendency to narrow focus down prematurely; discomfort with considering alternative options; skipping over key details	Tendency to rush this phase	Markedly poor listening skills hamper effectiveness of answers; bad pacing of one's presentation of self	Susceptibility to stress and drama; constantly putting out fires to the neglect of longer-range goals	Temptation to short-circuit the process; giving in to frustration and impatience

(Continued)

Appendix C

(Continued)

Ego	Choice of Career	Researching a New Job	CV	Interview	At Work	When Faced With a Setback
Alterior Ego	Guided by the advice and expectations of others	Little attention given to one's own drivers and motivators	Lack of compelling personal narrative	Failure to leave one's personal mark in the interviewers' memory	Lack of personal initiative; constantly worrying about approval from others	Over-reliance on other people's interpretation of what has gone wrong
Salter Ego	Setting one's sights too low; feeling pressurised into going for a particular job	Defensive attitude – mental picture of a hostile world that doesn't want one to succeed	Allowing a defensive tone to creep into covering letter and summary of past roles	Giving out about previous job(s); tensing up at questions perceived as hostile	Lack of scrupulosity about own tasks; tendency to envy or feel threatened by more dynamic colleagues	Dwelling on why this happened and who's to blame rather than how to sort it out

(Continued)

324

(Continued)

Ego	Choice of Career	Researching a New Job	CV	Interview	At Work	When Faced With a Setback
Exalter Ego	Driven by ego rather than values and meaningful goals	Having a blind spot to genuinely interesting opportunities	Overselling oneself	Coming across as smarmy, cocky, sleek, over-competitive, over-ambitious; raising flags as to ability to work in a team	Full of oneself and competitive; insincere	Bawling out the person beneath one
Voltaire Ego	Something which will not impinge on life outside of work even if it means boredom and repetition in role with no scope for development	Being guided *exclusively* by questions like, 'Is this role close to home?'; 'What's the annual holiday entitlement?'; 'What are the working hours?'; Comfort-zone priorities rule out chances of finding stimulating work	Bland, factual, no compelling narrative; marked lack of training and upskilling due to reluctance to leave home in the evening to invest in a course	Displaying unease at mention of new tasks in role, i.e. 'uncharted territory'; too quick to focus on working conditions and how secure the company is	Watching the clock; zero initiative; problems with punctuality	Clueless; 'Not my problem/fault'

Appendix D: The Career Appointers at a Glance

Ego	Choice of Career	Researching a New Job	CV	Interview	At Work	When Faced With a Setback
Faulter Ego	Being careful and judicious; factoring in worst case scenarios; having a realistically modest sense of one's talents and qualifications	Healthy suspicion of employers' recruitment pitches; not romanticising a prospective job; looking carefully before leaping; factoring in worst-case scenarios	Not overselling one's abilities	Coming across as thoughtful and realistic	Conscientious-ness and alertness to problems	Not fleeing into Polyanna mode

(Continued)

(Continued)

Ego	Choice of Career	Researching a New Job	CV	Interview	At Work	When Faced With a Setback
Walter Ego	Allowing oneself to think big and not settle for a life in Mediocristan	Thinking laterally; not going with the safest or most obvious option; being guided by how excited one feels regarding a career direction	Coming across as dynamic, enthusiastic and not restricted to comfort-zone thinking	Showing one's imaginative and creative side; making a real impression	Not allowing each day be a photocopy of the last; bringing fresh thinking to things	Optimism that, with a bit of creative strategising, the setback can be mounted
Halter Ego	Not fleeing basic financial commitments; willingness to advance in baby steps	Patient accumulation of data; not rushing into things	Thoroughness in research and preparation	Conveying a sense of unostentatious reliability; coming across as a good team player	Reliable and collegial; not hunting for glory all the time	Ability to think the problem through slowly and systematically

(Continued)

(Continued)

Ego	Choice of Career	Researching a New Job	CV	Interview	At Work	When Faced With a Setback
Altar Ego	Not being afraid to ask oneself if this role will meet one's deeper needs and values as a person	Keeping an eye out for opportunities; having trust that things will come right in the end	Coming across as a thoughtful and rounded person	Being reflective and not given to getting lost in procedural matters	Viewing one's role as more than just a means to an end; investing it with value and meaning	Taking the broad view
Vaulter Ego	Having little tolerance for drift	Impulse to seal the deal rather than get lost in endless reflection	Being brief and to the point	Being brief and to the point; giving the impression that one is enthusiastic about getting going in this new role	Doesn't mess about; gets things done; places a premium on delivery and meeting deadlines	Focus not on analysis but on (pro)action

(Continued)

Appendix D

(Continued)

Ego	Choice of Career	Researching a New Job	CV	Interview	At Work	When Faced With a Setback
Alterior Ego	Considers the opinion of others before jumping	Canvasses a wide range of viewpoints	Is constantly asking oneself, 'What impression am I making here?'	Highly alert to the verbal and body language reactions of interviewers	Excellent team player; knows how to liaise; doesn't impose own viewpoint all the time	Casts around for solutions and picks the best
Salter Ego	Sensitivity to one's own emotions makes one demand a job that is genuinely enjoyable	Always measures data against personal needs	Comes across as a human not a robot	Sensitive to needs and perspectives of interviewers	Notices when colleagues are not having a good day; is in touch with own feelings and moods	Sense of fair play – will stand up to bullies and defend scapegoats

(Continued)

(Continued)

Ego	Choice of Career	Researching a New Job	CV	Interview	At Work	When Faced With a Setback
Exalter Ego	Not afraid to aim high	Not shy about networking	Highly efficient; everything written for maximum impact	Infectious enthusiasm about what one can bring to this role and this organisation	High productivity and efficiency; fearless about thinking outside the box; constantly spotting possibilities others miss	Insists on no-nonsense trouble-shooting
Voltaire Ego	Not equating life with work	Being unapologetically fussy about work–life balance implications	Gives impressive sense of a personal 'hinterland', i.e. this person is more interesting than any job	Reassuringly normal, BS-free and *un-desperate about getting the job*; isn't promising the world at interview, so may actually deliver what's asked	Does what one says on the tin; low maintenance; not an attention seeker; not obsessed with status, because personal centre of gravity lies outside of workplace	Refuses to exaggerate magnitude of problem; 'At the end of the day, no one's died'; often a lone sane voice when everyone else is losing all perspective and getting completely stressed out

Career–Related Websites

(with thanks to Paul Mullen at www.measurability.ie)

Career/Interview Coaching and CV Re-Design

- Clearview Coaching Group – www.clearviewcoachgroup.com – Jane Downes' career coaching practice and career coach training company in Dublin
- CV Solutions – www.cvsolutions.ie – CV writing service in Ireland; CV tips and advice
- Interview Solutions – www.interviewsolutions.ie – Interview tips, techniques and skills; interview service in Ireland
- Interview Success – www.interview-success.com – Top tips and advice from an expert in the field
- Interview Questions – www.interviewquestions.biz – Complete guide to interview questions by profession
- CV Writing Service – www.cv-service.org – Curriculum Vitae (CV) and CV writing services with CV examples; expert advice, tips and help by Mike Kelley at First Impressions
- Job Interview – www.job-interview.com – Interview skills, techniques and sample interview questions and answers
- CVizz – www.cvizz.ie — Video CV builder and hosting service for graduates and employers

Irish Blogs – Careers, Jobs, Interviews, CVs and News

- Careers and Jobs – www.careersandjobs.ie – Blog about Irish jobs and careers
- HR and Recruitment – www.hrandrecruitment.ie – Blog for Irish employers about HR and recruitment issues
- CVs and Interviews – www.cvsandinterviews.ie – Blog with useful CV and interview advice
- CV 4 Jobs – www.cv4jobs.ie – Blog with useful CV and interview advice
- Jobs News – www.jobsnews.ie – Irish jobs and job market news
- SEO Consultant – www.seoconsultant.ie –Search engine optimisation consultant blog
- Outplacement Services – www.outplacementservices.ie – Outplacement services and outplacement consultants; 'outplacement' means career advice, guidance and coaching for people who are being made redundant
- Psychometrics – www.psychometrics.ie – Psychometric testing and psychometric tests
- RSS Jobs – www.rssjobs.ie – RSS feed of jobs currently available in Ireland

Irish Job News and Advice

- EirJobs.com – www.eirjobs.com/news – News about the latest jobs in Ireland
- NewToTown.ie – www.newtotown.ie – Answers questions typically asked by people coming to Ireland to work or live
- Work at Home Ireland – www.workathomeireland.com – An information resource for those looking to work from home in Ireland and the UK

Irish Job Listings and Resources

- IrishJobs.ie – www.irishjobs.ie – Jobs, vacancies and careers in Ireland
- Jobs.ie – www.jobs.ie – Jobs, vacancies and careers in Ireland
- Emotional Intelligence Ireland – www.EIIreland.com – Europe's first Assessment and Development Centre for Emotional Intelligence
- Employ Ireland – www.employireland.ie – Irish jobs, vacancies, job opportunities and careers in Ireland
- JobShop.ie – www.jobshop.ie – Irish jobs, vacancies, job opportunities and careers in Ireland
- RocketJobs.ie – www.rocketjobs.ie – Irish jobs, vacancies, job opportunities and careers in Ireland
- SalesJobs.ie – www.salesjobs.ie – Irish sales job listings
- ComputerJobs.ie – www.computerjobs.ie – Computer jobs, IT jobs listings
- IrelandHotelJobs.com – www.irelandhoteljobs.com – Hospitality jobs, chefs and tourism jobs
- AdminJobs.ie – www.adminjobs.ie – Offers administration jobs, office jobs, temp jobs and much more
- RetailJobs365.ie – www.retailjobs365.ie – Retail jobs site
- MidlandJobs.ie – www.midlandjobs.ie – Jobs in the Midlands: Mullingar, Athlone and Tullamore
- Hospitality Jobs Ireland – www.hospitalityjobsireland.com – Hospitality and travel jobs, events and training
- Jobs2Ireland.ie – www.jobs2ireland.ie – Jobs in Ireland and Northern Ireland
- Hook Head Software – www.hookhead.com – IT jobs in Dublin
- Flexitimers – www.flexitimers.com – A people-2-people platform connecting freelancers, contractors, small businesses and jobseekers to companies with flexible projects – part-time, freelance, interim, contract and telework

Sales Training, Marketing and HR Services

- Lucid Solutions – www.lucidsolutions.ie – Irish/UK solutions consultancy specialising in delivering intelligent and innovative IT, HR and insurance solutions
- Beyond the Boardroom – www.btbtraining.com – Irish business consultancy and training provider
- HR SOS – www.hr-sos.ie — HR consultancy
- 3R Sales and Marketing – www.3r.ie – Business growth and marketing consultants

International Careers, HR, Recruitment and Training Sites

- Positive Success Group – www.positivesuccessgroup.com – Executive coach training and career coach training in Ireland, the UK and Poland
- Cummins Mellor – www.cummins-mellor.co.uk – A specialist multidisciplinary recruitment agency for jobs in the north-west of the UK for temporary and permanent roles within a wide range of disciplines, including accountancy, administration, customer service, HR, sales and marketing, supply chain, manufacturing and industrial, and specialising in the hotel and catering industry
- Chefs Jobs UK – www.chefsjobsuk.co.uk – An established UK agency offering a chef recruitment service that provides permanent and temporary chef jobs, hotel, catering and chef recruitment
- CRB checks – www.personnelchecks.co.uk – UK-based agency offering CRB (Criminal Records Bureau) check services and criminal record disclosure applications
- Wilkinson Hindle Rec2Rec – www.wilkinsonhindle.co.uk – A Recruitment2Recruitment jobs specialist; for recruiters looking for recruitment positions

- Tag44 Management Consultants – www.tag44.com – US-based management consultants offering jobs in software development, food and beverage, accounting and finance, manufacturing and other sectors
- Orient – www.orientgold.co.uk – Offers apprenticeships and advanced apprenticeship programmes in the UK
- Growing Careers – www.growing-careers.com – A UK-based free vacancy service to job hunters seeking a 'career with a difference', and a cost-effective vacancy advertising service to employers and other organisations
- Hewitt Graduate – www.hewittgraduate.co.uk – Graduate actuarial careers at Hewitt UK
- Bankston Partners – www.bankstonpartners.com – A specialised American recruiting and consulting firm dedicated to connecting top professionals in accounting and finance, information technology, project management, and sales and marketing with emerging, mid-market, and *Fortune* level companies on a direct hire, project and contract basis
- NaukriHub – www.naukrihub.com – Online job search portal in India

Pre-Interview Company Research Online

- CorporateInformation – www.corporateinformation.com – Contains links and information on how to research companies worldwide. It also gives you profiles of other sites matching the search terms you entered.
- Yahoo's Business and Economy – dir.yahoo.com/Business and Economy – Also an excellent resource for researching companies worldwide.
- The Vault – www.vault.com – The Vault reports are insider guides to companies, including many anonymous interviews

with current and past employees to find out what it is really like in there.

- Ireland Business Directory – www.irelandbusinessdirectory. com – The most comprehensive directory for business in Ireland. Serving all counties in Ireland across all business sectors, covering retail, services, wholesale, etc.
- Industry Watch – www.industrywatch.com – An excellent tool for finding out everything you need to know about the company. It contains a lot of details, including an overview of the company, key executives, key competitors, quarterly and annual financials, stock quotes, a link to the homepage, and access to buy their credit report. You can view lists by industry or do a keyword search for a particular company.
- Last but not least a visit to the company's own website is absolutely mandatory.

A Select List of Further Books You Might Be Interested in Checking Out*

Adamson, Rachel and Soule, Mandy (2009), *Tough Interview Questions and How To Answer Them*, London: Which? Publishing.

Bronson, Po (2004), *What Should I Do With My Life? The True Story of People Who Answered the Ultimate Question*, London: Vintage.

Clayton, Bob (2005), *The Career Warranty Plan*, BGS Publishing.

Conrad Levinson, Jay and Perry, David E. (2009), *Guerrilla Marketing for Job Hunters 2.0: 1,001 Unconventional Tips, Tricks and Tactics for Landing Your Dream Job*, Hoboken, NJ: John Wiley and Sons.

Craddock, Maggie (2004), *The Authentic Career: Following the Path of Self-Discovery to Professional Fulfillment*, Novato, CA: New World Library.

---

* I hasten to point out that I don't necessarily endorse or agree with *everything* that is said in *all* of these books. They are merely the ones I do find myself spontaneously mentioning to clients with particular frequency.

Crofts, Neil (2003), *Authentic: How to Make a Living by Being Yourself*, Chichester: Capstone.

Dowd, Karen O. and Gong Taguchi, Sherrie (2003), *The Ultimate Guide to Getting the Career You Want and What To Do Once You Have It*, New York, NY: McGraw-Hill.

Gong Taguchi, Sherrie (2006), *The Career Troubleshooter: Tips and Tools for Overcoming the 21 Most Common Challenges to Success*, New York, NY: AMACOM.

Hall, Richard (2005), *Success: The Need to Succeed Is in your Genes, The Way to Succeed Is in this Book*, Harlow: Pearson Education.

Hayden, C.J. and Traditi, Frank (2005), *Get Hired Now! A 28-Day Program for Landing the Job You Want*, Point Richmond, CA: Bay Tree Publishing.

Hogshead, Sally (2005), *Radical Careering: 100 Truths to Jumpstart Your Job, Your Career, and Your Life*, New York, NY: Gotham Books.

Jansen, Julie (2006), *You Want Me to Work with Who? Eleven Keys to a Stress-Free, Satisfying, and Successful Work Life – No Matter Who You Work With*, New York, NY: Penguin.

Jay, Ros (2008), *Brilliant Interview: What Employers Want to Hear and How to Say It*, Harlow: Pearson Education.

Lees, John (2008), *How to Get a Job You'll Love 2009–10: A Practical Guide to Unlocking Your Talents and Finding Your Ideal Career*, Maidenhead: McGraw-Hill Education.

Manahan, Rowan (2004), *Where's My Oasis? The Essential Handbook for Everyone Wanting that Perfect Job*, London: Vermilion.

Moses, Barbara (2009), *What Next? Find the Work That's Right for You*, London: Dorling Kindersley.

Robinson, Jonathan and McConnell, Carmel (2003), *Careers Un-Ltd: Tell Me, What Is It You Plan to Do with Your One Wild and Precious Life?*, Harlow: Pearson Education.

Toms, Michael and Willis Toms, Justine (1999), *True Work: Doing What You Love and Loving What You Do*, New York, NY: Bell Tower.

Trunk, Penelope (2007), *Brazen Careerist: The New Rules for Success*, New York, NY: Warner Business Books.

Williams, Nick (2009), *The Work We Were Born To Do: Find the Work You Love, Love the Work You Do*, London: HarperCollins.

Index

Index

Index

Index

tips, 289
transferable skills, 297–298
types of, 293–297
Wheel of Success interviewing, 303
Irish marketplace, 257–260
non-traditional methods for facing, 259–260
traditional methods for facing, 258–259
irrational impatience, 126
IT skills, 267–268

Joanne, 36–37
job applications, 126
job exhibitions/fairs, 258–259
job sites, 258
job specification, creating your own, 260
job websites, 258
jobs
changing of, 234
creating a good impression in your new, 305–308
in new field, 208
putting into perspective, 223, 230
in same or related field, 208
staying in present job, 207, 229
Julia, 183–187
Julie, 142–145

Kierkegaard, Søren, 69
Killian, 140–142

laughing at oneself, 72

Lauren, 74–79
learning to drive, 73
Liam, 135–138
limits
excessive, 82
real-life, 82
LinkedIn, 260
listening skills, 243
literacy, 86
looking at oneself, 72
luck, 113–116

Maria, 48–49
marketplace, 257–260
Mary, 130–131
measured risks, 247–248
misplaced impatience, 123
Mitty, Walter, 57
see also Walter Ego
motivation, 225, 227–234
tips, 227–234
motivators in your work, 218, 231
multi-tasking, 242

negative tapes, 231–232, 250
negative visualisation, 58
negotiation skills, 242
networking, 220, 252, 259–260
neuro-linguistic programming (NLP), 57–58
New Age ethos, 105–106
new role, creating a good impression in your, 305–308
newspaper advertisements, 259
Niall, 113–120

Index

Index